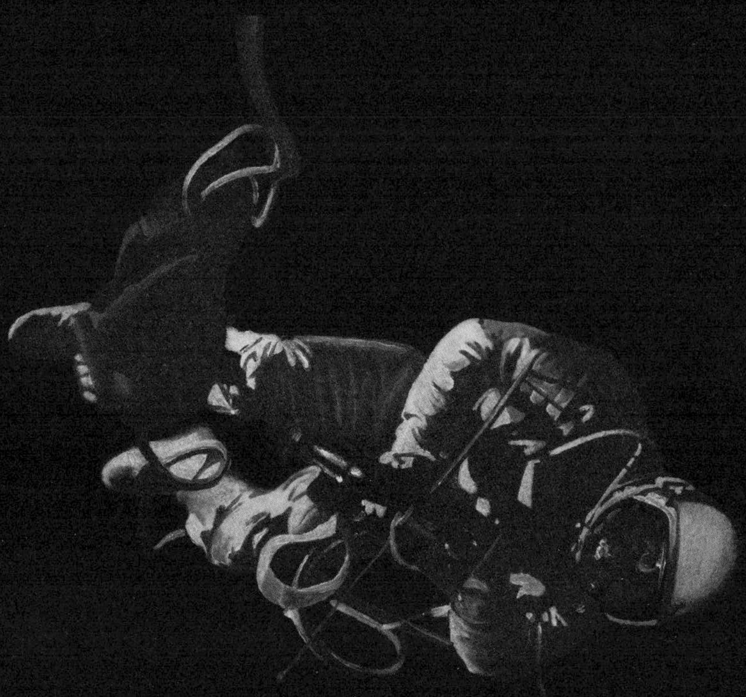

DISAPPEARING—

CALIFORNIA C. 1970

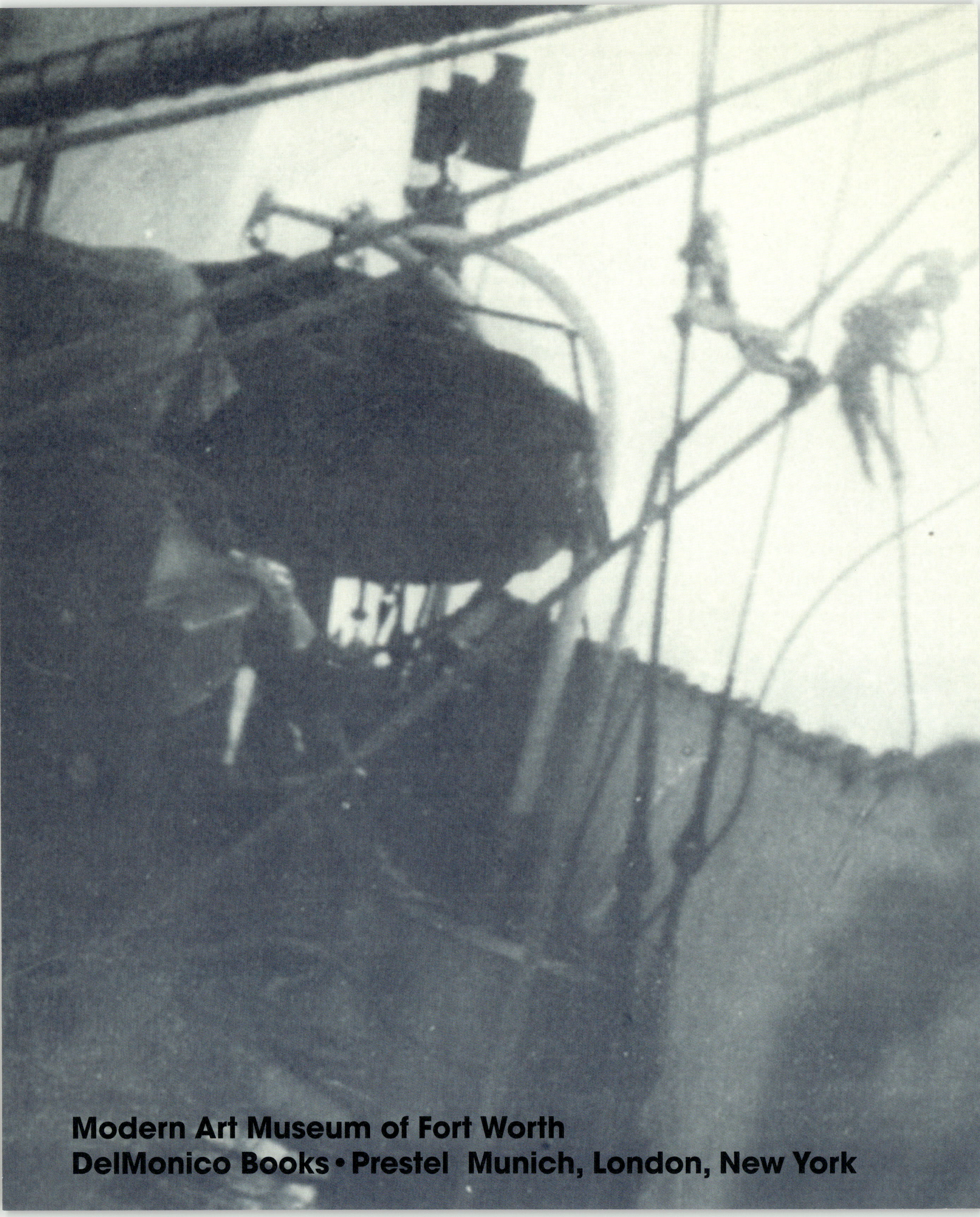

Modern Art Museum of Fort Worth
DelMonico Books • Prestel Munich, London, New York

DISAPPEARING—

BAS JAN ADER

CHRIS BURDEN

JACK GOLDSTEIN

PHILIPP KAISER

CALIFORNIA C. 1970

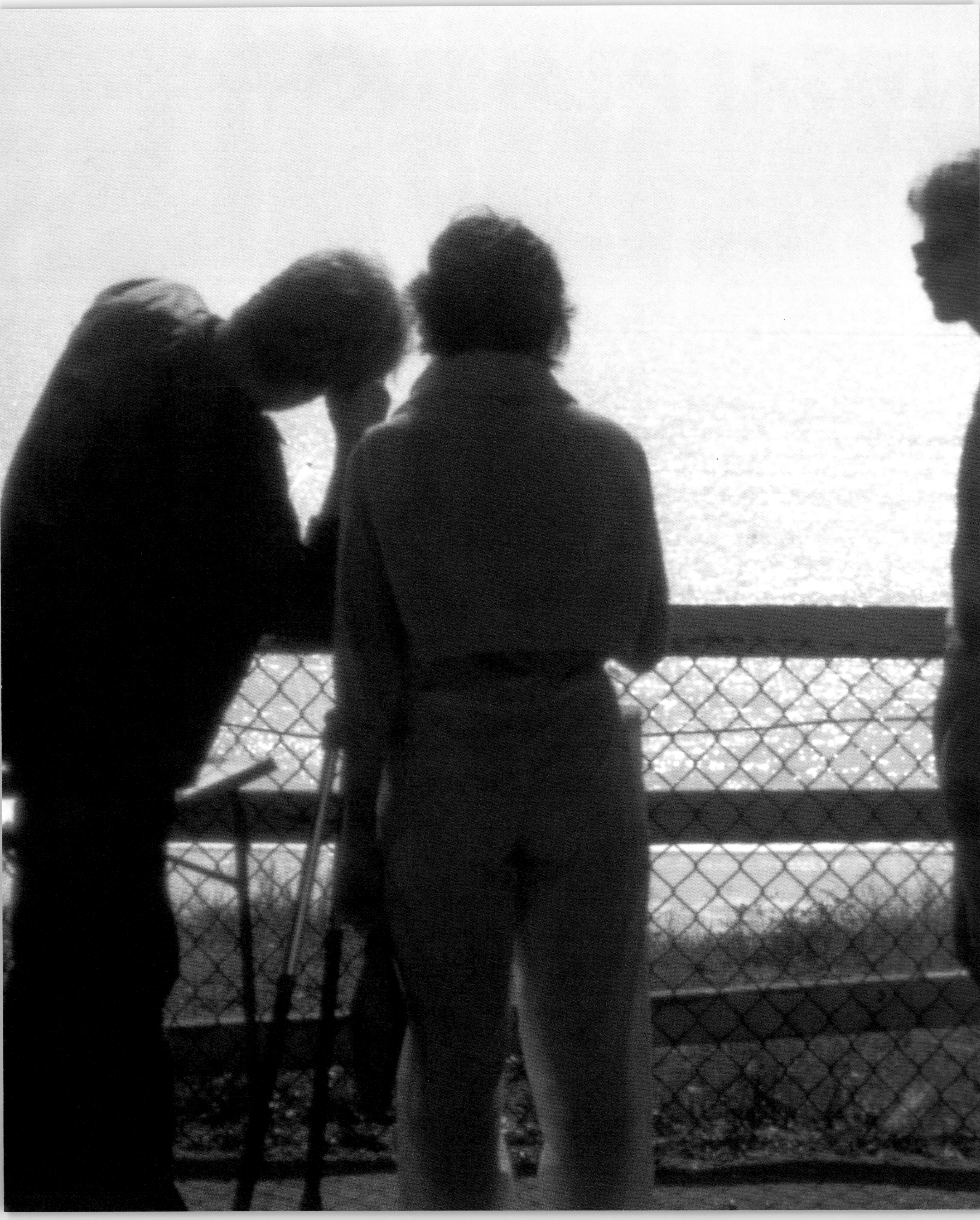

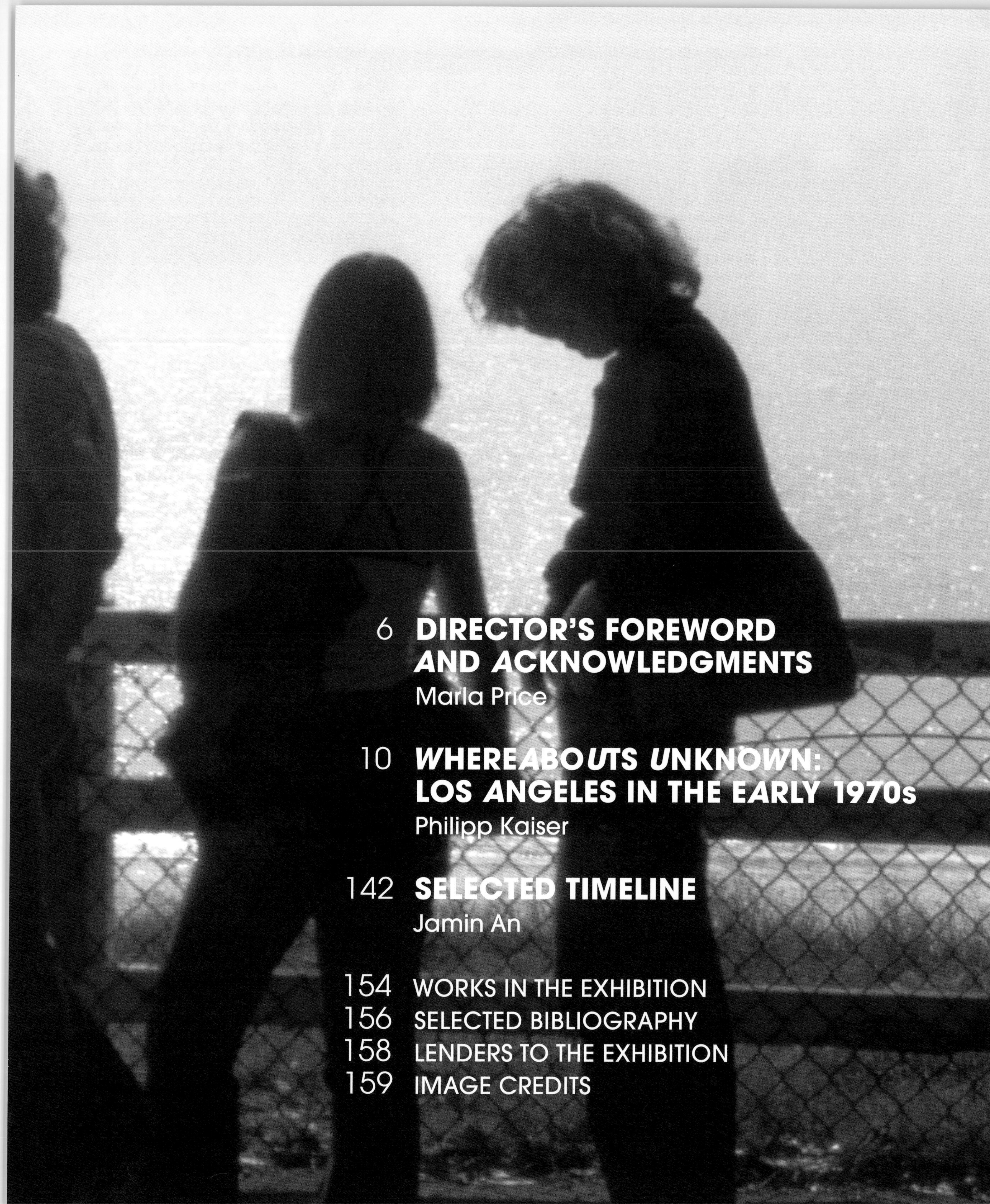

DIRECTOR'S FOREWORD AND ACKNOWLEDGMENTS

Shortly after Chris Burden performed *White Light/White Heat*, 1975, spending twenty-two days perched atop a suspended platform out of sight from viewers in the gallery below, film critic Roger Ebert interviewed the artist for the *Chicago Sun-Times*. Ebert's inquisitive profile captured Burden's reflections on *White Light/White Heat* and other recent performances, such as *Shoot*, 1971, and *Trans-Fixed*, 1974, that had quickly garnered the young artist from California wide attention. "Some of his pieces have been almost mystical experiences," Ebert learned. "During the 21 days [*sic*] he was invisible on the platform in the art gallery, people tried to climb up the walls to see if he was really there." Burden elaborated:

> My close friends in the art world knew I was there. For other people, it was really an experience. Some of them thought it was a put-on. I could hear everything they were saying. One person said to his friend that being in that room was almost spiritual—because I could hear them and didn't respond, and that colored how they spoke and thought.[1]

Dynamic oppositions were at stake with Burden's disappearing body. Crucially, he was not alone. Engaged with the interplay between artist and audience, absence and presence, reality and illusion, terrestrial and spiritual, Burden and fellow artists in Southern California found fertile ground in their own self-effacement. Disappearance formed a nucleus of interest, both a topos and strategy, which befitted the vexing extremes of the 1960s and 1970s.

Disappearing—California, c. 1970: Bas Jan Ader, Chris Burden, Jack Goldstein takes a focused look at disappearance in a groundbreaking period of California art through the works of three interconnected figures: Bas Jan Ader, Chris Burden, and Jack Goldstein. The importance of their individual legacies is without question. As "artists' artists," their respective examples have inspired many and defined innovations in conceptual art, performance, postmodern art, and public art. Though active in the same time and place, they were only loosely connected. Yet, all three cultivated a sustained attention to the disappearance of their selves, the artist's hand, and the traditional work of art. Moving chronologically over the course of the 1970s, this exhibition simultaneously offers a monographic examination of each featured artist and presents thought-provoking points of synthesis between their works. *Disappearing—California, c. 1970* asks us to consider Ader, Burden, and Goldstein's shared exploration into the meaning of disappearance in an age of violent conflict, social upheaval, and technological transformation.

The exhibition in Fort Worth is accompanied by a special presentation of Chris Burden's *Ode to Santos Dumont*, 2015. A helium-filled flying machine, this monumental performance sculpture takes inspiration from the Brazilian-born pioneer aviator Alberto Santos-Dumont, whose dirigible famously flew around the Eiffel Tower in 1901. *Ode to Santos Dumont* glides and circumambulates a vast, empty sixty-foot-diameter space without human control. As Burden's final work before his death in the same year, the kinetic sculpture's luminous shape and graceful, meditative flight provide a poignant epilogue to the exhibition.

Independent curator Philipp Kaiser organized *Disappearing—California, c. 1970*. We have found in Kaiser a generous visionary whose deep commitment to and kinship with artists resonate with the Modern's own. His depth of knowledge into the art of the 1960s and 1970s, as well as the spirit of Southern California, offers our audiences a new encounter with Ader, Burden, and Goldstein. This Museum has a long history of collecting and exhibiting work by California artists; in fact, two former directors went on to head major museums there. We are thankful for Kaiser's insights and passionate leadership extending this tradition.

This publication seeks to capture the convergences and divergences at the heart of the exhibition. Kaiser's essay provides a primer on the three artists and the complex constellation of concerns surrounding disappearance. As a creatively conceived surrogate of the exhibition, this book richly illustrates the astounding work of Ader, Burden, and Goldstein and evokes their assembly in the exhibition. In doing so, this catalogue serves as a document of Kaiser's curatorial gesture and strives to express the gestalt of the artists' shared disappearance.

We owe special thanks to Senior Curator Andrea Karnes and Jamin An. Karnes invited Kaiser to conceive a project for the Modern and provided instrumental counsel. Jamin An assisted Kaiser in Los Angeles and played a pivotal role throughout the exhibition's development. He served as a critical interlocutor for the exhibition's curatorial and scholarly interventions in addition to expertly managing the myriad details that brought this project together.

An exhibition such as this would not be possible without the vital partnership of the artists' estates. Their unfaltering commitment to the legacies of Ader, Burden, and Goldstein inspires our work. At the Estate of Bas Jan Ader, we are grateful to Mary Sue Andersen Ader, as well as Michael Briggs and Anna Meliksetian of Meliksetian | Briggs. Nancy Rubins of the Chris Burden Estate has nourished this project from the very beginning. For their above-and-beyond assistance, we especially recognize the Burden Estate's John Biggs, Liza McLaughlin, Erica Mercado, Rich Sandomeno, Joel Searles, and Matthew Teti. Last, but most certainly not least, Rebecca Donelson of the Estate of Jack Goldstein has been a tireless supporter.

Testifying to the broad significance these three artists hold, the works in this exhibition are brought together through the generosity of museums and private collections from throughout the United States and Europe. We are indebted to the following lenders who have entrusted us with their works: Philip Aarons and Shelley Fox Aarons; the Nicolas Berggruen Charitable Foundation; Galerie Bruno Bischofberger; Joanne Heyler and The Broad Art Foundation; Brian Butler and 1301PE; Larry Gagosian; Jasper Johns; Nicole Klagsbrun Gallery; Christoph Becker and Mirjam Varadinis and Kunsthaus Zürich; Raymond Learsy; Thierry Ollat and Musée d'Art Contemporain, Marseille; Kathryn Kanjo and the Museum of Contemporary Art, San Diego; Glenn Lowry and Ann Temkin and The Museum of Modern Art; Jane McCarthy and Regen Projects; Ronald Feldman Gallery; Paul and Yvonne Schimmel; Gilbert B. and Lila Silverman; BZ and Michael Schwartz; James Welling; David Zwirner Gallery; and those lenders who wish to remain anonymous. We also appreciate the financial support of the Kleinheinz Family Endowment for the Arts and Education.

Just as this exhibition brings California to Texas, realizing this project required the contributions of teams and supporters between Los Angeles, Fort Worth, and beyond. Lorraine Wild and Xiaoqing Wang of Green Dragon Office lent their immense talents to this book's design. At the Modern, editor Leslie Murrell was instrumental in shepherding this publication to completion. We appreciate Sheryl Conkelton and Elizabeth Tucker for their editorial support. To artists Judy Chicago, Suzanne Lacy, Allen Ruppersberg, Barbara T. Smith, and James Welling, we express gratitude for sharing their keen insights into the period. And for their special assistance to the exhibition, we also thank Brian Butler, Deborah McLeod and Rani Singh of Gagosian Gallery, Jessica Silverman, and Helene Winer.

We also wish to recognize our team at the Modern who handled this exhibition's logistical, technical, and programmatic needs. Appreciation goes to Jessica Jernigan, Associate Registrar; Brent Mitchell, Head of Exhibition and Collection Management; Terri Thornton, Curator of Education, and the entire education department; Kendal Smith Lake, Director of Marketing; Derrick Saunders, Graphic Designer; Tony Wright, Head, Design and Installation, and his team; and everyone at the Museum who contributed to the success of this project.

Dr. Marla Price
Director
Modern Art Museum of Fort Worth

1 Roger Ebert, "Art of Fear and Pain," *Chicago Sun-Times*, April 8, 1975.

dedicated to rk,
who disappeared
last year

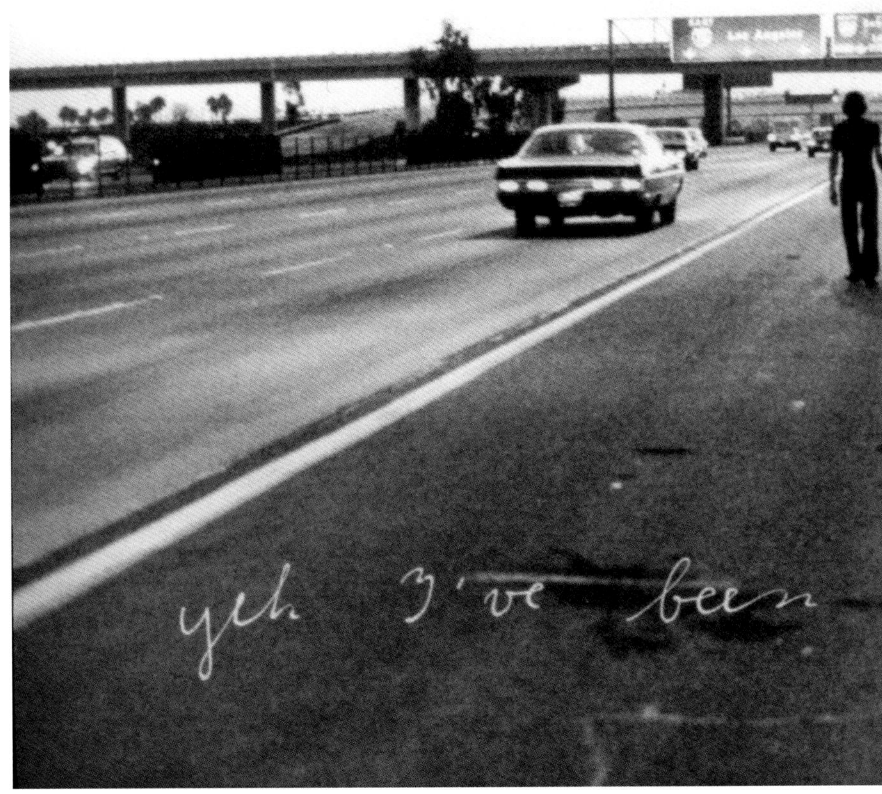

Bas Jan Ader, *In search of the miraculous (One night in Los Angeles)* (detail), 1973

WHEREABOUTS UNKNOWN

PHILIPP KAISER

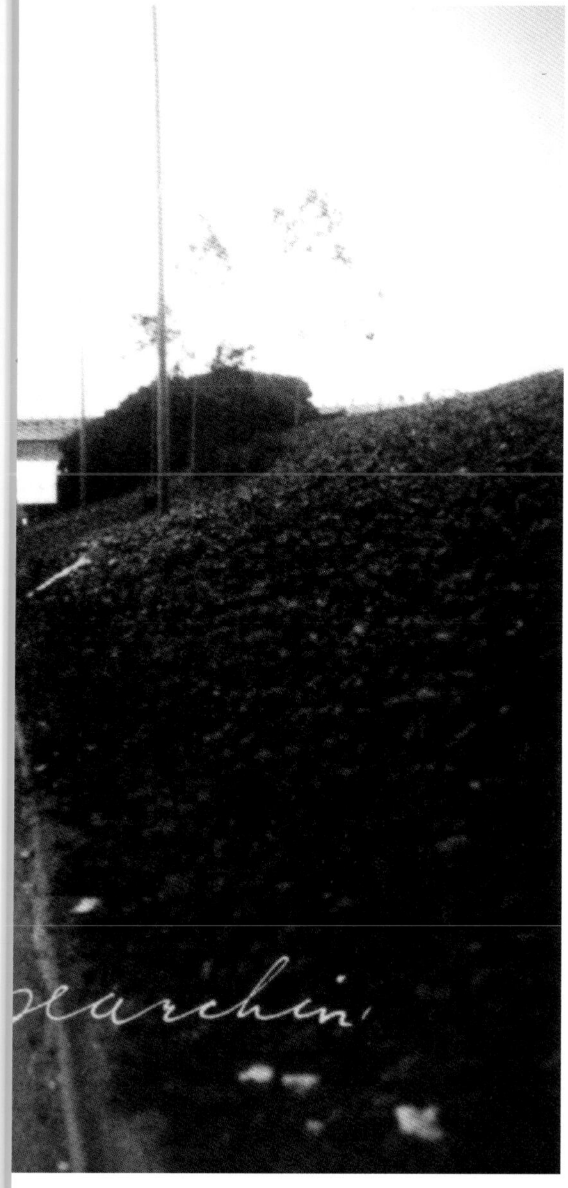

LOS ANGELES IN THE EARLY 1970s

When Chris Burden suddenly vanished for three days in 1971, his absence was probably most apparent to his wife at the time, Barbara. After his return on Christmas Eve, his disappearance was declared a work of art and subsequently commemorated with a relic (pages 30–31). Burden made a Plexiglas box with a silk-lined bottom and added a museum-style label with the following text: "DISAPPEARING. December 22–24, 1971. I disappeared for three days without prior notice to anyone. On these three days my whereabouts were unknown." The materialization of the work corresponded with its narration, similar to a short story or a rumor—then a genre commonly taken advantage of by artists[1]—and transmogrified Burden's disappearance into a poignant, symbolic action. Only a few months prior, Burden had graduated from the recently established MFA program at University of California, Irvine, with his spectacular and much-discussed *Five Day Locker Piece* (pages 60–63). Burden had himself shut into a locker two feet high, two feet wide, and three feet deep, where he stayed for five consecutive days without food. The locker above contained a five-gallon water tank, while the locker below held an empty tank of equal size. Beginning on a Monday at 8 am and ending on Friday at 5 pm, *Five Day Locker Piece* brought the artist's labor to the fore in the best materialist sense; at the same time, it visualized, by means of the minimalistic locker structure, the institutional constraints to which Burden saw himself subjected.[2] The complexity and radicality of his performative gesture, which also evoked the infamous "tiger cages" of the Vietnam War, can hardly make us forget that the revocation of the body, a visual disappearing, was being staged with utmost theatrical force.

At exactly the same time that Burden made this work, Jack Goldstein, in his final year at the newly opened California Institute of the Arts in Valencia, was executing quasi-private performances, both in his studio and outside, in urban spaces of Southern California. "I am always disappearing in my performances," he stated years later. "It's strange how personal my work is."[3] His early performative actions also occasionally resemble pictorial short stories, whose radical simplicity could be of a symbolic or allegorical nature: "A figure, dressed in white, walks along the white line in the middle of the highway. He becomes visible only when sporadically lit by the headlights of on-coming cars."[4] For his MFA thesis the following year, in 1972, Goldstein had himself buried alive. In a wood coffin equipped with a breathing tube, he disappeared under the earth; promptly at sunset, his teacher, John Baldessari, and friends assembled on the CalArts campus, high above the freeway. In the dark, only a blinking red light could be seen, which reproduced the artist's heartbeat twenty feet away.[5] "The movies and performances became symbolic of my disappearance, just as my final show at CalArts [did],"[6] said Goldstein, since "I've always worried about disappearing, and I did. I have

1 With respect to Land Art, in 1969 Dore Ashton described how spatially remote works, whose status can scarcely be verified by a public, are sustained: "The orchid in the jungle does not go unseen. If it is not actually seen, it is photographed, reproduced, talked about, documented ad absurdum." Dore Ashton, "Exercises in Anti-Style: Six Ways of Regarding Un, In, and Anti-Form," *Arts Magazine* 43, no. 6 (April 1969): 45–47.

2 On Burden's *Five Day Locker Piece*, see Matthew Teti, "Occupying UCI: Chris Burden's *Five Day Locker Piece* as Institutional Critique," *RACAR (Revue d'art canadienne/ Canadian Art Review)* 43, no. 1 (2018): 39–52.

3 Goldstein, quoted in Richard Hertz, *Jack Goldstein and the CalArts Mafia* (Ojai, CA: Minneola Press, 2003), 18.

4 *Untitled* (Highway Piece), 1971, by Goldstein, as described in Jack Goldstein and John Miller, *Jack Goldstein: Films, Records, Performances and Aphorisms, 1971–1984*, Christopher Müller and Daniel Buchholz, eds. (Cologne: Walther König, 2003), 68.

5 John Baldessari recalled Goldstein's *Burial Piece*: "It was one of the most risky pieces I have ever seen. . . . Jack said he was trying to give up something organic to make a symbolic statement." Hertz, *Jack Goldstein and the CalArts Mafia*, 65.

6 Hertz, *Jack Goldstein and the CalArts Mafia*, 93.

disappeared. I mean, I literally disappeared for ten years."[7] Goldstein's success in the 1970s and early 1980s in New York came to an end abruptly in the early 1990s, when his drug use got the better of him and his work began to change and fell into the background. Goldstein came back to San Bernardino Valley, where he lived in a trailer without electricity or water, and tragically ended his life in 2003.[8] The artist's heartbreaking rise and fall nourished an insufferably romantic mythos that was hardly conducive to Goldstein's reception and appreciation, and it lent mystery to his biography and his work.

A similarly dominant narrative has also overshadowed the reception of the artist Bas Jan Ader, who was born in the Netherlands and died early. A friend of Goldstein who concluded his studies in art and philosophy in the late 1960s and lived in Claremont, not far from Los Angeles, Ader vanished on the high seas in 1975 when he was only thirty-three years old. His modest, poetic body of work was initially concentrated in performances that were recorded in photographs and films. In the film *Nightfall*, realized in 1971, like Burden's *Disappearing* and Goldstein's highway proposal, the artist can be seen in his garage, lit by two light bulbs on his left and right, for a duration of four minutes (pages 54–57). As if enacting a ritual, Ader slowly picks up a rock, raises it above his head, and throws it at one of the lights, which goes out, and then throws it at the other, so that he finally vanishes in the dark and into the black of the projection.[9] The media-reflexive element of *Nightfall* should not obscure the fact that Ader had already dealt with the subject of falling the previous year, in his films *Fall 1, Los Angeles* and *Fall 2, Amsterdam* (pages 46–49). Ader spoke very little about their philosophical dimension during his life, but his friend, the artist William Leavitt, with whom he published the magazine *Landslide*, commented that the connection between the words "fall" and "fail" was always highly significant for Ader's work. As Ader himself said in one of his rare interviews, "I have always been fascinated by the tragic. That is also contained in the act of falling; the fall is failure."[10] In *Fall 1, Los Angeles*, a short, slapstick-esque, black-and-white 16 mm film, we see the artist sitting on the roof of his suburban house in Claremont, until he falls off and disappears down an embankment. In *Fall 2, Amsterdam*, the artist rides his bicycle along a canal, then falls, intentionally or not, into the water and disappears, whereupon the film starts over again. Ader's decided interest in loss of control and self-determination has been connected with the tragic death of his father, and emphasized repeatedly. His father, a practicing Protestant pastor who was part of the resistance during the German occupation of the Netherlands, helped to save many Dutch Jews until he was captured and executed by a firing squad. Falling, and thereby vanishing, is omnipresent in Ader's work, no matter how poetically or farcically this aspect may present itself.

7 Goldstein, quoted in Meg Cranston, "Over Here: Interview with Jack Goldstein," in Philipp Kaiser, ed., *Jack Goldstein × 10,000* (Newport Beach, CA: Orange County Museum of Art, 2012), 207.

8 See Hertz, *Jack Goldstein and the CalArts Mafia*, 194 ff.

9 Christopher Müller, "Bas Jan Ader," in Müller, ed., *Bas Jan Ader. Filme, Fotografien, Projektionen, Videos und Zeichnungen aus den Jahren 1967–1975* (Cologne: Verlag der Buchhandlung Walther König, 2000), 68.

10 Ader, quoted in Alexander Dumbadze, *Bas Jan Ader: Death is Elsewhere* (Chicago and London: University of Chicago Press, 2013), 17. Dumbadze's monograph is the most comprehensive and accomplished contribution on Ader to date.

Now, it cannot be a coincidence that the early works of Ader, Burden, and Goldstein overlapped and amplified each other—they almost seem to comment on one another. Belonging to the same generation, although they were socialized in different educational contexts, the three artists knew one another and, to an extent, were friends, though they were not members of any kind of closed artists' group.[11] Their staged disappearances cropped up in the early 1970s in Southern California in a perplexing manner, such that a specific moment in art seemed to be condensing, its motivations and contexts demanding examination. A few years ago, Thomas Crow traced some of these staged disappearances in Southern California, and it seems that in the scholarship on contemporary California art there has been increasing interest in this particular phenomenon.[12]

The exhibition *Disappearing* is, to an extent, a case study of a vernacular California conceptualism of the 1970s. It focuses on an artistic moment, brings together the works of three notable artists, and asks the question: Why did these three white male artists make themselves disappear at precisely this point in time? Certainly, *Disappearing* could also have been developed into a thematic exhibition with the wider scope of a period overview, yet it seems important now to focus on Ader, Burden, and Goldstein, who not only staged disappearing in single works, but also each established it as the nucleus of their whole practice, thereby setting themselves radically apart from many other artists of the time.

11 I remember a conversation with Chris Burden in Topanga Canyon leading up to preparing the reconstruction of his installation *Exposing the Foundation of the Museum*, 1986, which was first on view at Temporary Contemporary, the original outpost of the Museum of Contemporary Art, Los Angeles. In response to my question regarding the significance of disappearance in Jack Goldstein's work and why their two bodies of work overlapped, he seemed not to want to have anything to do with Goldstein. According to Helene Winer, Goldstein and Burden knew each other in passing, and Goldstein was strongly influenced by Burden's work, which he considered deeply impressive. Winer, in conversation with the author, Palm Springs, February 6, 2018. Burden spoke about Ader in an unpublished interview that Matthew Teti from the Burden Estate made available to me; Burden was much more fascinated by Ader's work than he ever acknowledged. Ader, however, was displeased by Burden's dismissive attitude. See the section "Disappearance and Death" in this essay.

12 During the preparation of the retrospective exhibition *Jack Goldstein × 10,000*, which I organized in 2012, it was a revelation to me that Goldstein's work anticipated and, above all, celebrated his own disappearance. See Philipp Kaiser, "Why not use it? Painting and Its Burden," in *Jack Goldstein × 10,000*, 125 ff. That same year, for the exhibition *It Happened at Pomona: Art at the Edge of Los Angeles, 1969–1973*, Thomas Crow published the essay "Disappearing Act," which first described this phenomenon in its full breadth. Interestingly, for Bruce Nauman's most recent retrospective at Schaulager in Basel and The Museum of Modern Art in New York, which bears the title *Disappearing Acts*, Kathy Halbreich took inspiration from Crow's essay, though without giving it any mention. As is well known, Nauman resided in Pasadena for a time, beginning in 1969, yet the title appropriated by Halbreich seems unsuitable in our context. Nauman's work may focus on absence(s), but less on disappearance.

DISAPPEARANCE AND
DEMATERIALIZATION

The standard narrative of Los Angeles as an art center generally begins with the opening of Ferus Gallery in 1957, which not only established the so-called Cool School but also served as a platform for artists such as Ed Kienholz and Ed Ruscha and presented Andy Warhol's first solo exhibition, *Campbell's Soup Cans*. The role of the Pasadena Museum of Art in the 1960s and the founding of the new Los Angeles County Museum of Art in 1965, as well as the many activities of galleries, belied how young and, at times, provincial the art scene was then. Not until 1970, when the Chouinard Art Institute was merged with the California Institute of the Arts (which had been founded several years before by Walt Disney) and artists such as Baldessari and Allan Kaprow were engaged as teachers, did Los Angeles gain recognition as an art center—by artists and critics in the city itself and increasingly elsewhere.[13] Baldessari invited numerous artists from Europe and New York and, with his Post-Studio classes, created an attractive educational model without a fixed curriculum. The radical pedagogy of CalArts drew young artists such as Troy Brauntuch, Matt Mullican, Hirokazu Kosaka, and James Welling. And, in 1972, Judy Chicago moved her Feminist Art Program from Fresno to Valencia and CalArts to join Miriam Schapiro. From the outset, CalArts established itself as a center of conceptualism and feminism, and its significance cannot be overestimated. At the same time, other programs developed, such as the previously mentioned UC Irvine and the colleges in Claremont. For the establishment of the vernacular conceptualism that is the subject of discussion here, it is precisely the exchange between the different curricula that seems to have been decisive. The photographer Lewis Baltz wrote about the small college he attended for graduate work, in the town of Claremont, "This wasn't like CalArts, a scheme to be a certain thing, or Irvine, where they really had an objective. It didn't seem to work that way. It seemed just to happen."[14]

Relevant to this context is Helene Winer, who took over the Pomona Art Center in Claremont in 1970 and, during her brief tenure of two years as director, not only established the new epicenter of California conceptualism but also showed Ader, Burden, and Goldstein, each for the very first time. Their exhibitions in the sleepy college town were relevant enough that Baldessari drove with his CalArts students in a VW Bus to attend each of them.[15] Winer, who previously worked at the Los Angeles County Museum of Art, noticed when she took up the position that the more interesting exhibitions were taking place in small museums or university galleries outside Los Angeles, and not, as one would assume, in the city itself.[16] Her exhibition program focused on

13 See Douglas Eklund, ed., *The Pictures Generation, 1974–1984* (New York: The Metropolitan Museum of Art, 2009), 22 ff.

14 Baltz, quoted in Rebecca McGrew-Yule, "Opening Things Up: Why and How It Happened in Pomona," in McGrew-Yule and Glenn Phillips, *It Happened at Pomona: Art at the Edge of Los Angeles, 1969–1973* (Claremont, CA: Pomona College Museum of Art, 2011), 17.

15 See the conversation between Matt Mullican, John Baldessari, and Tracey Bashkoff in Rainer Fuchs, ed., *John Baldessari: A Different Kind of Order* (Cologne: Museum Moderner Kunst Stiftung Ludwig Wien, 2005), 58.

16 Winer, quoted in McGrew-Yule, 25.

performances and new California conceptualism, which distinguished itself from the rigid, primarily language-based conceptual art of the East Coast. The group of artists in Los Angeles, according to Winer, "was both closely allied to but made striking departures from this Conceptualist orthodoxy. The new work that I found utilized imagery, humor, cultural references, and wide-ranging content in varied mediums, including painting and drawing."[17] Winer, who was involved with Goldstein during and after her time in Pomona, met Leavitt and Ader through him, while Burden, whose work Goldstein followed and admired, realized a performance piece at Pomona at Winer's invitation.[18]

Baldessari's influence on the students at CalArts was powerful: he conveyed to them not only a new style but a completely new attitude toward the possibilities of art; art was not only an expression but also an investigation.[19] His unorthodox conceptualism united humor, language, mass-media iconography, and the history of art in an innovative, clever, and ironic way. His move from San Diego to Los Angeles in 1970 was an important turning point for him: not only did he start teaching at CalArts, he invented his new artist self in his *Cremation Project* that year (fig. 1). The paintings that he had made between 1953 and 1966 were burned in a crematorium in an event that was publicly announced and that, for its first exhibition presentation, was commemorated with a plaque bearing the range of the works' dates and the name John Anthony Baldessari. The incineration of his early, non-text-based paintings was, on the one hand, an ironic act, exaggerated by the artist's making cookies from some of the ashes, which were eaten and digested and finally

17 Winer, quoted in McGrew-Yule, 168.

18 See "Helene Winer: Burden at Pomona," in Lisa Phillips, ed., *Chris Burden: Extreme Measures* (New York: Skira Rizzoli in association with the New Museum, 2013), 164.

19 See Hertz, *Jack Goldstein and the CalArts Mafia*, 52, 55.

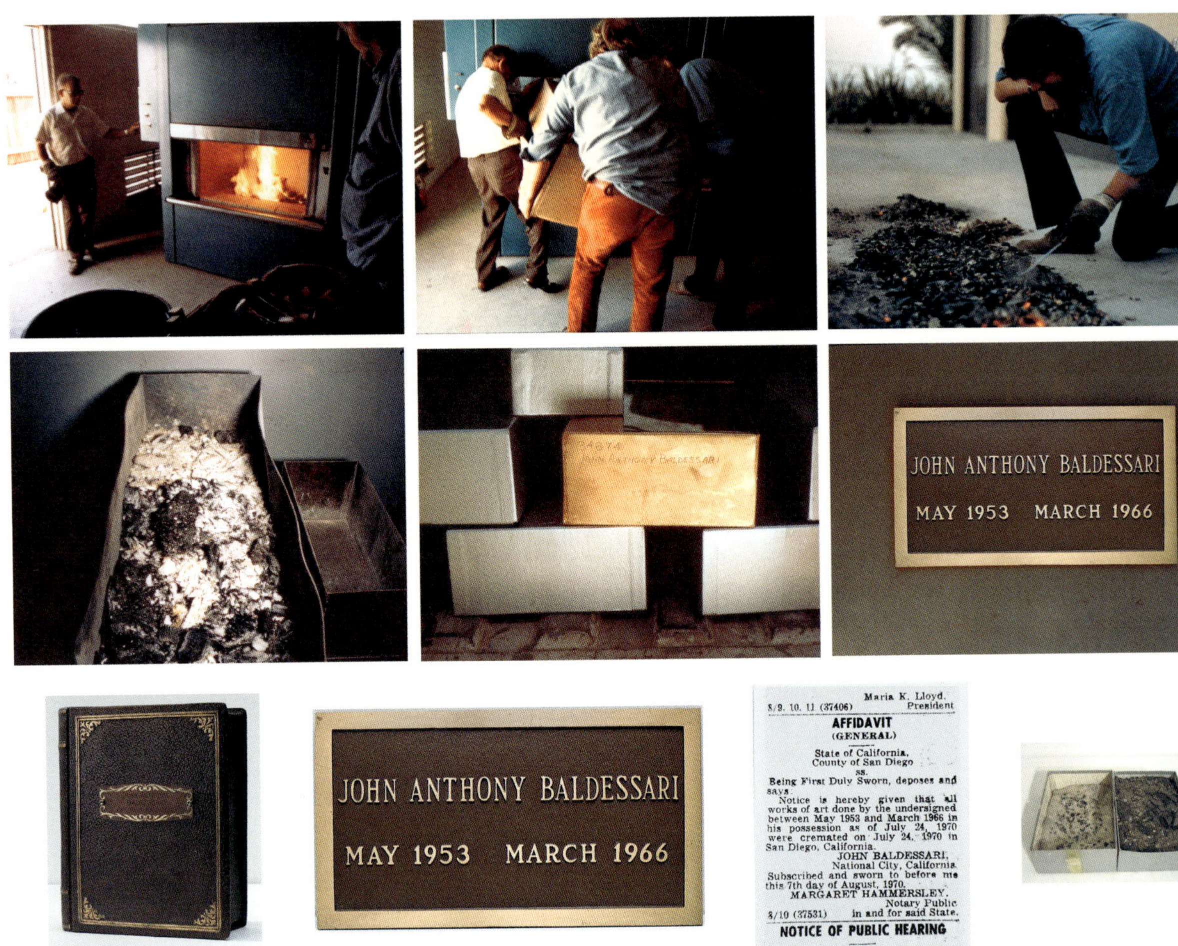

FIG. 1. **John Baldessari, *Cremation Project*, 1970**

ended in the earth. "Will I save my life by losing it?" Baldessari wrote about the loss of his old work. "Will a Phoenix arise from the ashes? Will the paintings having become dust become art materials again? I don't know, but I feel better."[20] On the other hand, the *Cremation Project* seems to be the expression of a radical nihilism that interred the partial subject John Anthony Baldessari. The elimination of the subject in the late 1960s was a necessary consequence of the dematerialization of the art object.[21] As has been observed, it was primarily conceptual practices that problematized the subject status of the artist, particularly the much-cited "death of the author," first announced by Roland Barthes in 1967 in *Aspen*.[22]

We can trace the influence of Baldessari's *Cremation Project* in Goldstein's performance *Burial Piece* at CalArts, although Goldstein's act was significantly more radical. This is not only because the artist subjected himself to the danger of being buried alive, but also because his whole artistic practice vehemently called authorial subjectivity into question. Goldstein depersonalized his pictures by removing his physical traces from the painting; he selected the source image and left the entire execution to his assistant. An airbrush—not a paintbrush—was used in order to avoid any handwork that might reveal artistic discretion, and Goldstein even went so far as to urge his studio assistants to sign the paintings.[23] Hardly any artist accomplished their own disappearance in their work with as much vehemence as Goldstein: he disappeared in his performances, films, paintings, installations, and in real life—first retreating into a trailer, and finally taking his own life.

DISAPPEARANCE AND DEATH

Less than a year after he vanished for three days, Burden was dead. During his *Deadman* performance in front of Riko Mizuno Gallery in Los Angeles, the artist lay covered with a tarpaulin on busy La Cienega Boulevard, flanked by two fifteen-minute flares positioned nearby, and mimicked an accident victim (pages 66–71). Just before the flares extinguished, a police car arrived. A group of onlookers gathered in front of the gallery and marveled at the police presence, especially in light of the tacit consensus that what was happening was art. Burden was arrested and booked for causing a false emergency to be reported. The trial took place in Beverly Hills. After three days of deliberation, the jury failed to reach a decision, and the judge dismissed the case. "Shakily,"

20 Baldessari, quoted in Meg Cranston and Hans-Ulrich Obrist, eds., *John Baldessari: More Than You Wanted to Know About John Baldessari*, vol. 1 (Zurich: JP Ringier, 2013), 98.

21 Interestingly, Lucy Lippard in her legendary publication only presented one part of *Cremation Project*, the notarized cremation document. See Lippard, *Six Years: The Dematerialization of the Art Object from 1966 to 1972* (New York: Praeger Publishers, 1973), 179.

22 Roland Barthes, "The Death of the Author," *Aspen*, nos. 5 and 6 (1967), http://www.ubu.com/aspen/aspen5and6/threeEssays.html#barthes. Sol LeWitt's "Paragraphs on Conceptual Art" (1967) were central in formulating a vocabulary for conceptual art on the East Coast, which in *Baldessari Sings LeWitt*, 1972, was ironically undermined in all its dogmatism.

23 "I can't stand to look at anything that my hand does. When I had studio assistants, I had them sign my name on the back of the paintings. I almost had to fire them to sign the paintings." Goldstein, quoted in Hertz, *Jack Goldstein and the CalArts Mafia*, 202.

wrote the art historian Frazer Ward, "*Deadman* generated a situation in which art was granted precedence over the legal authority of the LAPD."[24]

While the iconography of *Deadman* spoke in a clear language, the role of the spectators was more ambivalent. According to Ward, in Burden's work, the onlookers are the ones to whom control over the disaster is transferred and in whose hands the fate of the performance lies. In *Deadman*, however, art and life were destabilized. Many witnesses had to speak in court, among them Winer, who was presumably called to testify because she was not an artist and had a respectable job.[25] In addition, the artist Barbara T. Smith, who studied with Burden in Irvine, wrote a letter in his defense that was published in *Artweek*.[26] Only a week later, Goldstein had an exhibition at Mizuno's gallery, which he opened with a performance. Exactly seven days after *Deadman*, he presented an indoor version of his CalArts *Burial Piece*. He lay in a wood coffin while a flashing light simulated his heartbeat, rhythmically bathing the white walls of the gallery in a red glow. The explicit iconography of death in both performances is a morbid subtext for all the works discussed here, in one way or another.

Just as risky and therefore appropriate for comparison with Goldstein's *Burial Piece* were the journeys undertaken by Ader and Burden, for whom homecomings could not be assumed with any certainty. Regarding having himself dropped off in San Felipe in Baja California in 1973 for *B.C. Mexico*, in order to paddle southward to a remote beach where he endured 120-degree heat for eleven days, he said, "I didn't want to die but I wanted to come close, in a sense."[27] Burden's project was announced as an exhibition at Newspace in Newport Beach, where a simple note informed visitors about his absence (pages 79–81). Soon after, when he paddled back and was picked up, he presented a short film of his journey at the gallery and read excerpts from his diary. *B.C. Mexico* was an "act of survival" and simultaneously a metaphorical action, the point of which was to have been away.[28] The title reflects a distant realm: as the art historian Kristine Stiles later wrote, it "inverts the artist's initials, drawing the subject of the work into the deep time of the earth itself as it stretches at least 4.5 billion years into the past. The reference to Mexico evokes a place of advanced civilizations, which thrived long before the Conquest with its decimating diseases and limited perspective that dates history to the birth of Christ."[29]

Burden's *B.C. Mexico* was also a dark premonition of Ader's *In search of the miraculous*, the big sailing trip in the little Guppy, *Ocean Wave*, upon which the Dutch artist embarked in summer 1975 (fig. 2). Ader was familiar with Burden's work, and it can be assumed the following statement referred implicitly to him: "I do not make body sculptures, body art, or body works. When I fell off the roof of my house, or into

24 Frazer Ward, *No Innocent Bystanders: Performance Art and Audience* (Hanover, NH: Dartmouth College Press, 2012), 105 ff.

25 "Helene Winer: Burden at Pomona," 166. Winer observed that the case was ultimately dismissed since it was unclear which law had been broken.

26 Barbara T. Smith, "Art Piece Brings Arrest," *Artweek* (January 6, 1973): 3.

27 Burden, quoted in the documentary film *Burden*, directed by Richard Dewey and Timothy Marrinan (Screenprint Pictures, 2016), 90 minutes. See also Andrea Grover, ed., *Radical Seafaring* (Watermill, NY, and Munich: Parrish Art Museum and Prestel, 2016).

28 Müller, "Bas Jan Ader," 73.

29 Kristine Stiles, "Burden of Light," in *Chris Burden* (Chicago: University of Chicago, 2007), 32.

a canal, it was because gravity made itself master over me."[30] The blatant physicality and directness of Burden's work seemed foreign to Ader; he also did not understand his own actions as performances as "he thought performance art lacked the ability to discover philosophical truth."[31] In this sense, his work *In search of the miraculous*, which was originally structured as a trilogy and ultimately contained only two parts, cannot be understood as a performance. Two years before the Atlantic crossing, Ader realized an eighteen-part photo work, for which he walked across Los Angeles in the dead of night in search of something remote, ending up at the Pacific Ocean (pages 86–87). The second part was intended to be a "romantic, adventurous voyage across the Atlantic,"[32] from Cape Cod to Land's End, England. In his exhibition in spring 1975 at the Claire S. Copley Gallery in Los Angeles, Ader showed a slide projection with pictures of the UC Irvine chorus singing nineteenth-century sea shanties during the opening, as well as images of the first part of the intended trilogy (pages 88–93).

In recent years, much has been written about Ader's uncompleted work *In search of the miraculous*: about the fact that the voyage was planned to take sixty-seven days but Ader had with him provisions and water for 180 days; that he took film and photo cameras with him as well as a notebook; and that his wife, Mary Sue Andersen Ader, was waiting in England for him in late summer—in vain, as it would turn out. Ader's boat, *Ocean Wave*, was discovered one year later off the coast of Ireland by a Spanish fishing boat, and in the last forty years these events have produced many myths and inspired countless artists.[33]

Ader's and Goldstein's tragic disappearances in real life should by no means be retrospectively projected onto each artist's work. But, to some extent, these early disappearances do seem to be self-fulfilling prophecies since the artists were obsessed with their own disappearance, each in his own way. In *Untitled (Sweden)*, 1971, a less well-known, large-format double-slide projection Ader conceived for his exhibition in

30 Ader, quoted in *Avalanche* (Winter 1971): 3. In his biography on Ader, Dumbadze writes incorrectly that the statement was published in 1970, before Burden had executed a single performance; nevertheless, Dumbadze concludes that Ader must have been familiar with Burden's work. See Dumbadze, *Bas Jan Ader*, 38.

31 Alexander Dumbadze, "Of Passivity and Agency: Jack Goldstein," in *Jack Goldstein × 10,000*, 21.

32 Ader in a letter to Geert van Beijeren, quoted in Rein Wolfs, ed., *Bas Jan Ader: Please Don't Leave Me* (Rotterdam: Museum Boijmans van Beuningen, 2006), 103.

33 For a concise description of *In search of the miraculous*, see Dumbadze, 105 ff. Simon Starling, Ahmet Ögüt, and Tacita Dean are only a few of the artists who have been inspired by Ader's disappearance.

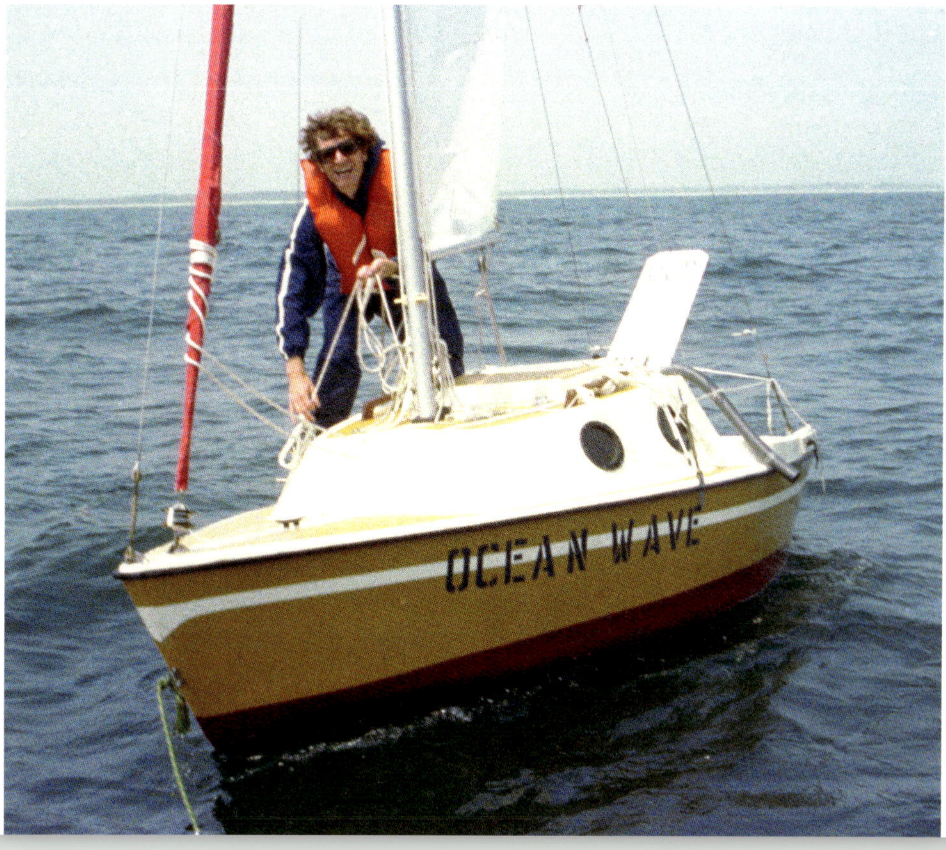

FIG. 2. Bas Jan Ader, Still from the launch of the *Ocean Wave*, Chatham Harbor, Chatham, Massachusetts, July 1975

Pomona, we see the artist in forest undergrowth, mimicking his surroundings (pages 32–35). In the image on the left he stands as erect as the trees, and in the one on the right he is lying on the ground, like the trees around him that have been cut down. The temporality between left and right, before and after, attests to the inevitability of time, and of death, and is especially harrowing because of Ader's destiny. The artist not only disappears in the undergrowth of the forest he mimics but also stages the inevitability of his fate.

DISAPPEARANCE AND THE SUBLIME

Before Ader's tragic last work, the adventurous journey across the Atlantic, the artist was already associated with a kind of romanticism. His works were termed "nostalgic," since the motifs are laden with yearning and his artistic use of the mediums was conspicuously old-fashioned.[34] Conceptualism harbors a residual romanticism, according to the artist Sol LeWitt: conceptual works always imply an acknowledgment of infinity. In this reading, a solitary nocturnal walk through Los Angeles to the Pacific, the singing of sea shanties, or the solitary crossing of the Atlantic are framed as expansive gestures toward infinity. "By foregrounding this evocative, suggestive, and open-ended quality of the conceptual gesture," the art critic Jan Verwoert concludes, "Ader shows how deeply indebted conceptual art is to the aesthetics of the sublime."[35]

Ader's connections to the sublime are numerous. In the photo work *Farewell to faraway friends*, 1971, which was made during the same trip to Scandinavia as *Untitled (Sweden)*, the artist can be seen from behind at sunset, positioned not unlike the figure in Caspar David Friedrich's *Monk by the Sea*, 1808–10 (pages 40–41). Through this more or less explicit quotation, Ader quite directly activated the idea of the sublime, the aesthetic category that generated great debate precisely during the period of early Romanticism. First described in aesthetic philosophy in the mid-eighteenth century, the sublime was linked to the "beautiful." The meaning of the sublime was transformed over the years, yet in the sense of Edmund Burke, the philosopher who originally described it, the sublime is an embodied response to overpowering grandeur. Landscapes that feature elements such as mountains or the sea, which until then had occupied a problematic position in the philosophy of aesthetics, took on entirely new connotations and were newly perceived. The subject, who is overwhelmed in the face of the totality of the phenomenon, sees him- or herself exposed to the infinite and must find new bearings. Ader's

34 Jan Verwoert, *Bas Jan Ader: In Search of the Miraculous* (London: Afterall Books, 2006), 5.

35 Verwoert, *Bas Jan Ader: In Search of the Miraculous*, 15.

disappearance at sea and Goldstein's lonely astronaut who vanishes into the solitude of night in *Untitled*, 1979, are ciphers of the sublime, just like those Caspar David Friedrich once inscribed. According to Rosetta Brooks, Goldstein's *Spacemen* are so small that one has to move closer: "*Spaceman* is perhaps a metaphor for Goldstein's desire to be lost in space and cut off from the flow of life, drifting in infinite space."[36] With its tiny figures, Goldstein's triptych draws the viewer into its vast expanse (pages 100–01). The work functions in a way not unlike Barnett Newman's "zip paintings," which, in their aggressive verticality, also draw the viewing subject closer, into the painting's infinite field.

As various as the definitions of the sublime, and as differentiated as subcategories of the sublime may have been in aesthetic theory, there was nevertheless the shared understanding that the experience of the sublime incorporated the sensation of being astonished and the enjoyment of the experience of losing oneself. Thus, Burden's affective and aggregative installations seem closely linked to the sublime, perhaps most clearly in his first, *The Reason for the Neutron Bomb*, 1979 (pages 120–23). A room-filling, rank-and-file arrangement of 50,000 shortened matches, each glued to a nickel, representing the 50,000 tanks the USSR then had stationed behind the Iron Curtain, formed a twenty-by-thirty-foot field over which a text proclaimed "The Reason for the Neutron Bomb." The work creates an impressive image of postwar apocalypse, and the substitution of ordinary objects for weapons powerfully represents the submergence—the collective, deliberate disappearance—of war's horrors behind capitalism.

DISAPPEARANCE AND MAGIC

Allen Ruppersberg, who was a student with Goldstein at the Chouinard Art Institute, opened a solo exhibition in Pomona on Halloween in 1972, the forty-sixth anniversary of the death of the great magician Harry Houdini. Among other works, Ruppersberg exhibited *Missing*, consisting of overdue notices for five books by or about Houdini checked out from the Los Angeles Public Library, and the photo series *The Disappearing Chinese Theater*, 1972, in which Grauman's Chinese Theatre vanishes into thin air and reappears as the Arc de Triomphe. The books that mysteriously disappeared and the fake magic trick "where you see the wires," as Ruppersberg put it,[37] attested to an exceptionally light touch in dealing with disappearance, an approach totally foreign to Burden and Goldstein at that time. However, probably the best-known work in Ruppersberg's

36 Rosetta Brooks, ed., *Altered States* (New York: Kent Fine Art and ZG Publications, 1988).

37 Ruppersberg, in an interview with Marie B. Shurkus, in McGrew-Yule, *It Happened at Pomona*, 227.

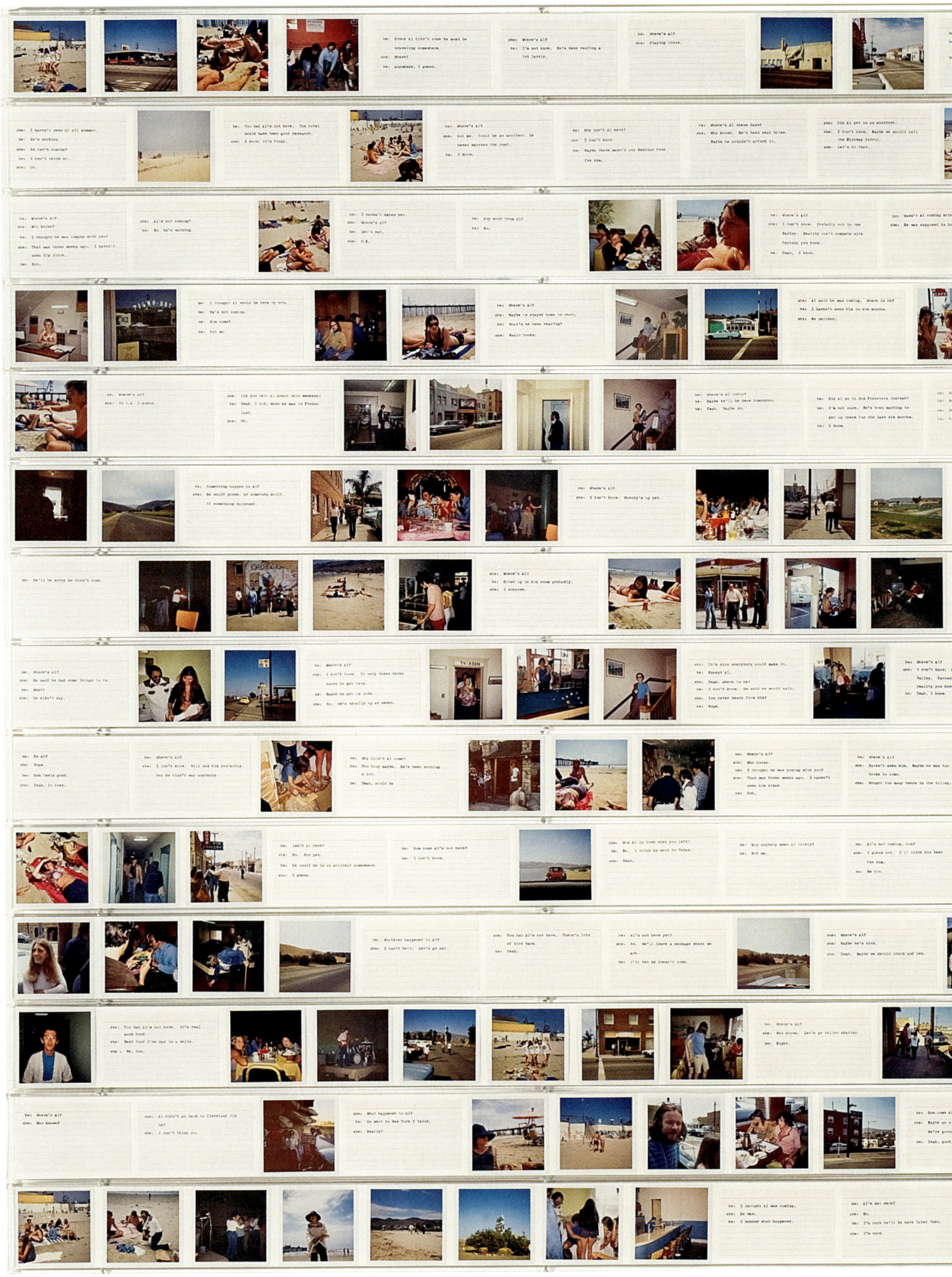

FIG. 3. **Allen Ruppersberg, *Where's Al?*, 1972**

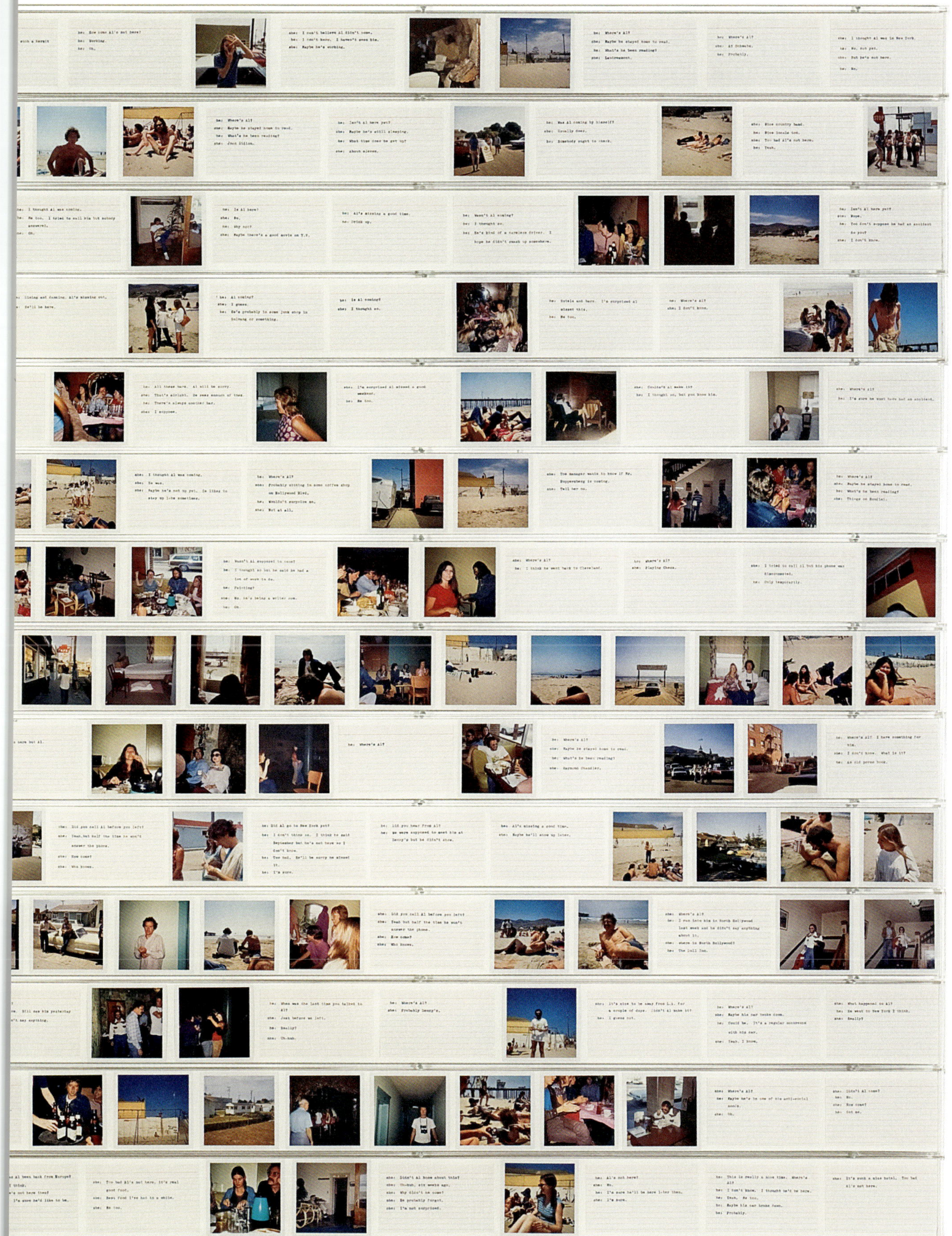

exhibition was the participatory piece *Where's Al?*, which covered a wall with push-pinned text cards and photographs (fig. 3).[38] The bits of text in connection with Ruppersberg's photographs suggest the dialogue of a film script:

> He: Where's Al?
> She: Probably sitting in some coffee shop on Hollywood Blvd.
> He: Wouldn't surprise me.
> She: Not at all.

Or,

> He: Where is Al?
> She: I don't know.[39]

Ruppersberg's interest in magic in general and Harry Houdini in particular may also call to mind the work of Tony DeLap, one of the California minimalist artists, who, as a professor at UC Irvine from the mid-1960s on, influenced many students, including Burden. DeLap's complex sculptural installation *Houdin's House*, 1967, (the title referring to the famous nineteenth-century French magician whose name Houdini appropriated) was included in the much-discussed exhibition *American Sculpture of the Sixties* at the Los Angeles County Museum of Art, where it was seen by Burden.[40] DeLap continued to play with the idea of magic: just a few years after the first presentation of *Houdin's House*, he added a levitating woman who appeared and disappeared from view by means of a projection reflected onto the glass, and in 1971, at the Marcel Duchamp Festival at UC Irvine, he presented his performance *A Spatial Occurrence, the Levitation of a Human Being* (fig. 4).[41] DeLap's interest in magic had considerable influence; Ruppersberg remembers an evening that he spent together with DeLap at the legendary Magic Castle in Hollywood.[42]

38 Originally created for the tenth wedding anniversary of his friends Terry Allen and Jo Harvey, the work had a participatory component, as the text cards and photos could be rearranged.

39 Allen Ruppersberg, *One of Many–Origins and Variants* (Cologne: Kunsthalle Düsseldorf, 2005), 109, 223.

40 Also worthy of mention here is the serial relief sculpture *Houdini*, which was made two years later. See Bruce Guenther, *Tony DeLap* (Newport Beach: Orange County Museum of Art, 2000), 27 ff.

41 On the festival, organized by Barbara Rose and Moira Roth, see Bonnie Clearwater, ed., *West Coast Duchamp* (Miami Beach: Grassfield Press, 1991), 115 ff.

42 Ruppersberg, in a phone conversation with the author, November 21, 2018.

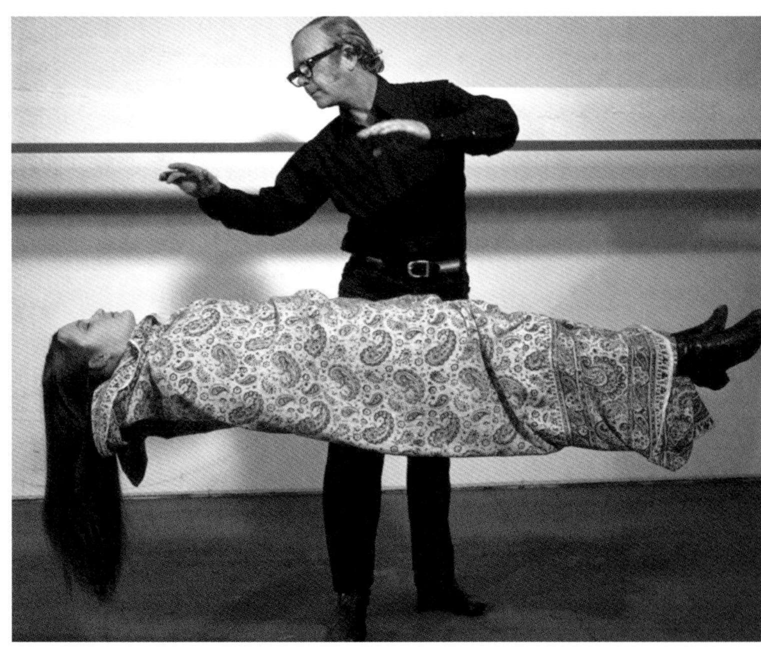

FIG. 4. Tony DeLap, *A Spatial Occurrence, the Levitation of a Human Being*, 1971

Goldstein had little to do with Ruppersberg's dandyish lightness, yet he, too, was interested in Houdini: his *Burial Piece* can be traced to Houdini, who almost lost his life during his "buried alive" stunts, through which he first became famous.[43] Yet, the question of who first took interest in Houdini should not stand in the foreground here. More important is the fact that magic was employed by these artists to "patch" the inexplicable into the fabric of conceptual art—a generally Californian attitude that would have been inconceivable for the conceptual art of the East Coast.

DISAPPEARANCE AND APPEARANCE

It can hardly be denied that the staged disappearances of Ader, Burden, and Goldstein occasionally had a morbid tone and that each of them portrayed, or at least evoked, death and its inescapability. In the early 1970s, death was omnipresent in the military infrastructure located in Southern California's industrial complex. As Thomas Crow wrote, "For a generation of young men under threat of being involuntarily enlisted in a futile war that few if any of them endorsed, infusing the work of art with themes of the artist's hidden, fugitive, or even entombed condition carried inescapable implications of genuine legal jeopardy and physical peril."[44]

While the realities of the militarization of Southern California and the trauma of the Vietnam War, which lasted until the mid-1970s, have often been connected to Burden's brutally direct performances, it should not be forgotten that, in the work of all three artists, we are confronted with an exaggerated theatricality. That theatricality did not contradict the veracity and authenticity that Burden pursued in his performances, however. In *White Light/White Heat*, 1975, for example, he lay on a minimalistic shelf placed high on a wall that made him invisible to the visitors to his New York gallery (pages 74–77). Subjecting himself to an extreme situation, he would stay there for the whole period of the exhibition, day and night.[45]

It quickly becomes clear how different the three artists' attitudes were on this point. If Ader had to pay for his last work with an extremely high price—his life—Goldstein had a completely different concept of veracity and authenticity: "The difference between Bas Jan and me is that I wouldn't have to take the boat trip; a flyer would have been enough. He came out of a time when the artist had to be involved in making a piece; he physically had to make the journey, while I would have

43 Ruppersberg cannot remember ever having talked about Houdini with his friend Jack Goldstein.

44 Thomas Crow, "Disappearing Act: Art In and Out of Pomona," in McGrew-Yule, *It Happened at Pomona*, 49.

45 In their veracity, Burden's early performances were often compared with Joseph Beuys's action *I Like America and America Likes Me*, 1974. As is well known, Beuys only spent time with the coyote while the gallery was open, after which the artist's workday was over. Burden's performance, the title of which refers to a song by John Cale about heroin addiction, to some extent became an artistic test of courage: "Burden achieved a similar, although non-narcotic state, reproducing some of these effects by remaining isolated, fasting, and drinking one six-ounce glass of celery juice a day." See Stiles, "Burden of Light," 23.

treated it as pure theater."[46] While it seems baffling that Goldstein would consign his friend, who was older by only three years, to a different generation, it nevertheless becomes explicit here how much Goldstein's practice operated on a symbolic level of representation and differed from Ader's and Burden's veristic approaches. Nevertheless, it was the case for each of the three artists that they were only able to stage their own disappearance in the knowledge that an audience, no matter how large it may have been, would witness it. In Burden's *Disappearing*, the rumor of his vanishing activated the work, transforming it into a symbolic action, while in Goldstein's *Burial Piece*, absence was staged with utmost theatrical force, ultimately in order to affirm Goldstein's presence as the artist. Yet, for Goldstein, the dialectical relationship of absence and presence was always ambivalent. This ambivalence was pointedly staged in his film *A Spotlight*, 1972, which takes place in his Los Angeles studio (pages 50–51). A spotlight calls attention to him while he simultaneously attempts to get away from it; following him in the darkness, the light continues to pester him with great persistence. The cone of light illuminates the artist like a rock star, yet to the same extent it styles him as hunted and pursued.

The synchronous disappearances of Ader, Burden, and Goldstein have been given various justifications: the desire for the dematerialization of (art-)object and (artist-)subject inherent to conceptualism; the omnipresence of death in the context of the Vietnam War; the temptation of magic's sleight of hand; and a fascination with the morbid and the sublime.

As much as these works can be described as the product of vernacular California conceptualism, we have to ask ourselves if it was a coincidence that the burst of staged disappearances took place right at the moment that feminism was beginning to establish itself in Southern California. In 1971, Judy Chicago brought her Feminist Art Program to the newly opened CalArts and drew substantial attention. The exchange between Baldessari's first Post-Studio class and the new feminist program was more extensive than is usually acknowledged. To be sure, the new feminist discourse first had to firmly establish itself, and therefore had to isolate itself to a certain degree from male-dominated conceptual art; in other words, it had to formulate its own conceptual rhetoric. However, the performance artists were close friends with one another. As Barbara T. Smith said, "We weren't competitive. We were just honoring of each other's pieces. And it was just a small group that was ever there."[47] This statement makes clear that many performative works—even those by Goldstein or Burden—could have taken inspiration from a feminist practice or, perhaps, were a "subconscious response" to it. In the words of Suzanne Lacy, a former student of Chicago's, "[The performances were] a response to the issues that women were bringing up. . . . They began like normal people reacting to the emerging

46 Goldstein, quoted in Hertz, *Jack Goldstein and the CalArts Mafia*, 23.

47 Smith, in an unpublished roundtable discussion with Judy Chicago, Suzanne Lacy, and Barbara T. Smith, moderated by Andrea Karnes and Philipp Kaiser, Santa Monica, July 8, 2018.

discourse."[48] Some of the feminist performances exposed bodies to violence and brutality, not unlike Burden's early performances. For example, Lacy and Chicago's cooperative project *Ablutions*, 1972, centered on conversations with rape victims (fig. 5).[49] It resembled a Happening, with activities such as bathing in blood and eggs and the arranging of bloody animal organs, engaging the vulnerability of the female body through an abject staging. As much as the performative artists supported each other, their agendas were quickly differentiated. In Chicago's words:

> I was trying to symbolically disappear the patriarchal and masculinist environment and structure, and these guys [Ader, Burden, Goldstein] were trying to disappear themselves. . . . I thought those performances were self-indulgent, because these men are acting like their bodies are at risk every day like women's are; you must be out of your mind. You get to inflict damage on your body as an act of choice. We are the subject of violence constantly; that has nothing to do with choice.[50]

We can only speculate to what extent the appearance of feminism was connected with the disappearance of the white male artist. In our case, the (male) disappearances were by no means timid—rather, perhaps, they can be read as heroic as they emphasized and restated the active subject. At times their actions were so heroic that we can detect some despair behind them, a despair that may have been grounded in fear generated by the political situation of the time but also certainly due to each artist's utmost desire to dematerialize themselves.

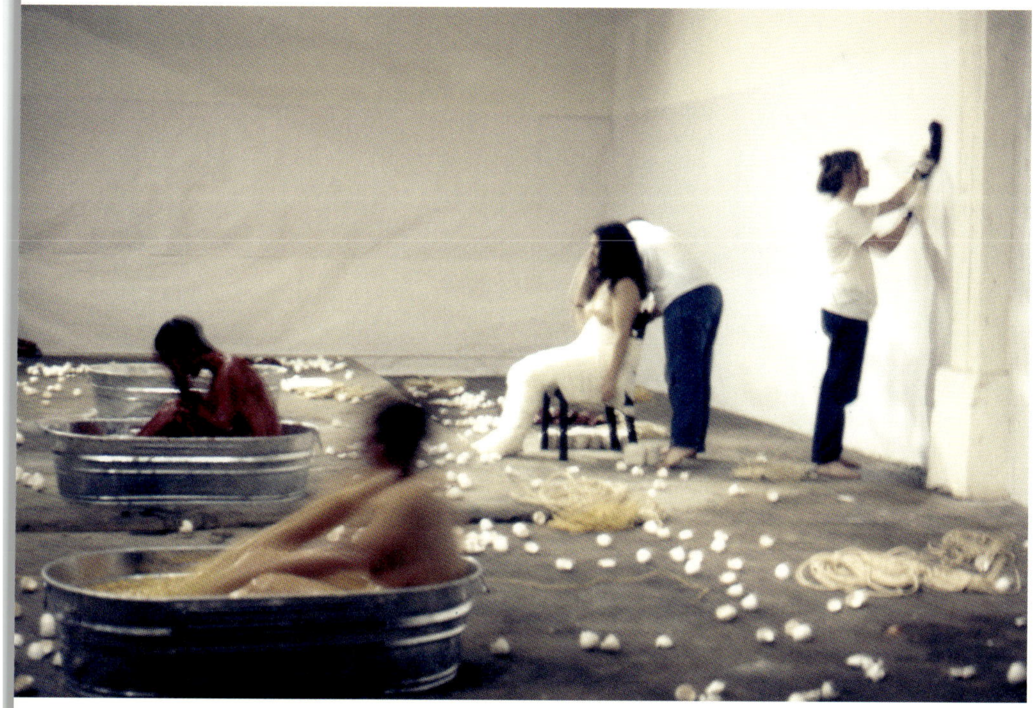

FIG. 5. ***Ablutions*, 1972. Performance by Judy Chicago, Suzanne Lacy, Sandra Orgel, and Aviva Rahmani**

48 Lacy, in an unpublished roundtable discussion with Chicago, Lacy, and Smith.

49 Sandra Orgel and Aviva Rahmani also participated in *Ablutions*.

50 Chicago, in an unpublished roundtable discussion with Chicago, Lacy, and Smith.

Disappearing
December 22–24, 1971

I disappeared for three days without prior notice to anyone. On these three days my whereabouts were unknown.

Chris Burden, *Disappearing*, 1971
Relic: Void (empty case)

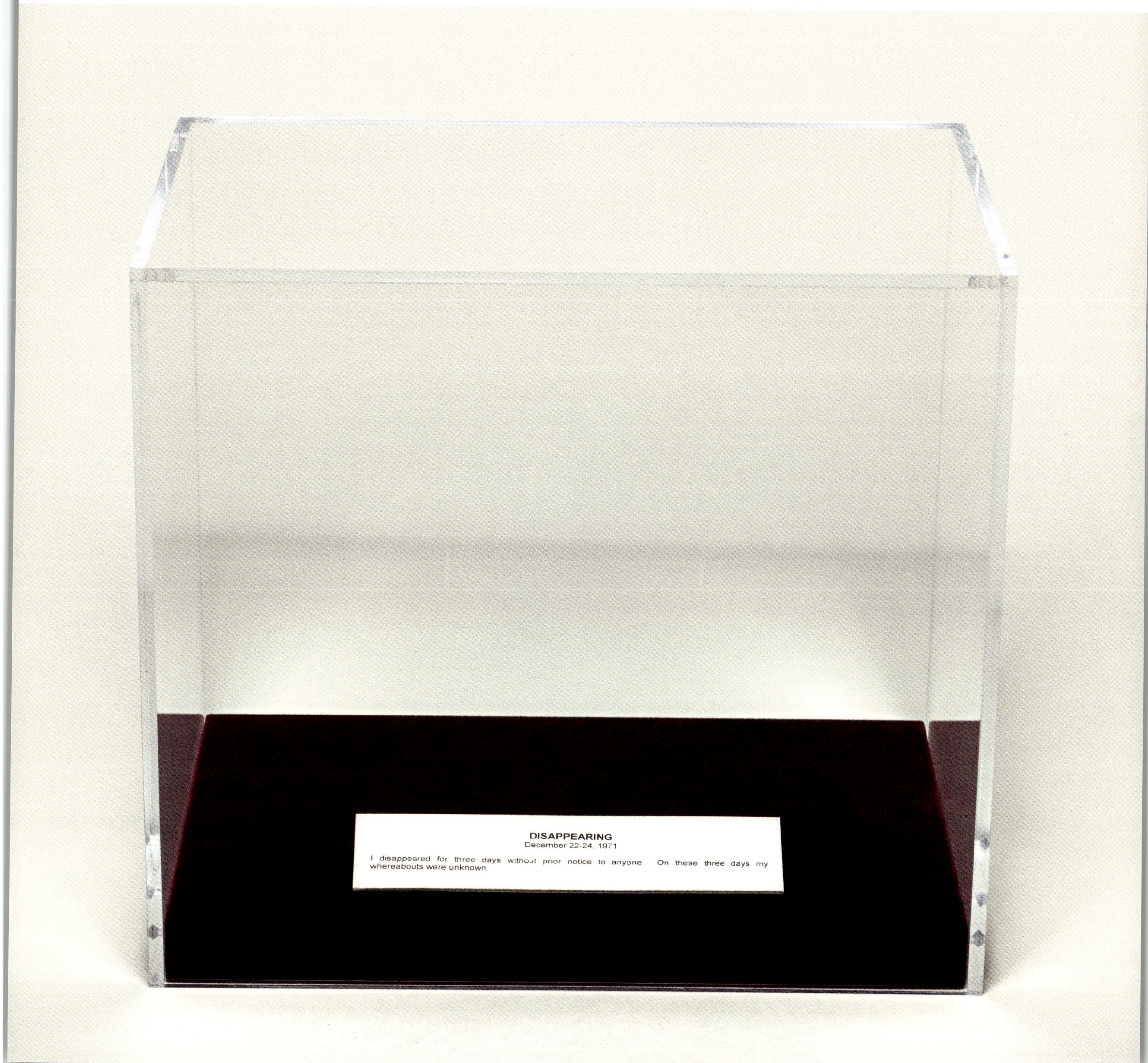
DISAPPEARING
December 22-24, 1971
I disappeared for three days without prior notice to anyone. On these three days my whereabouts were unknown.

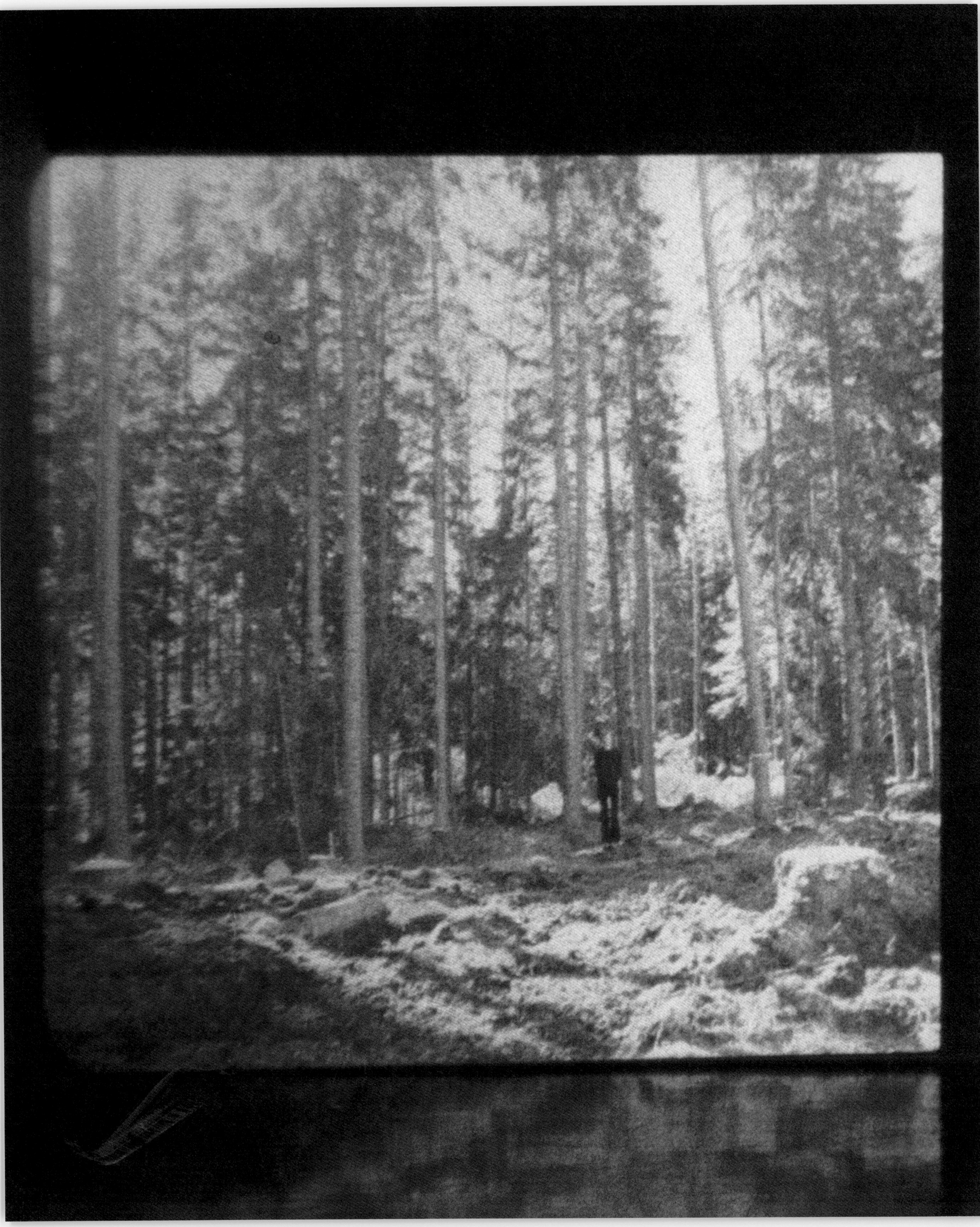

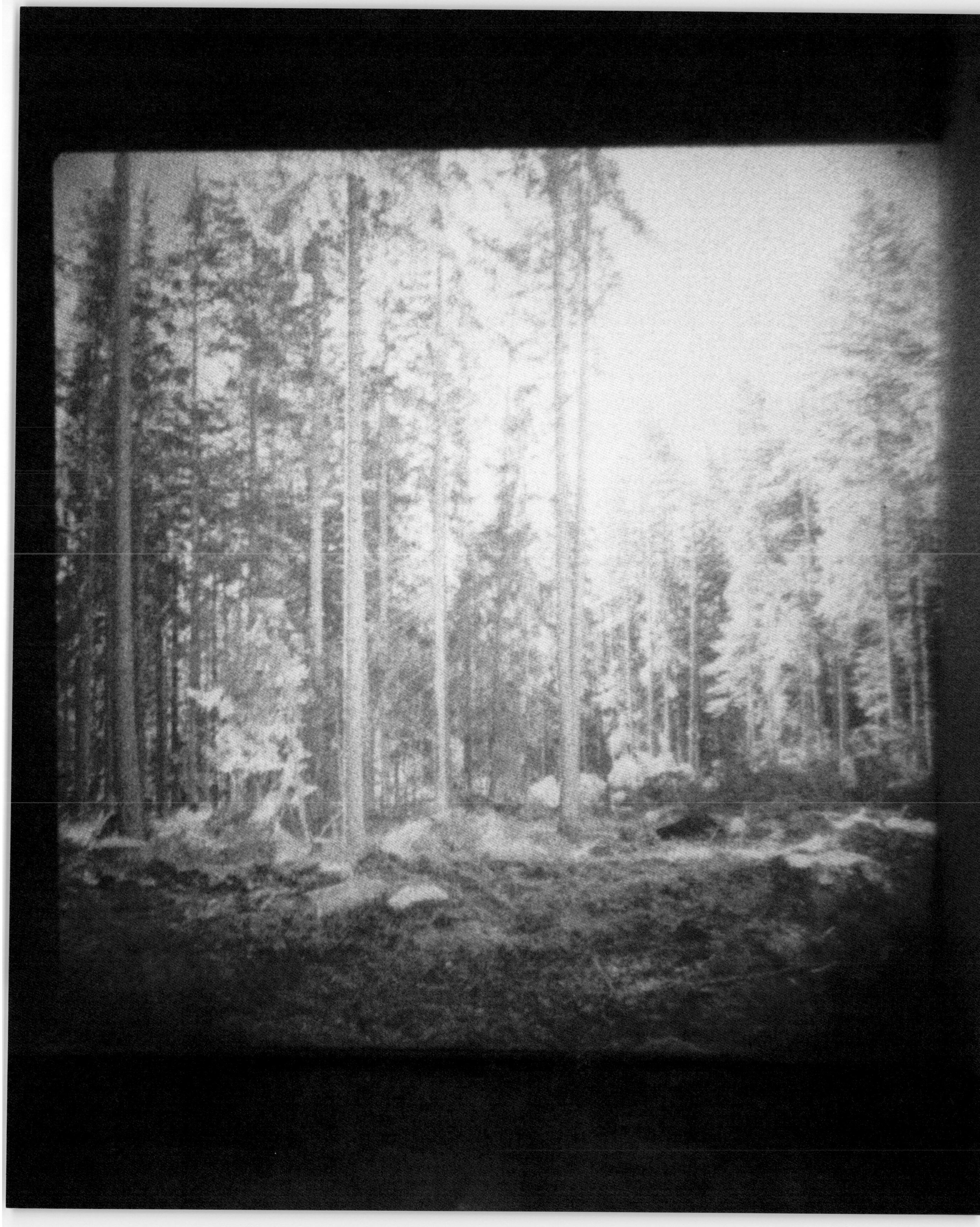

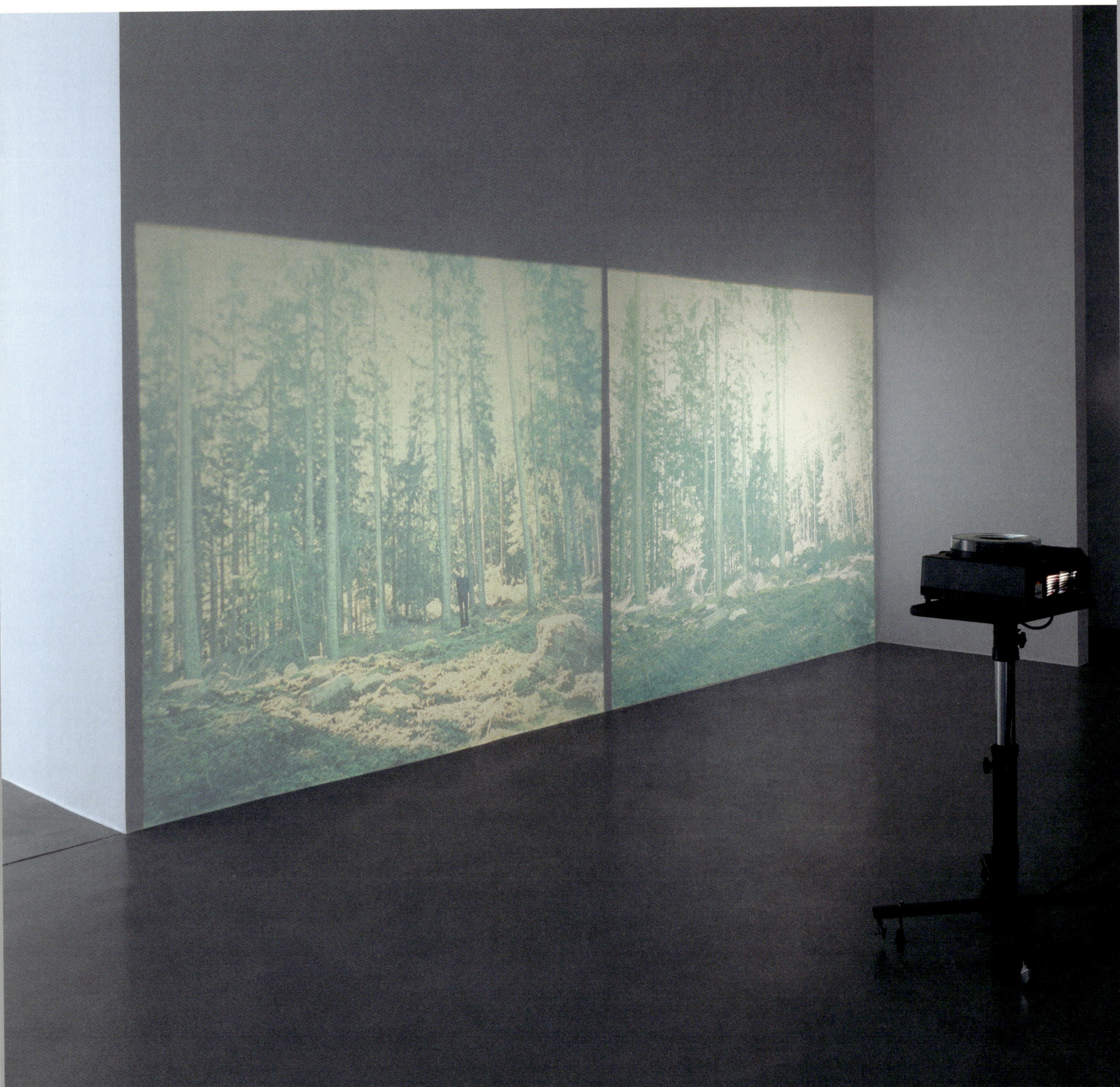

PREVIOUS SPREAD AND ABOVE
Bas Jan Ader, *Untitled (Sweden)*, 1971

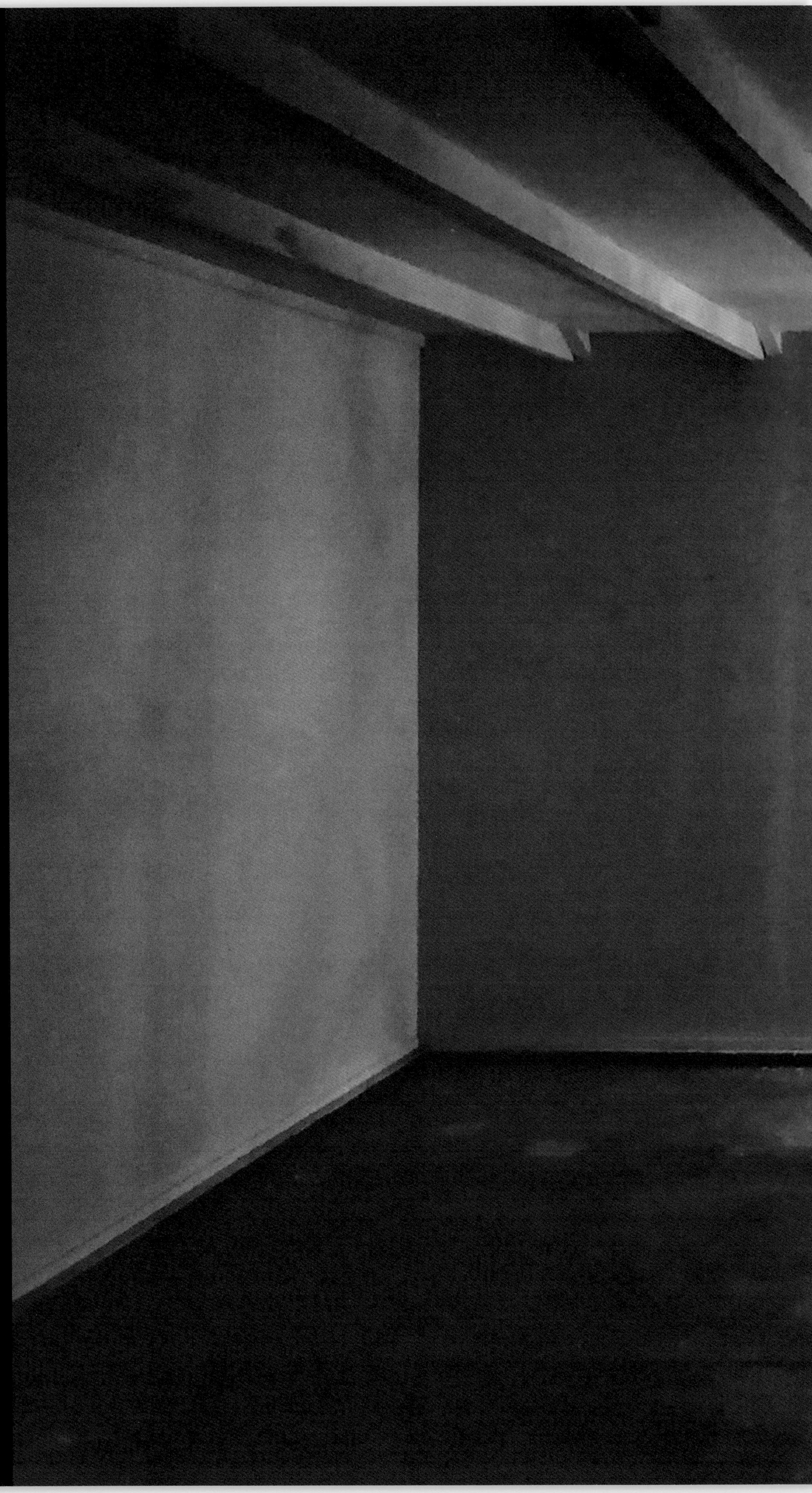

Bas Jan Ader, *Please don't leave me*, 1969

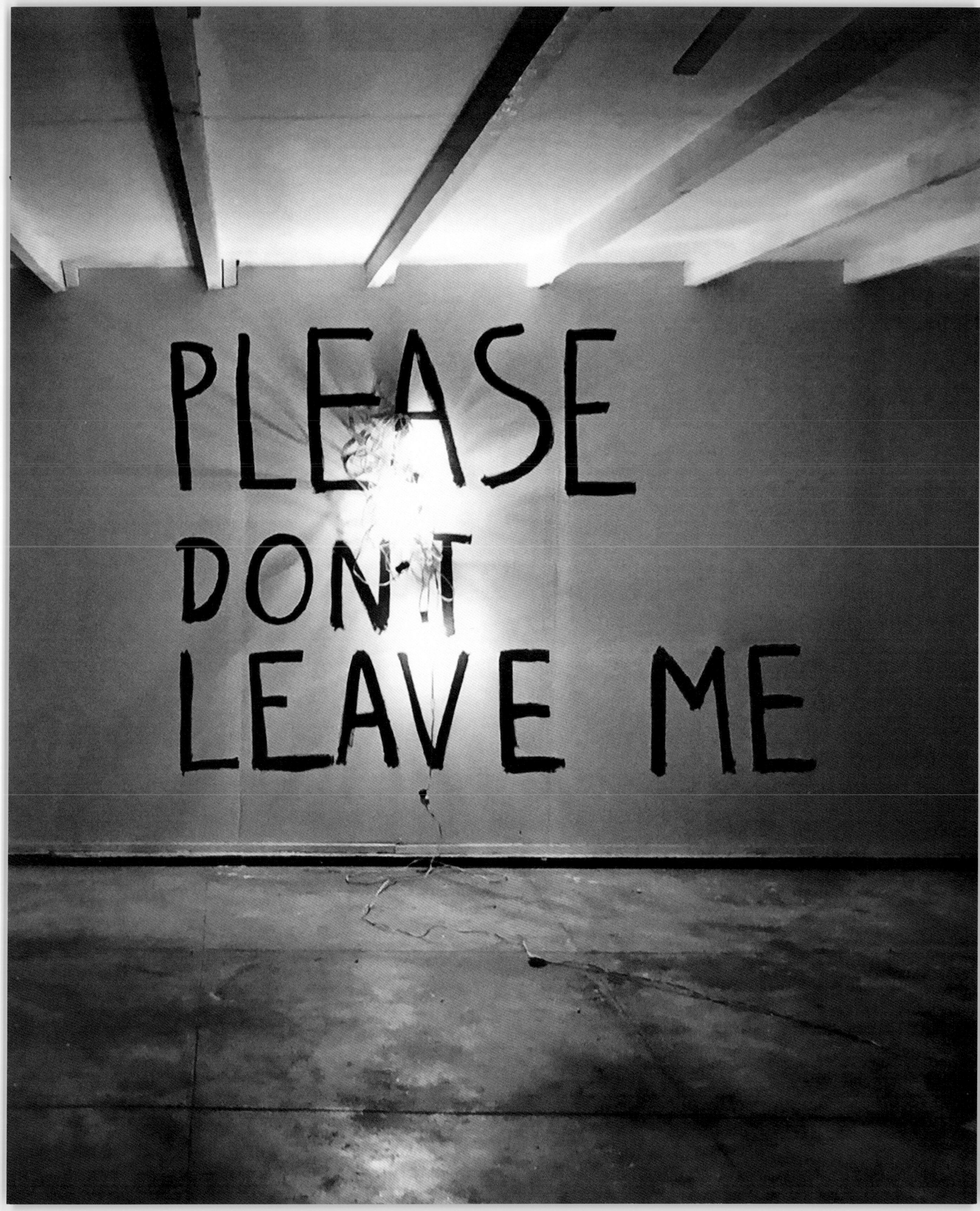
PLEASE
DON'T
LEAVE ME

Chris Burden, *Survival Kit*, 1979

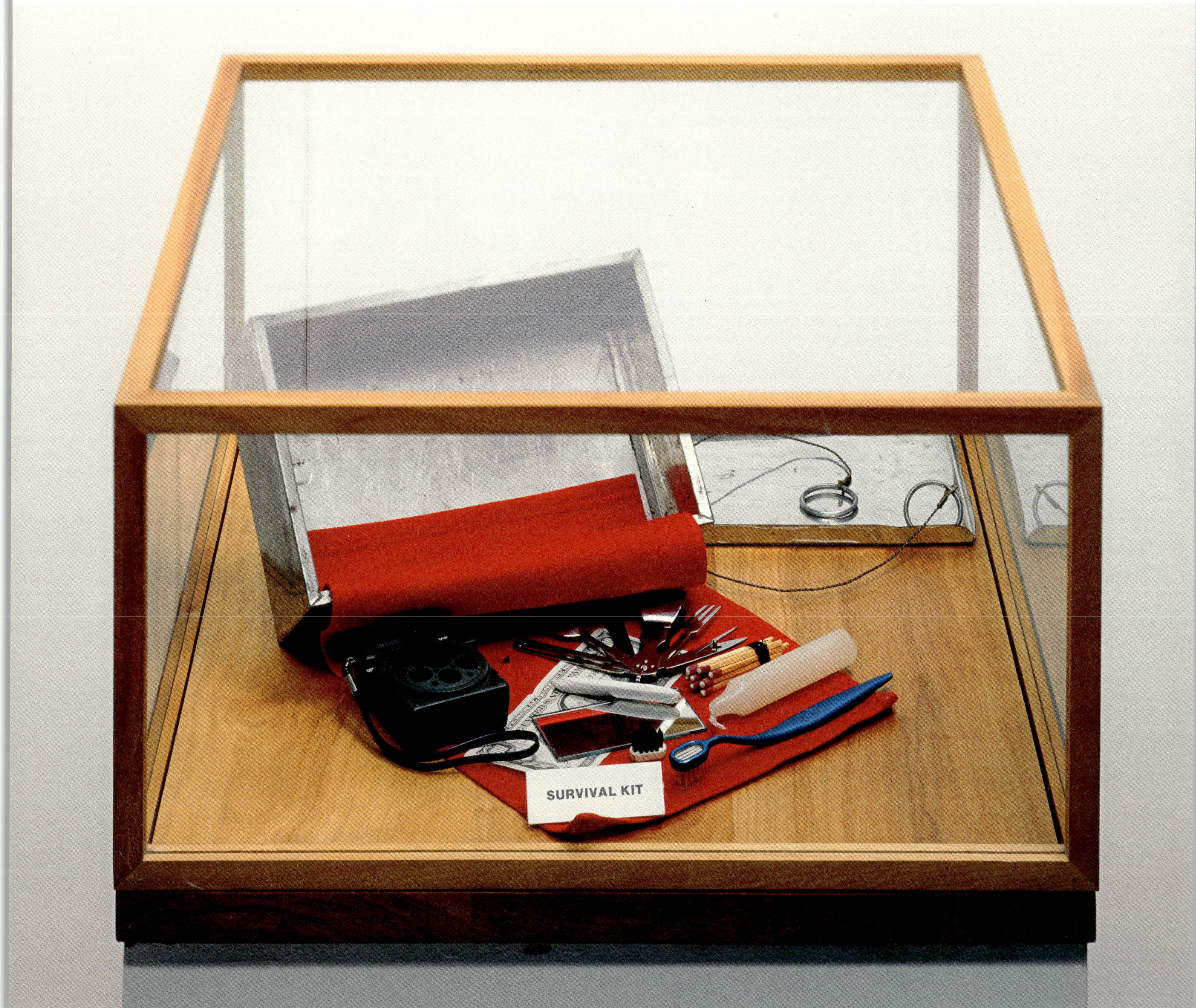
SURVIVAL KIT

Bas Jan Ader, *Farewell to faraway friends*, 1971

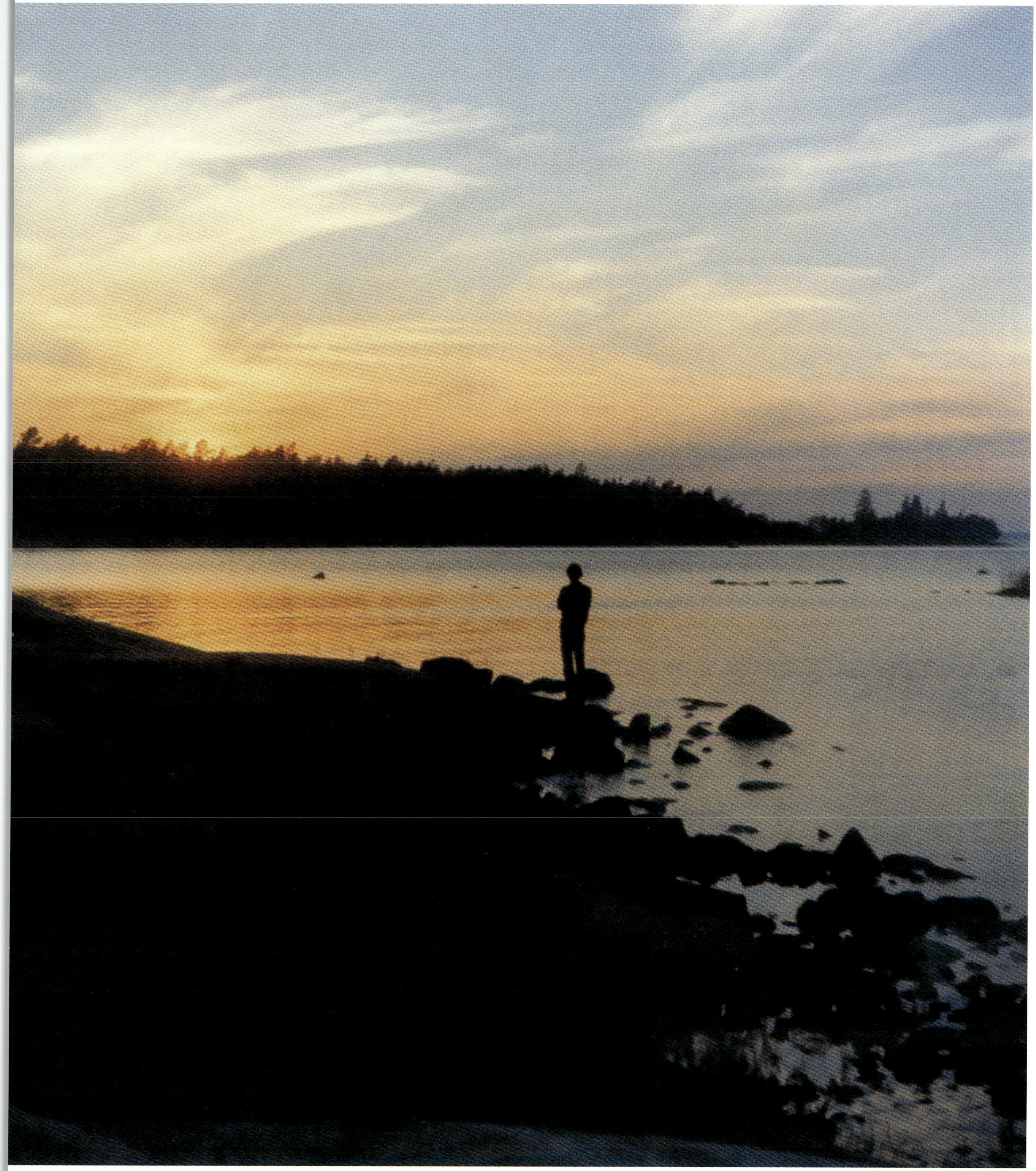

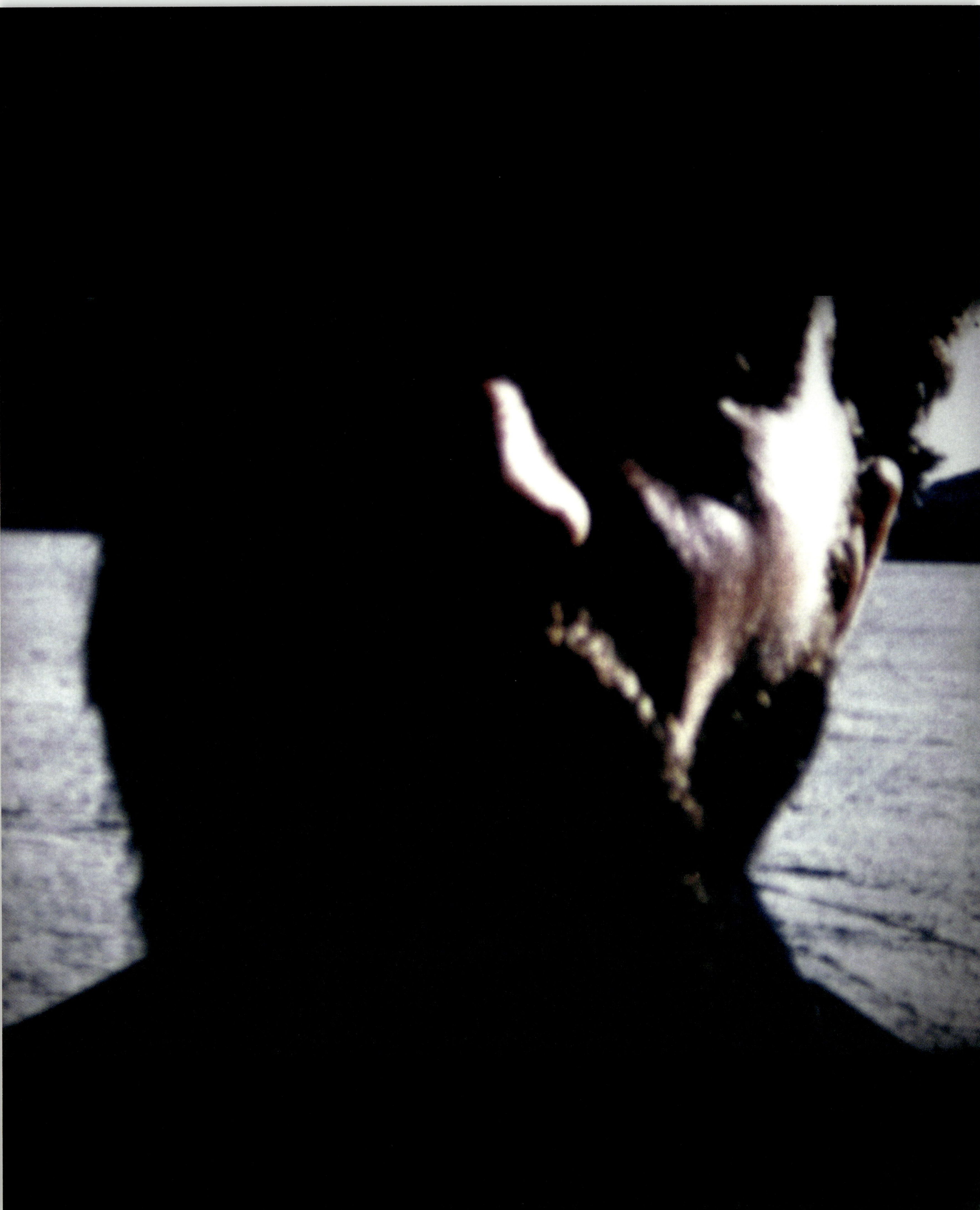

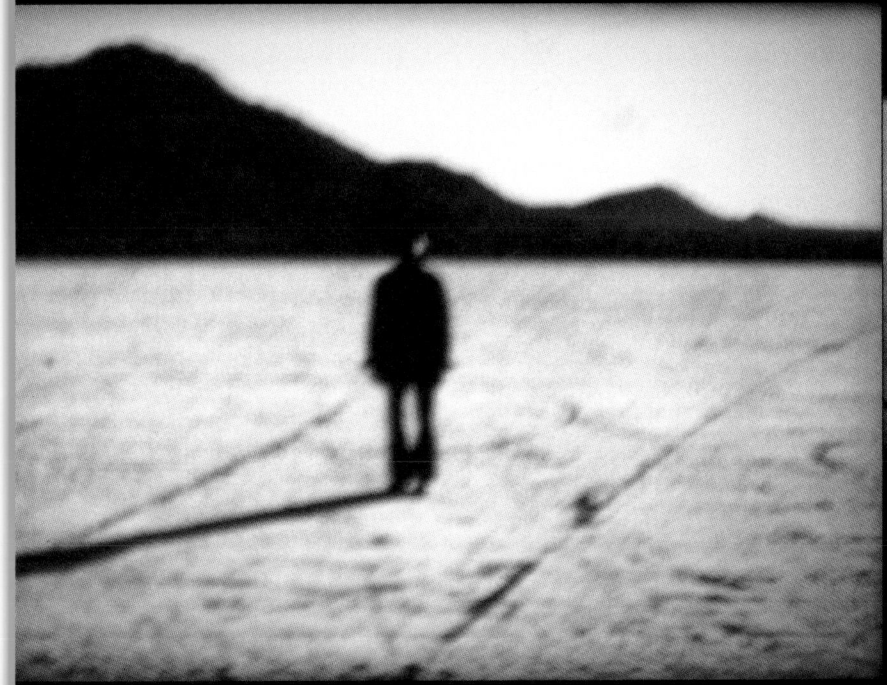

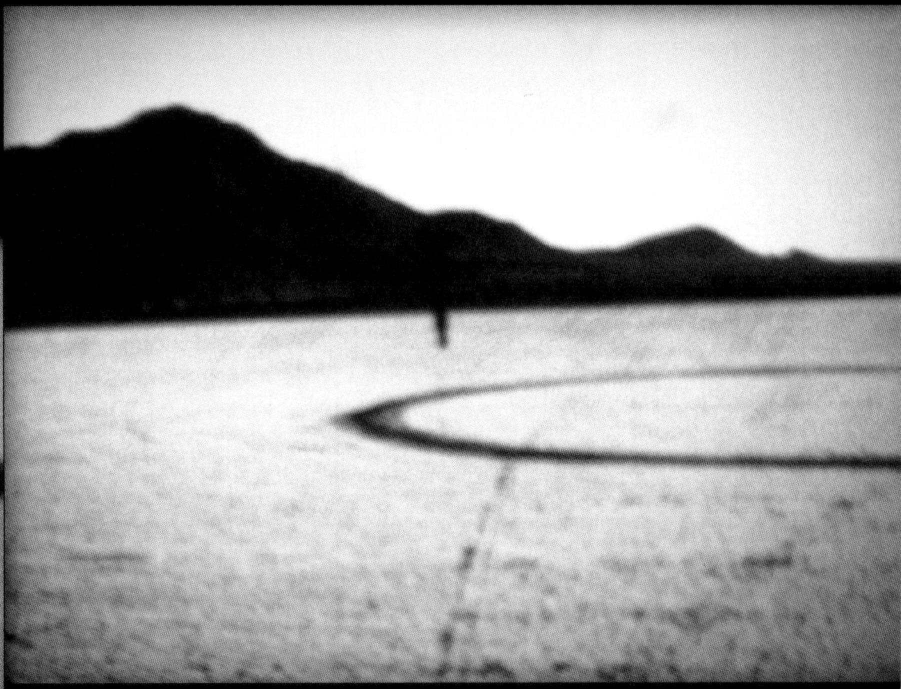

Stills from Jack Goldstein, *Jack*, 1973

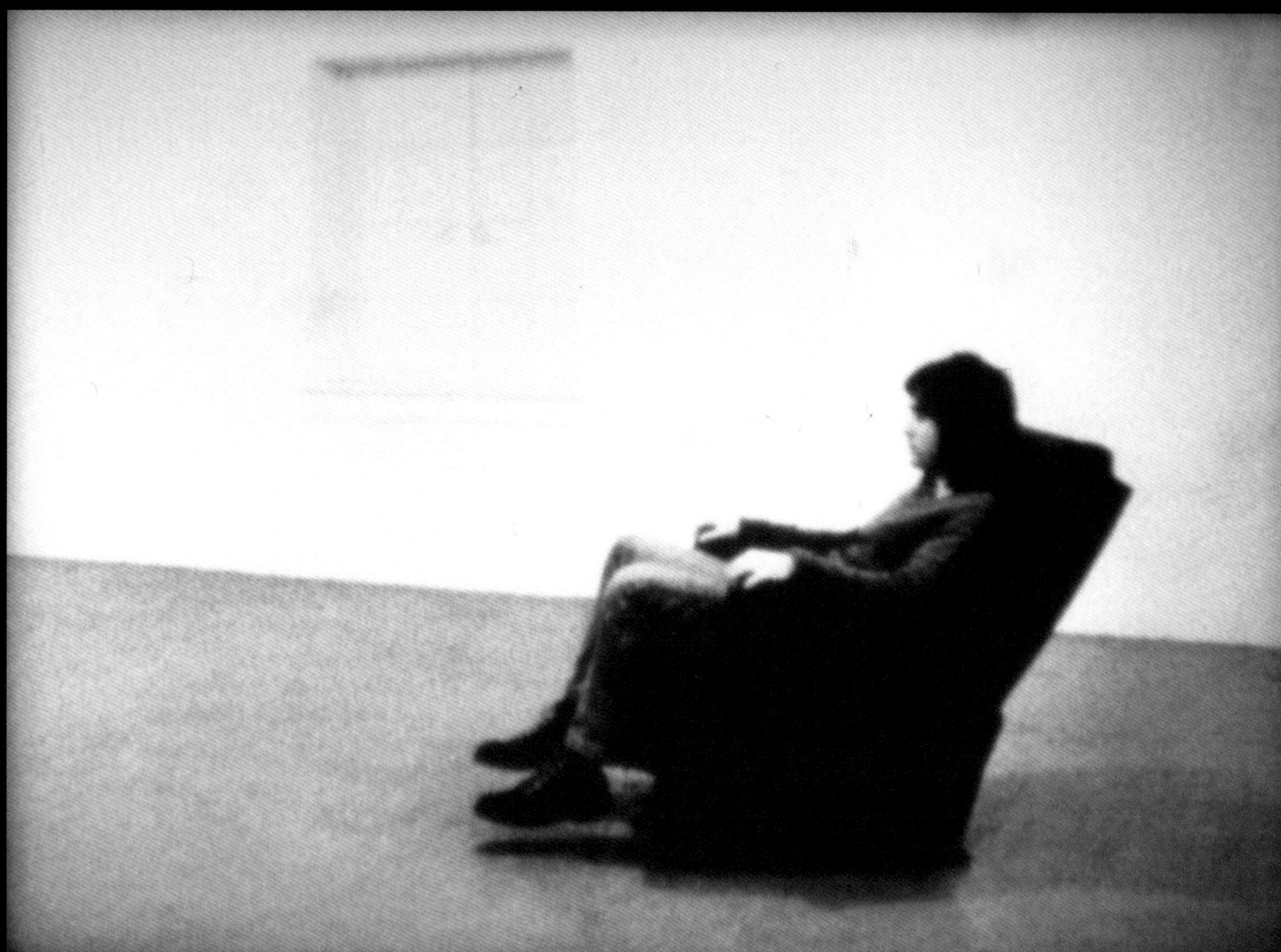

Stills from Jack Goldstein, *Rocking Chair*, 1972

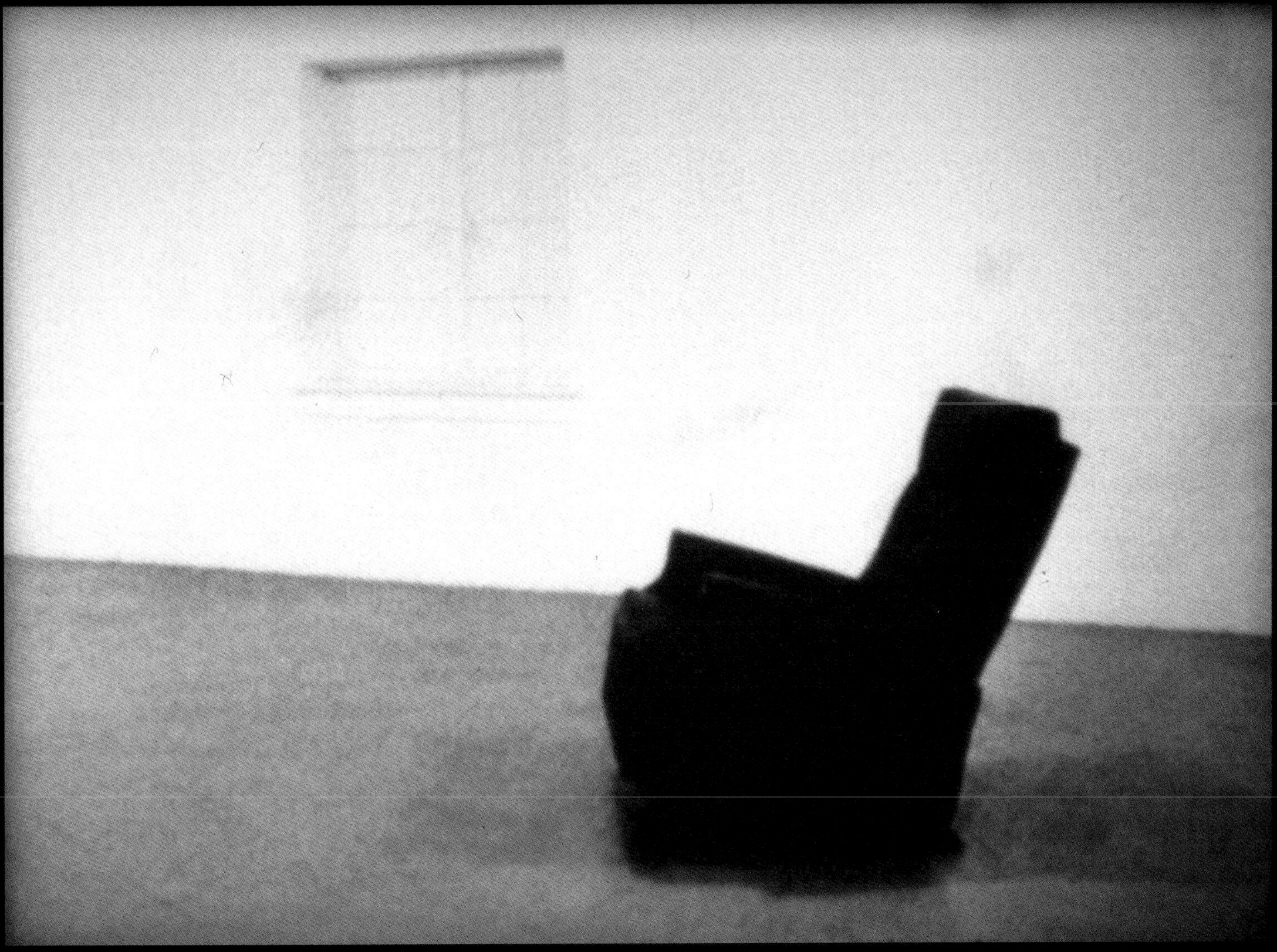

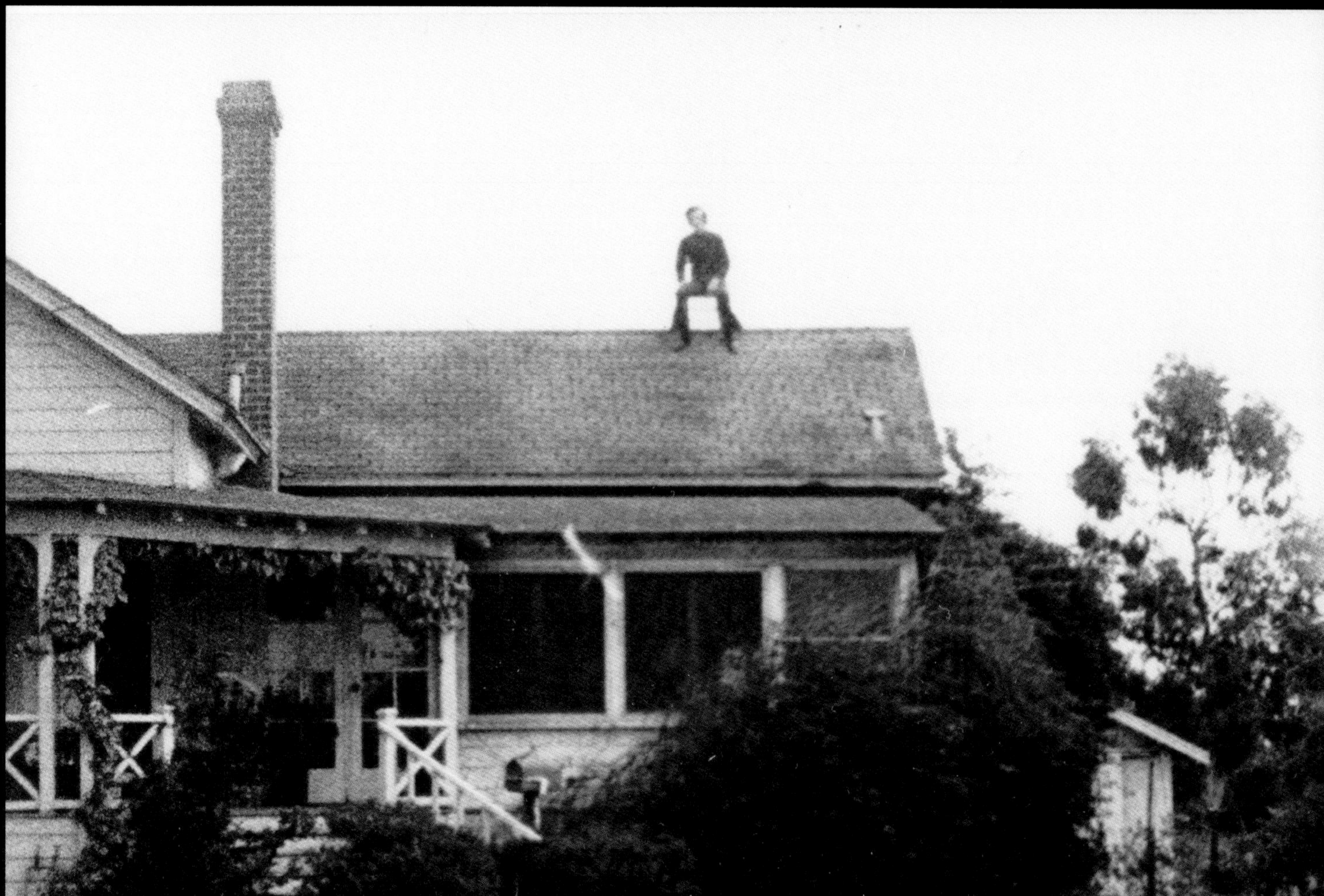

Stills from Bas Jan Ader, *Fall 1, Los Angeles*, 1970

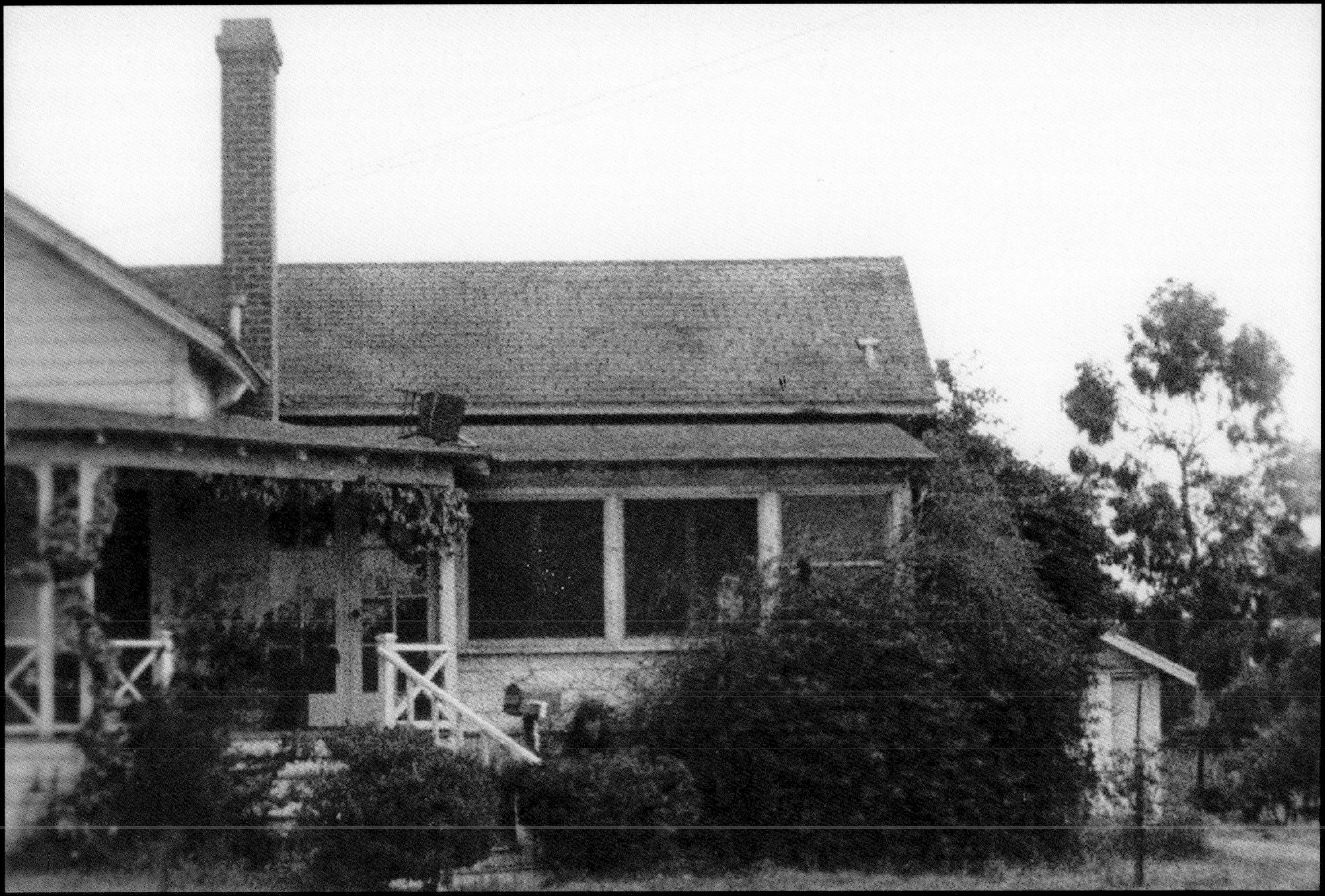

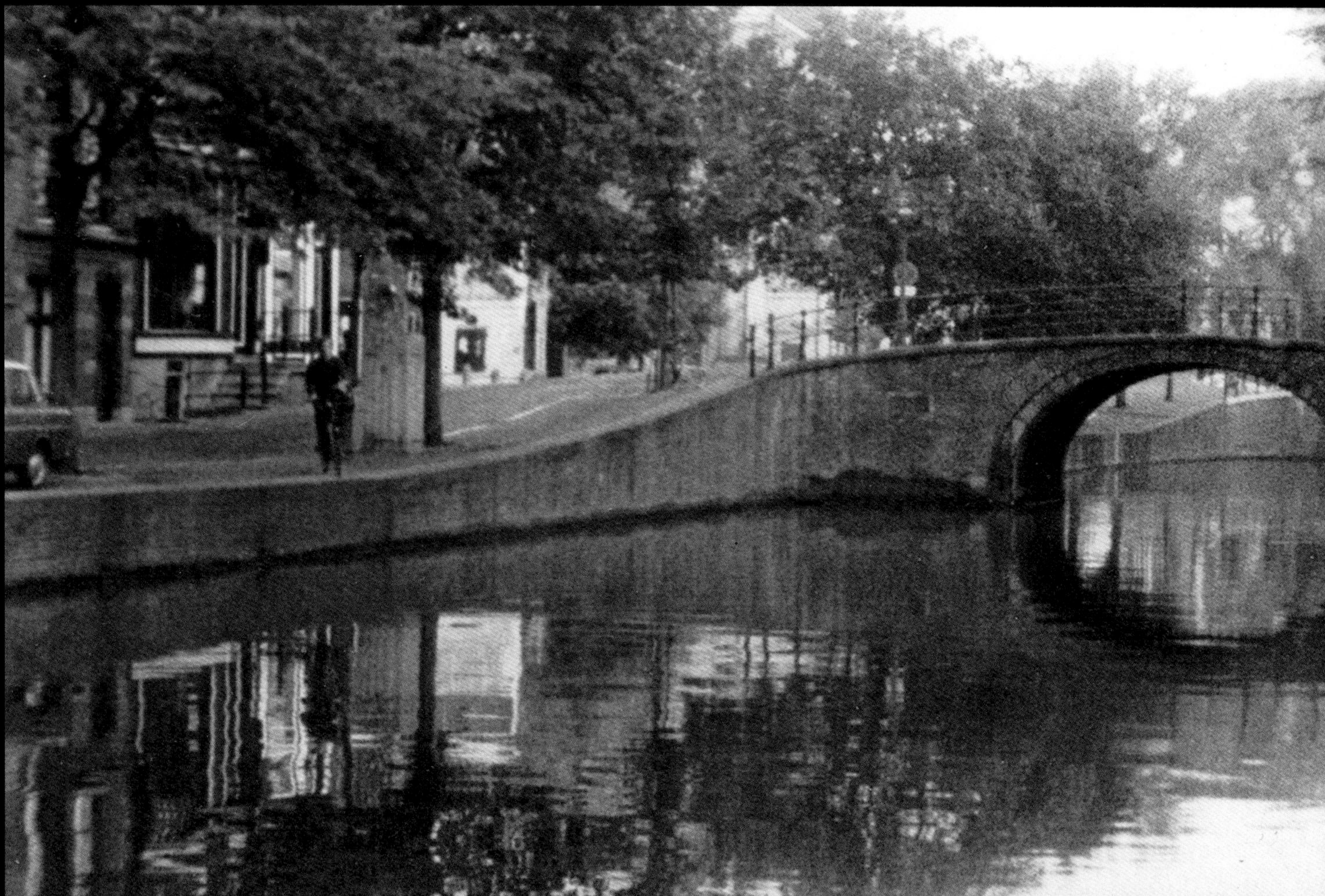

Stills from Bas Jan Ader, *Fall 2, Amsterdam*, 1970

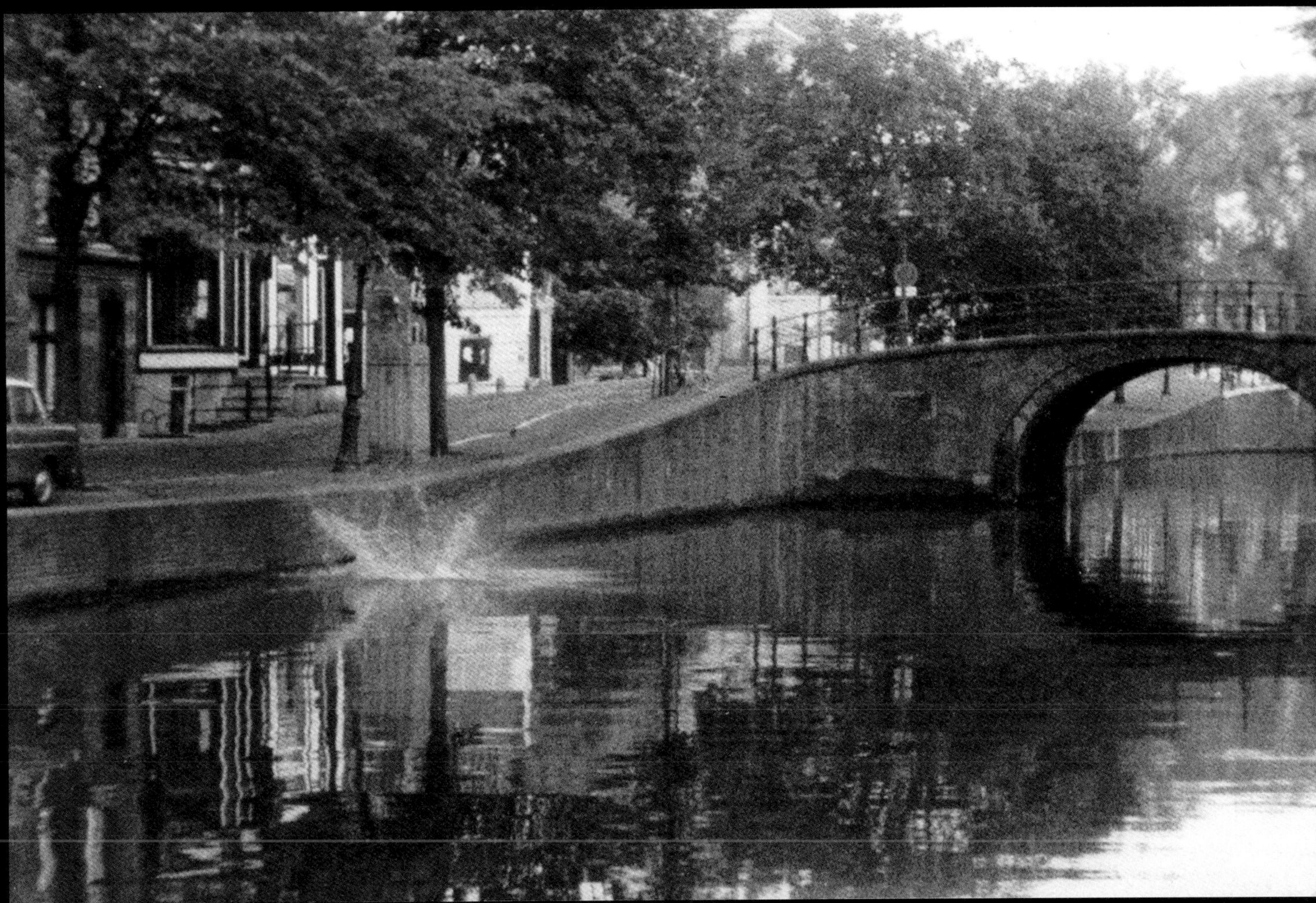

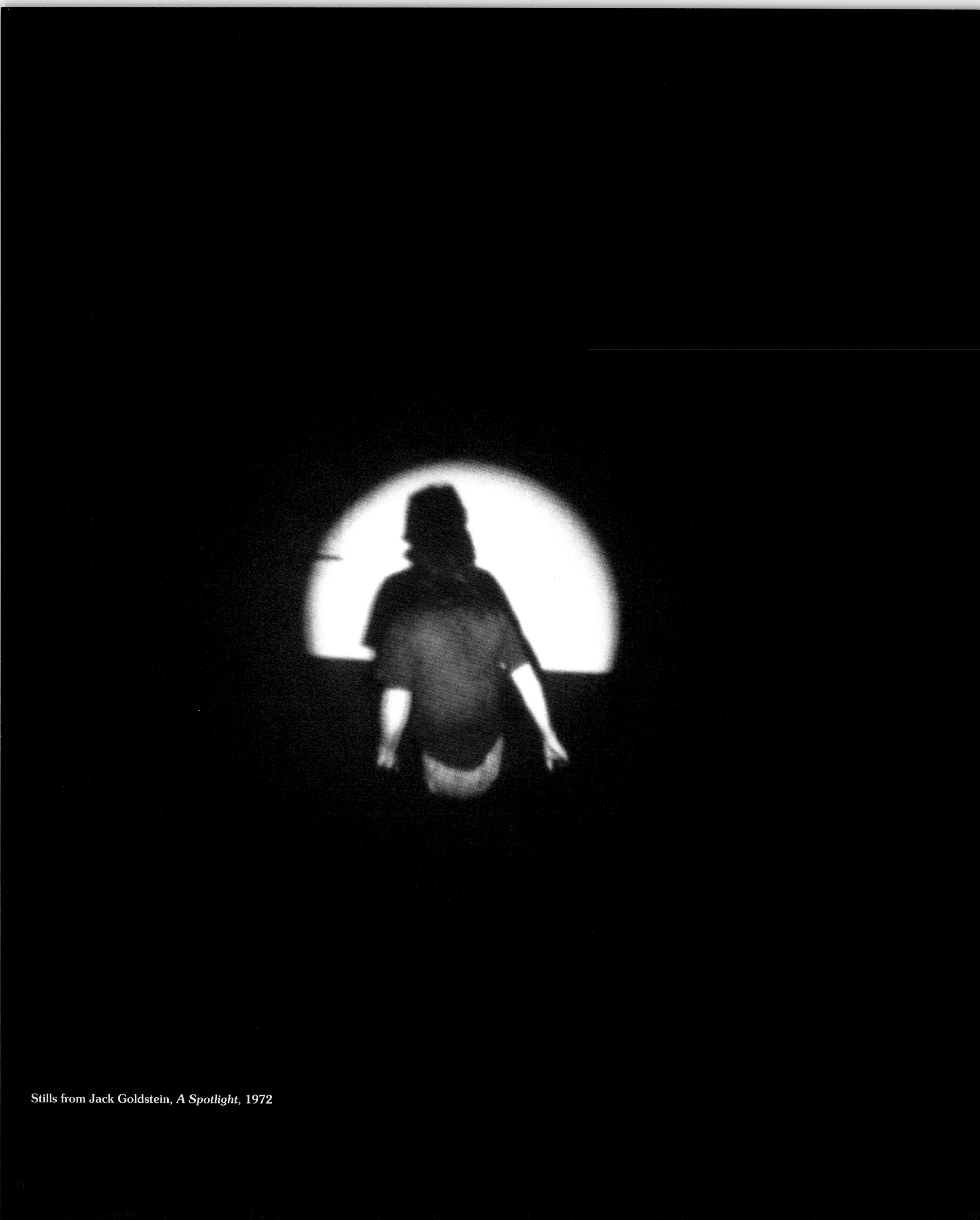

Stills from Jack Goldstein, *A Spotlight*, 1972

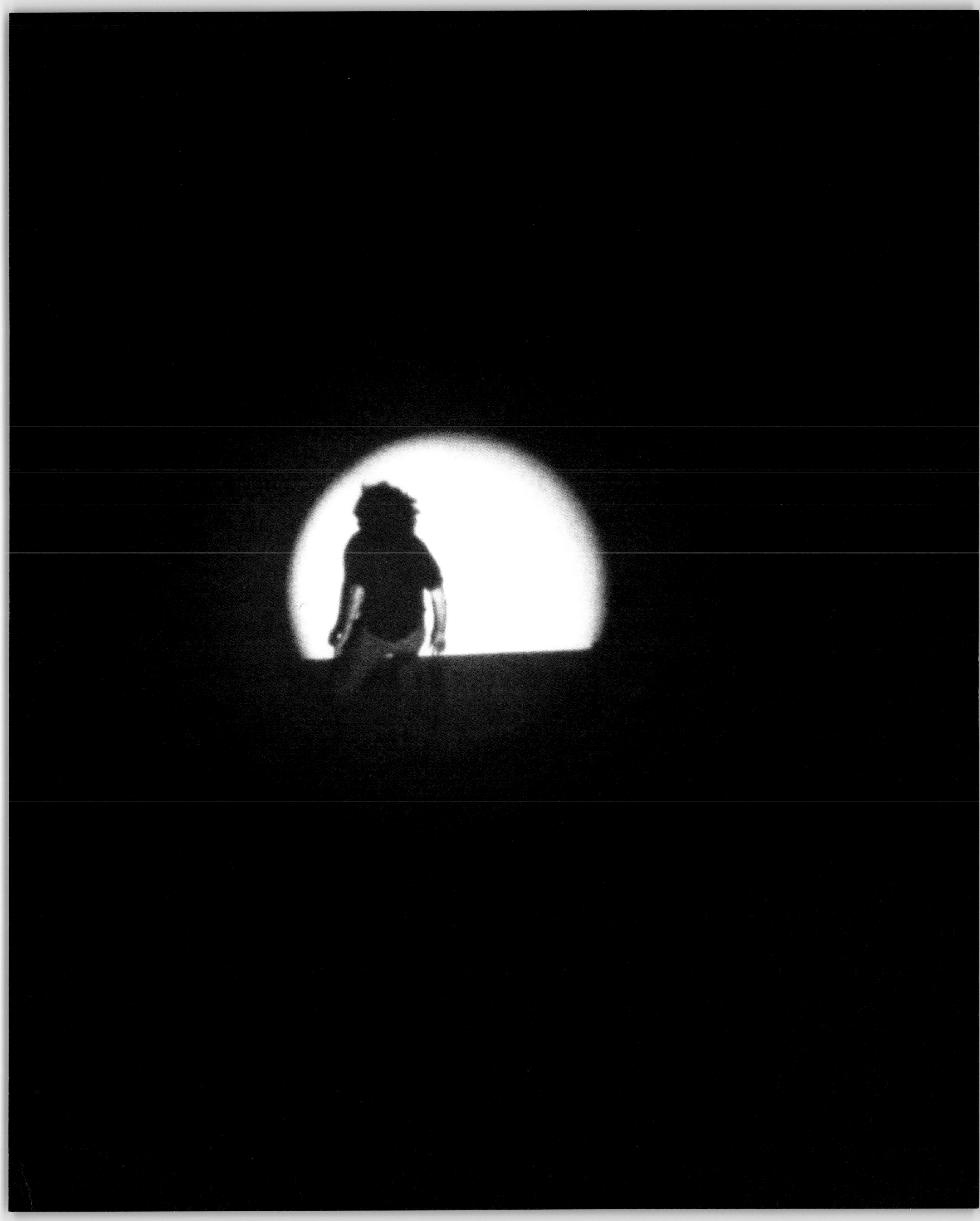

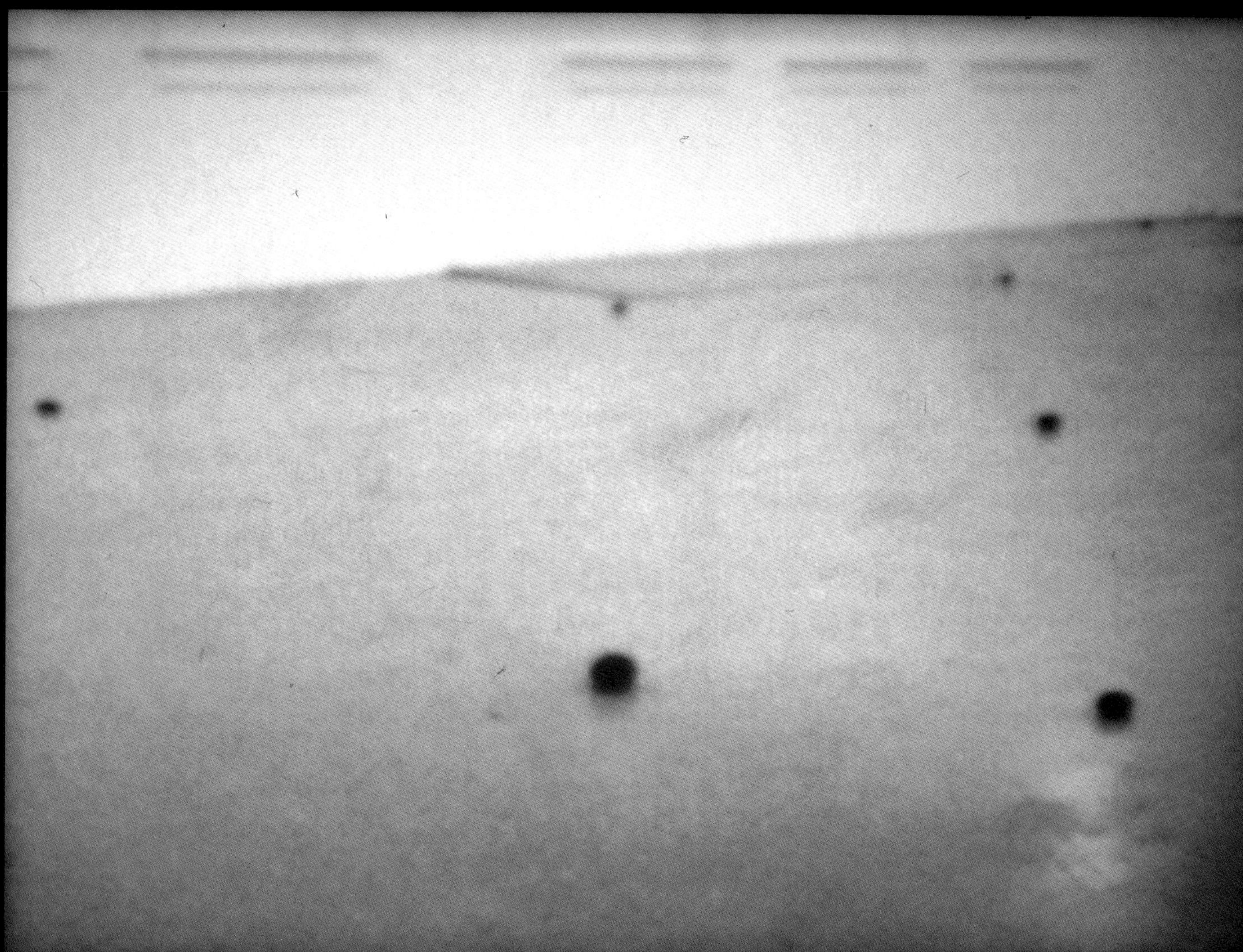

Stills from Jack Goldstein, *Here*, 1973

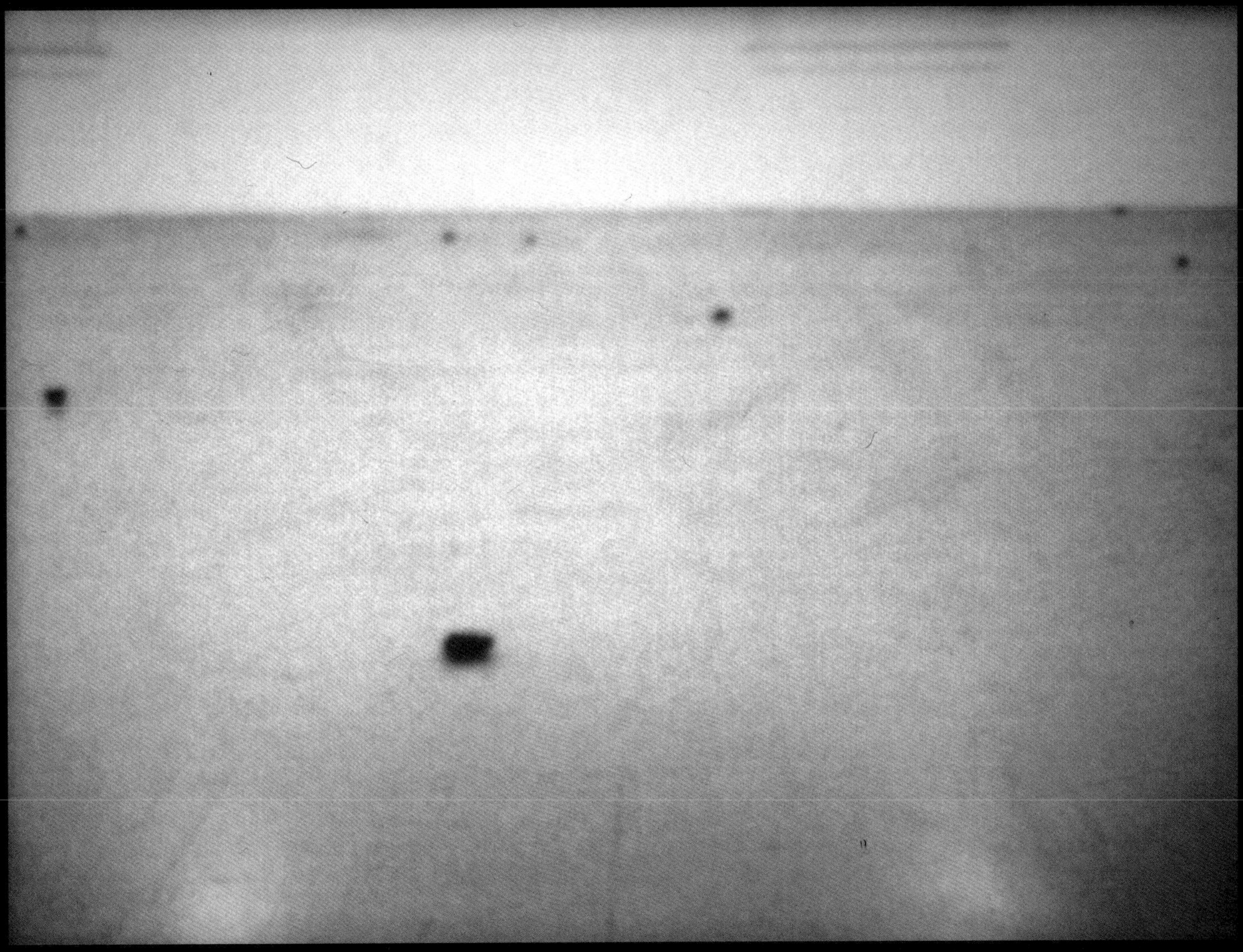

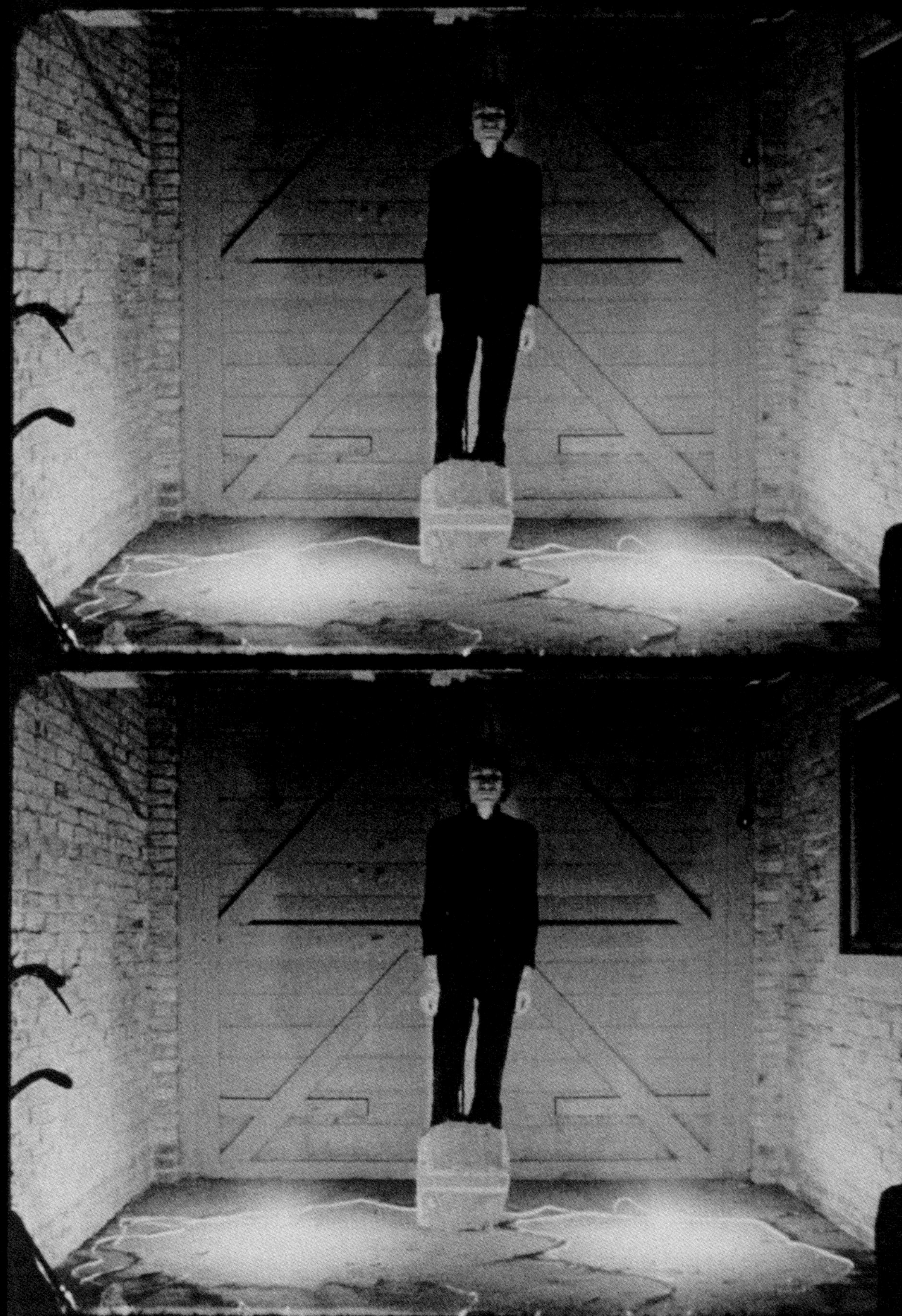

ABOVE AND FOLLOWING SPREAD
Stills from Bas Jan Ader, *Nightfall*, 1971

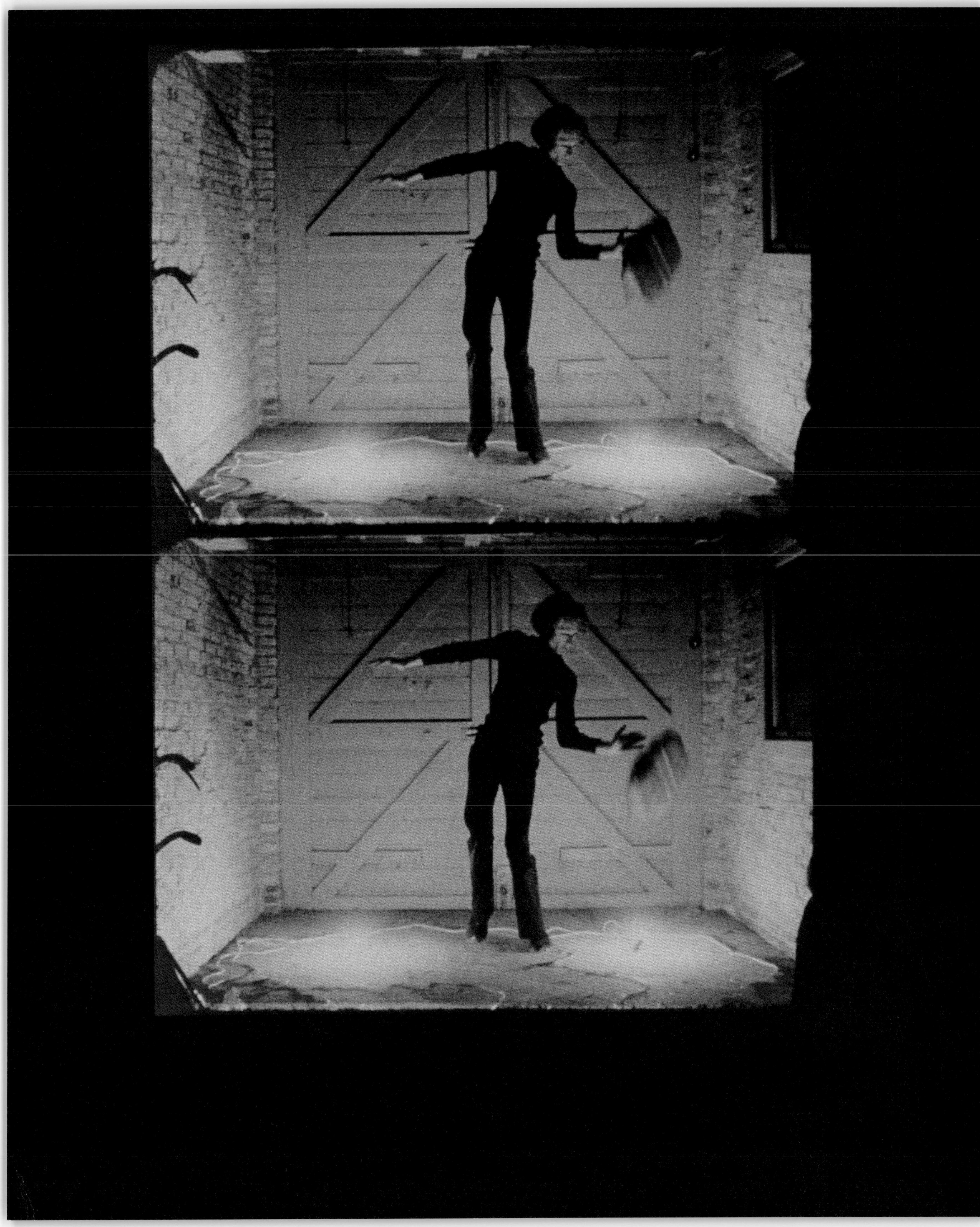

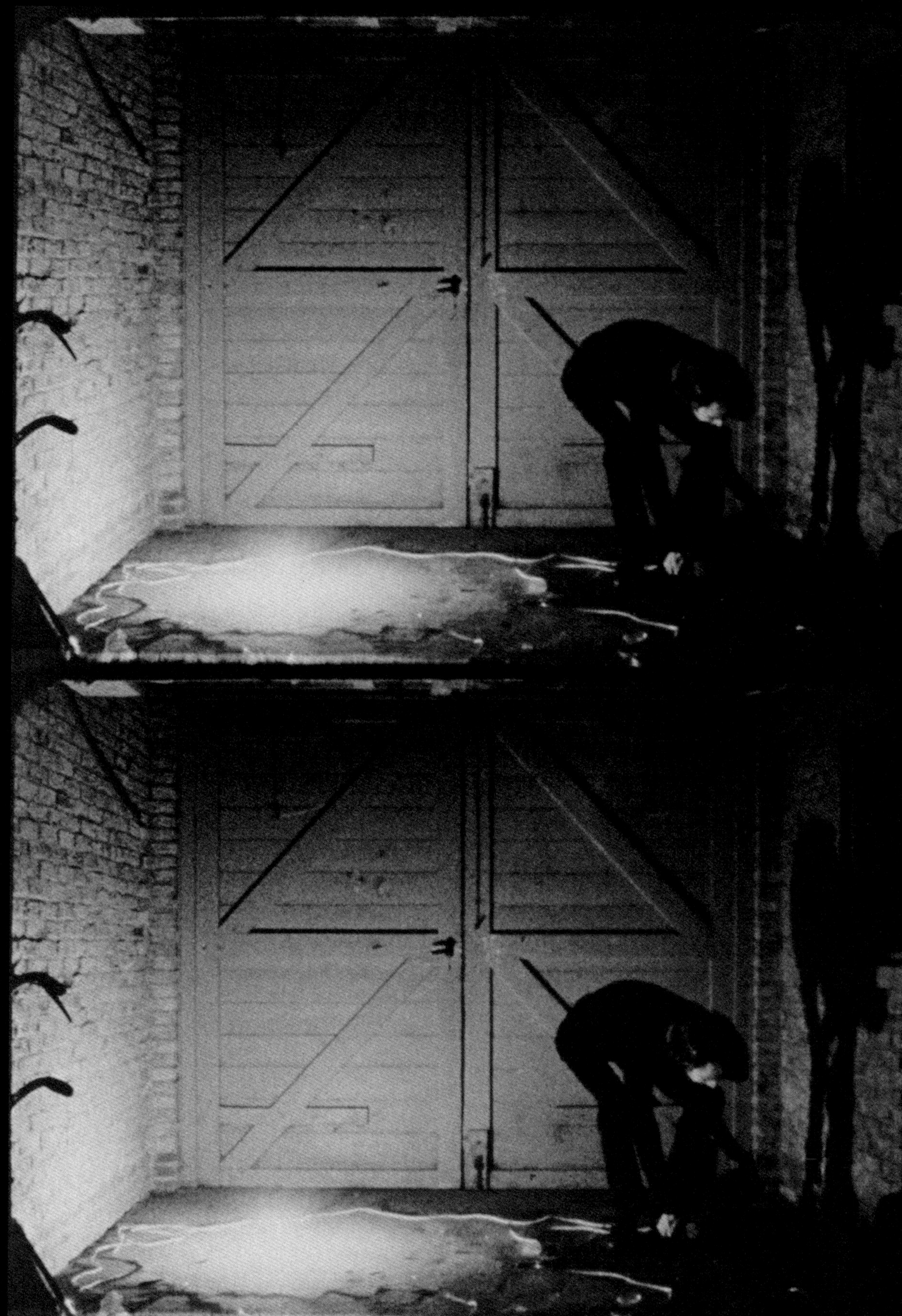

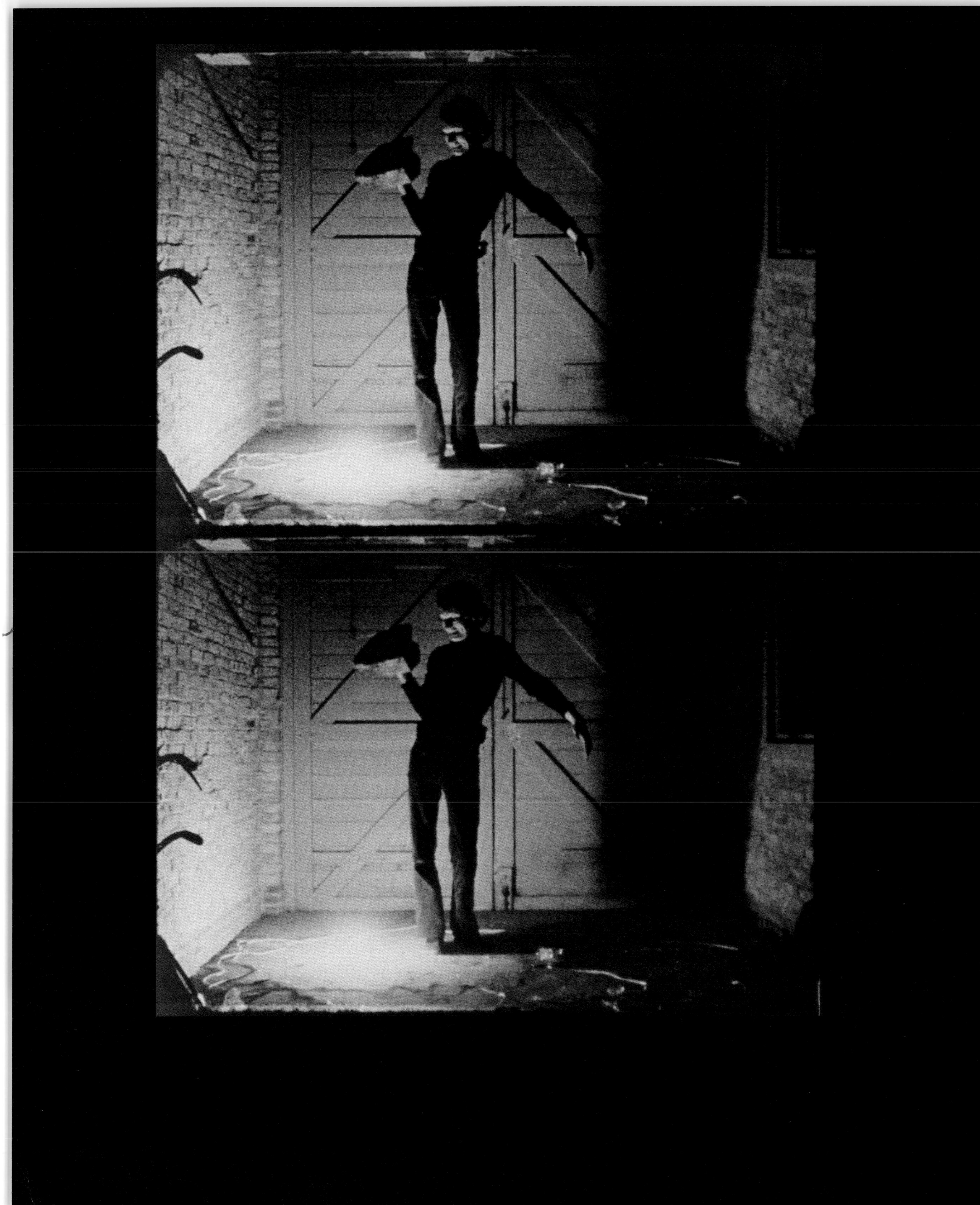

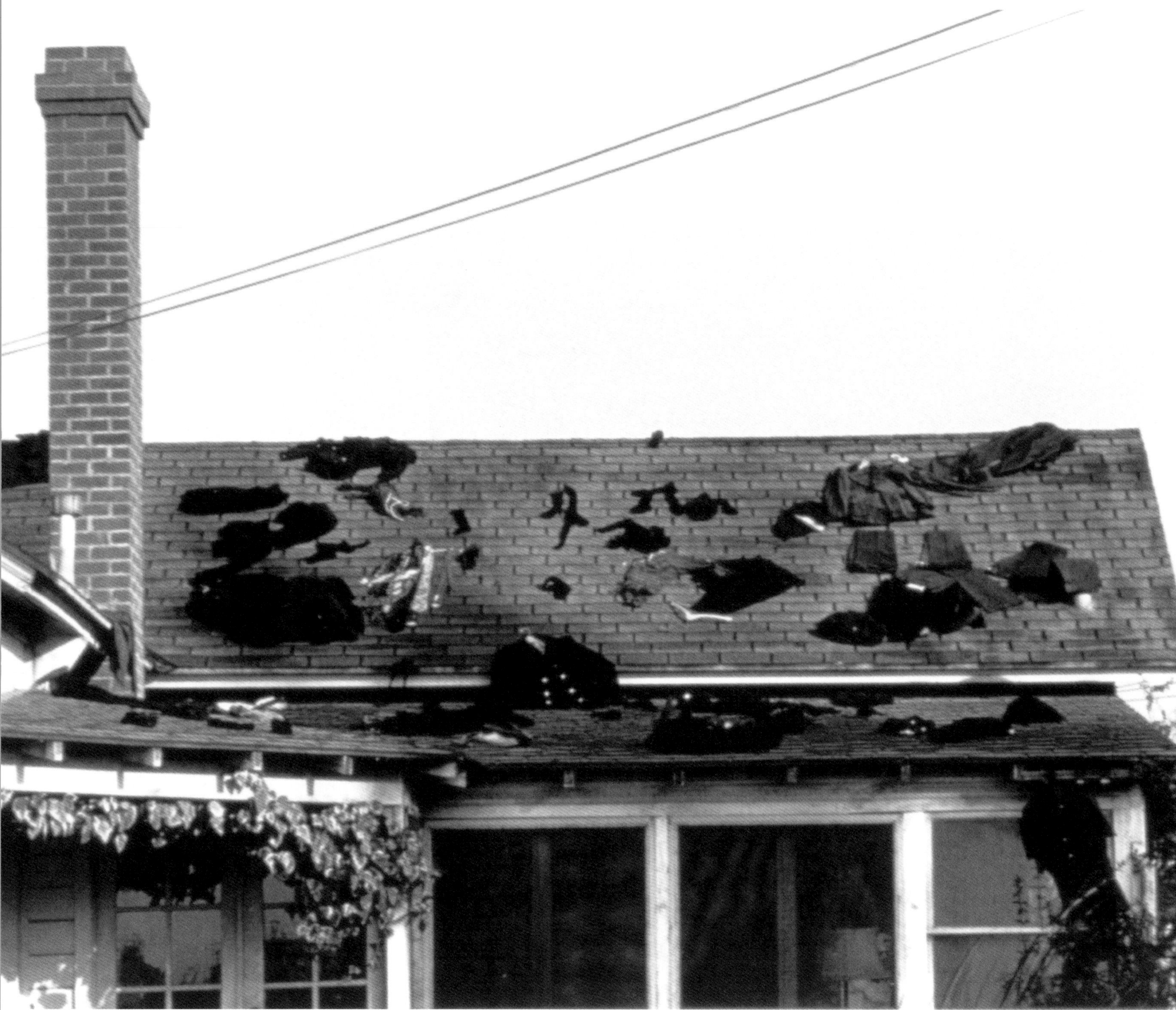

Bas Jan Ader, *All my clothes*, 1970

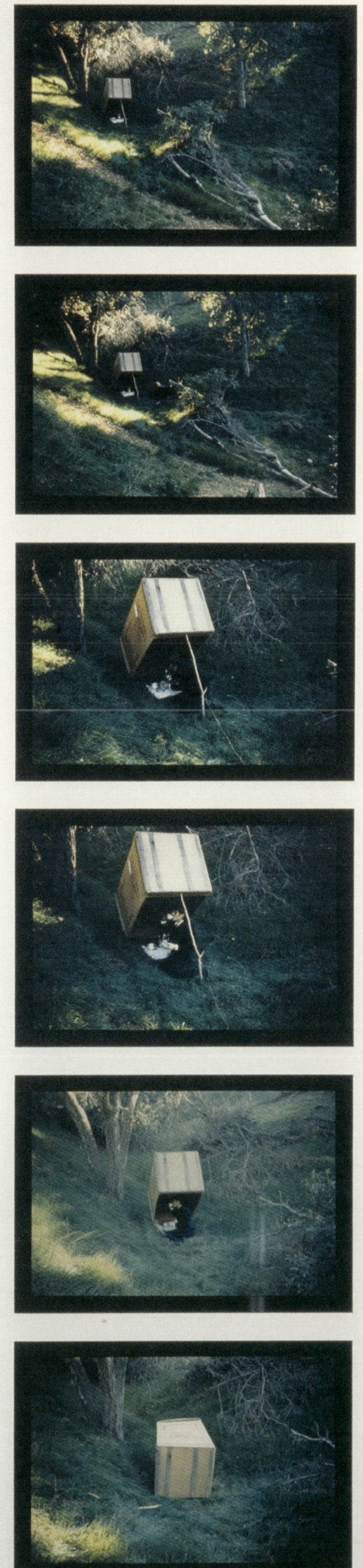

Bas Jan Ader, *Untitled (Tea party)*, 1972

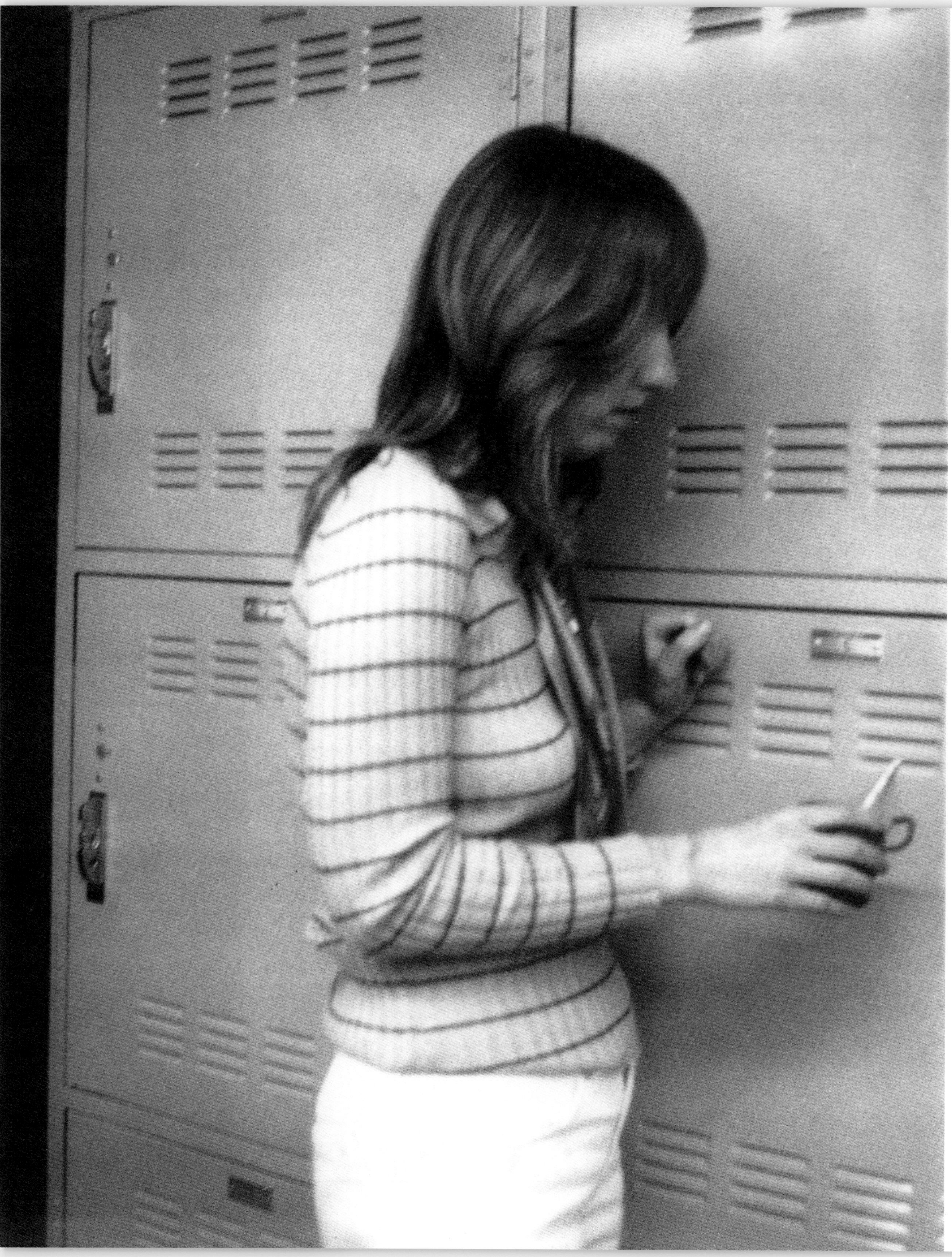

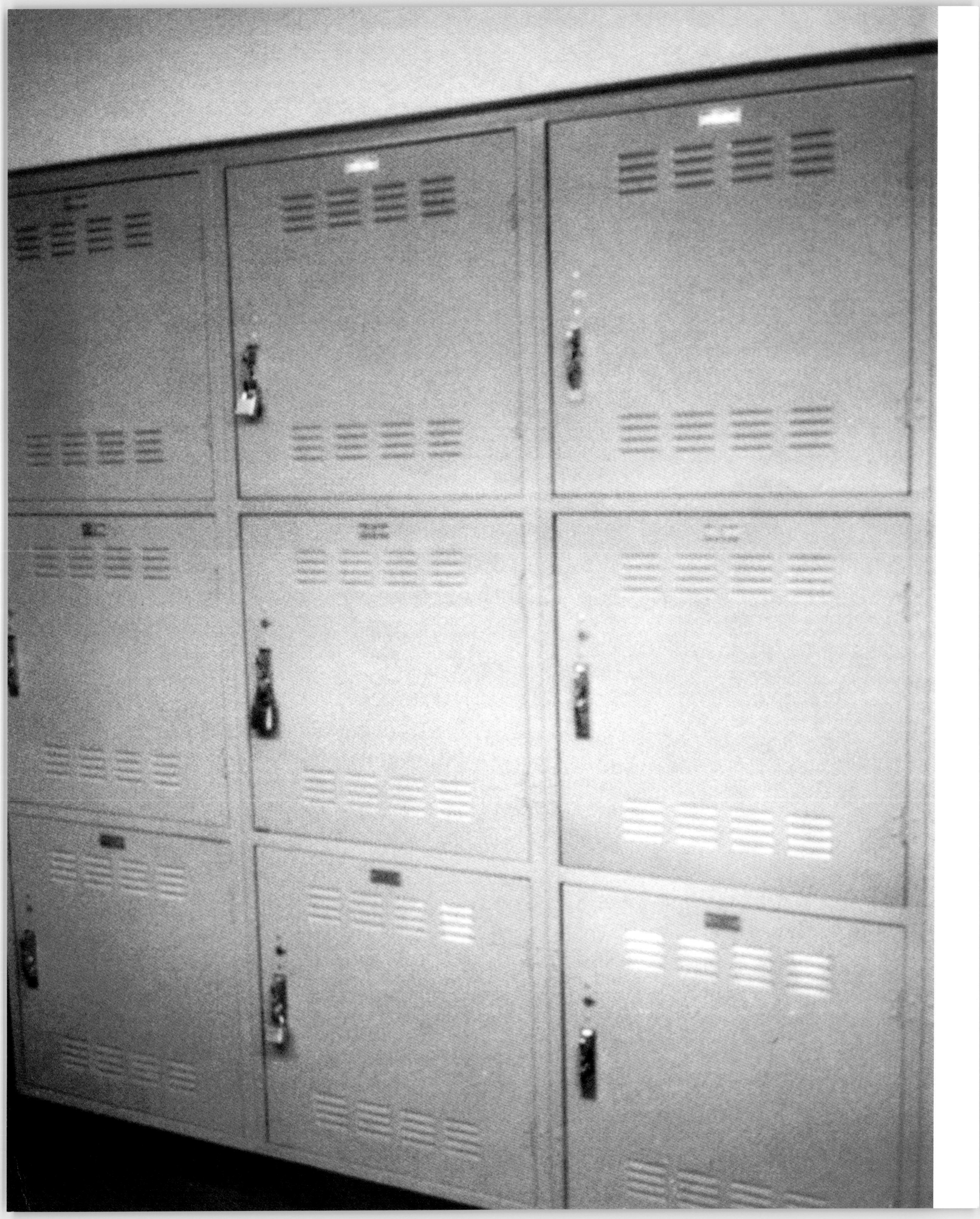

Five Day Locker Piece

University of California, Irvine: April 26–30, 1971

I was locked in locker number 5 for five consecutive days and did not leave the locker during this time. The locker measured two feet high, two feet wide, and three feet deep. I stopped eating several days prior to entry. The locker directly above me contained five gallons of bottled water; the locker below me contained an empty five gallon bottle.

PREVIOUS SPREAD
Chris Burden, *Five Day Locker Piece*, 1971
University of California, Irvine: April 26–30, 1971

RIGHT
Chris Burden, *Five Day Locker Piece*, 1971
Relic: Padlock

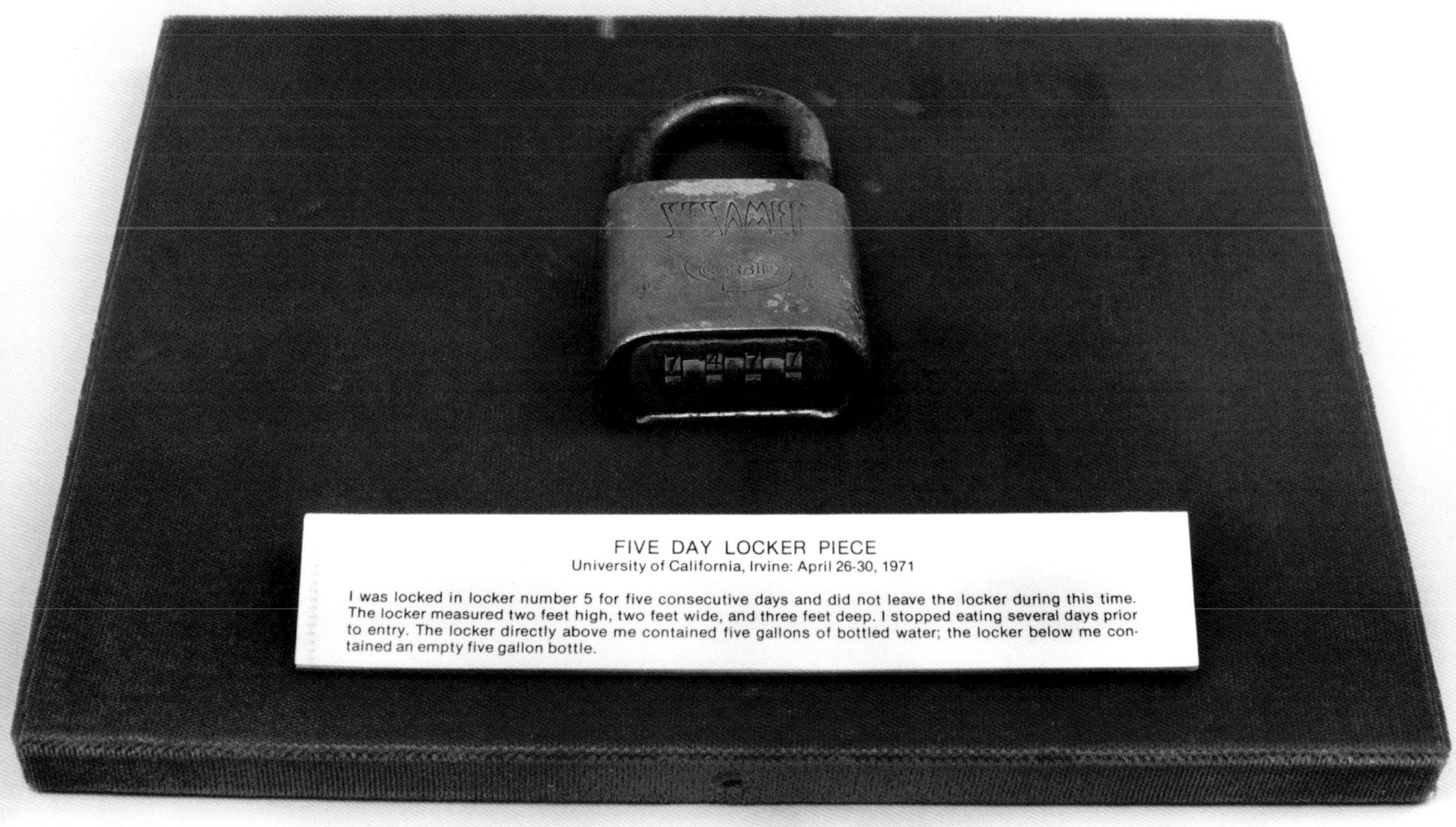
FIVE DAY LOCKER PIECE
University of California, Irvine: April 26-30, 1971
I was locked in locker number 5 for five consecutive days and did not leave the locker during this time. The locker measured two feet high, two feet wide, and three feet deep. I stopped eating several days prior to entry. The locker directly above me contained five gallons of bottled water; the locker below me contained an empty five gallon bottle.

You'll Never See My Face in Kansas City
Morgan Gallery, Kansas City, Missouri: November 6, 1971

For three hours I sat without moving behind a panel which concealed my neck and head. No one could see behind the panel; a piece of board sealed the underside of the space. In conjunction with the performance, I wore a ski mask at all times during my stay in Kansas City from November 5–7, 1971.

Chris Burden, *You'll Never See My Face in Kansas City*, 1971
Relic: Ski mask

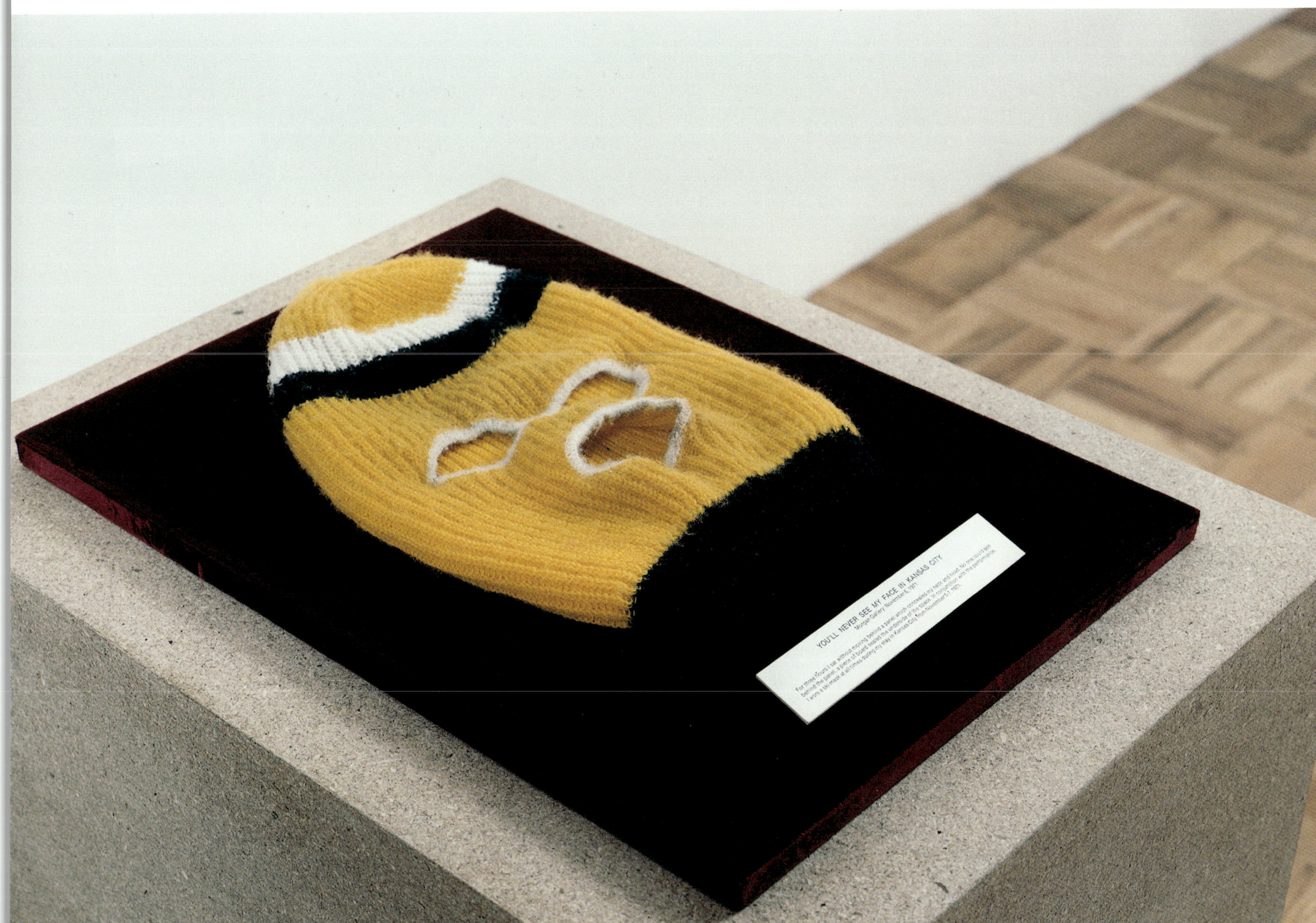
YOU'LL NEVER SEE MY FACE IN KANSAS CITY
Morgan Gallery, November 6, 1971

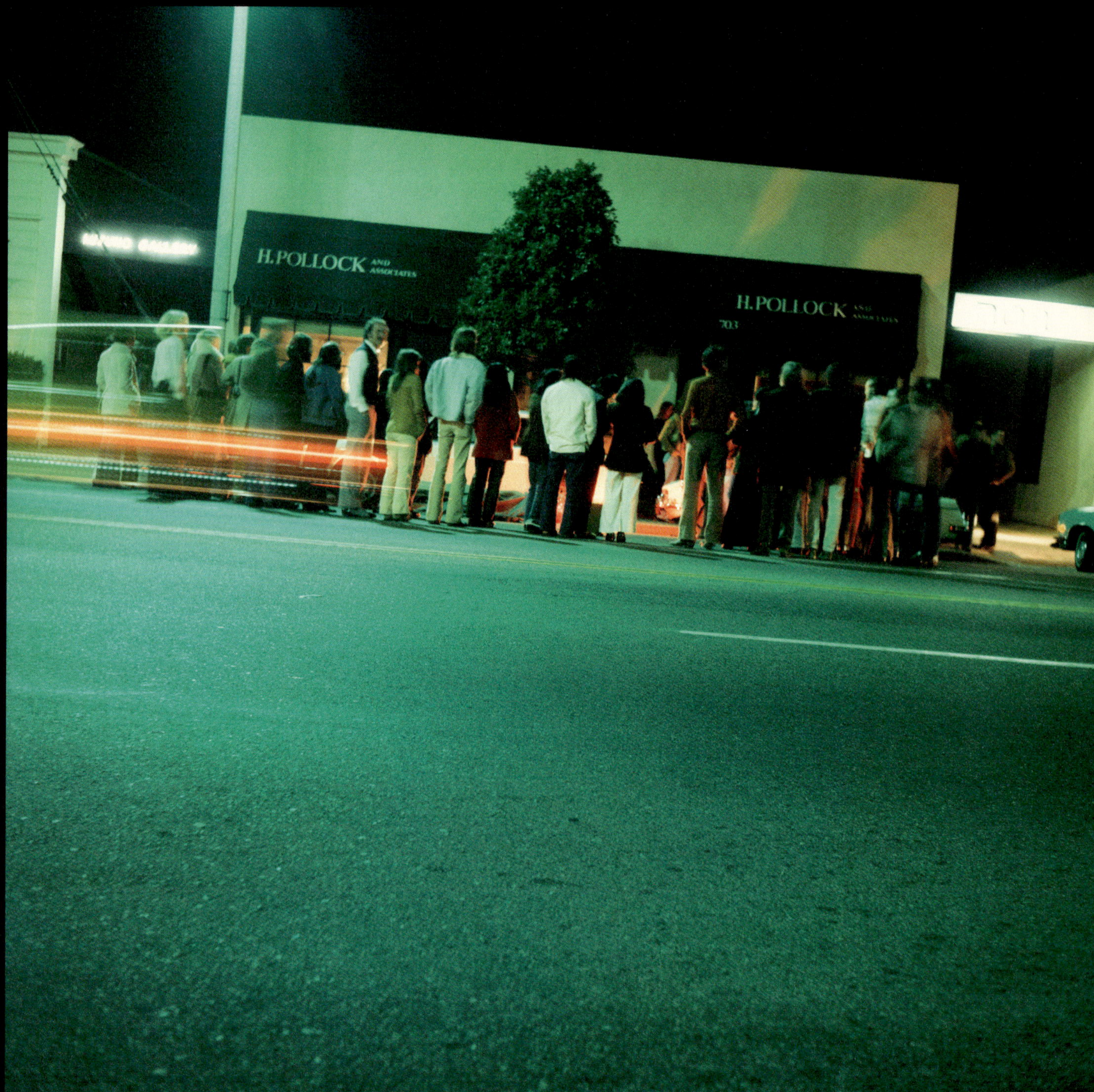
H.POLLOCK AND ASSOCIATES
H.POLLOCK
703

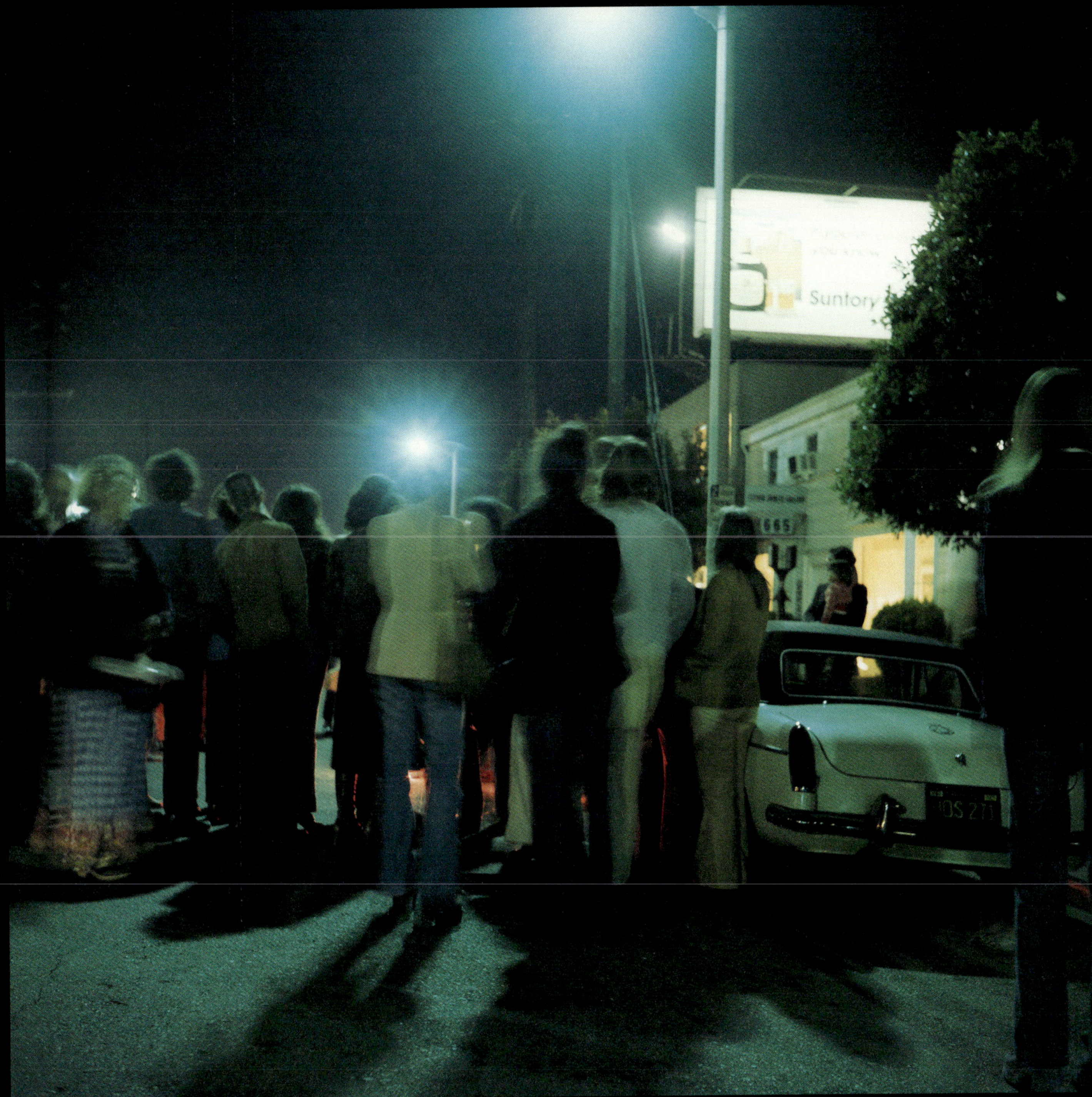
Suntory

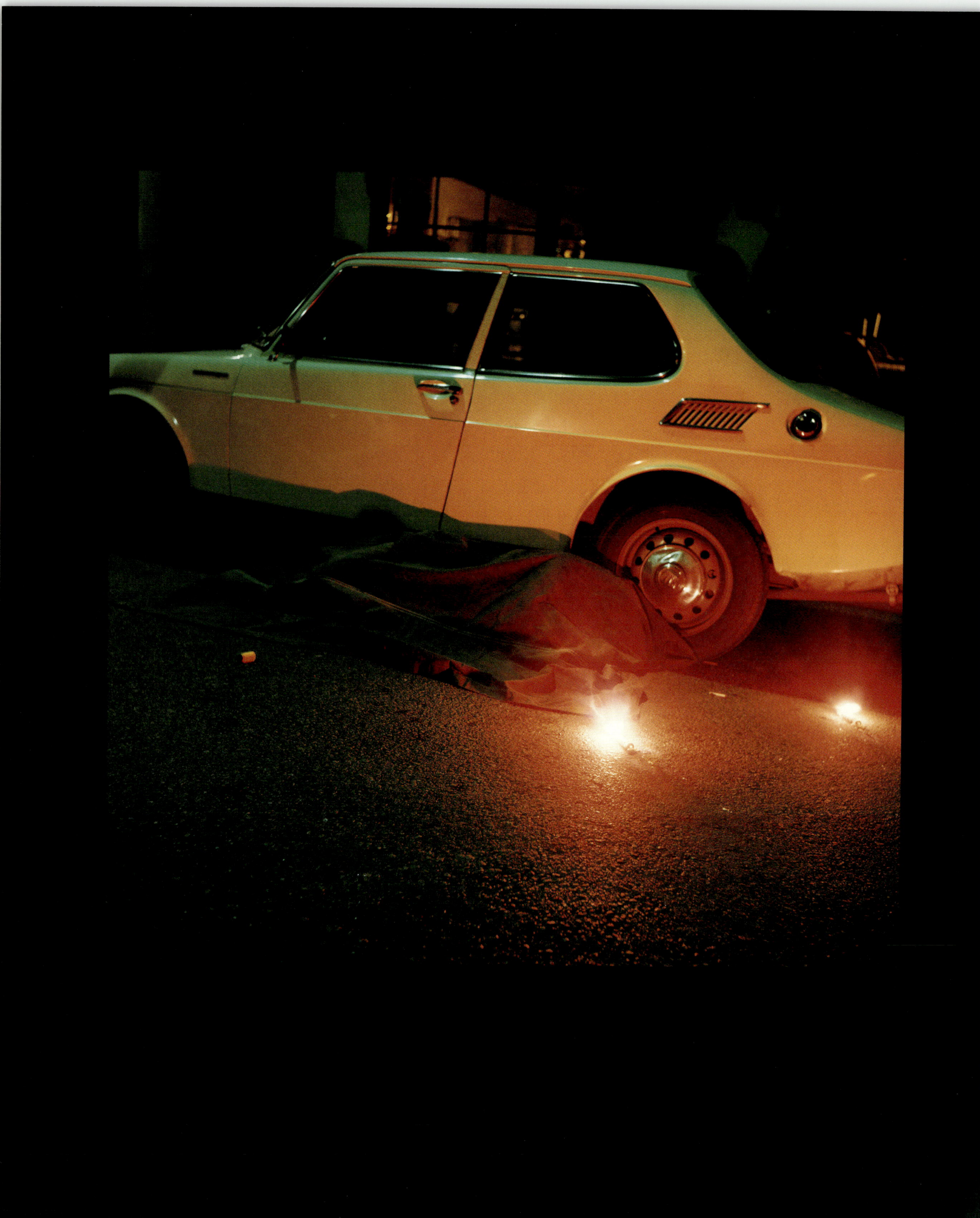

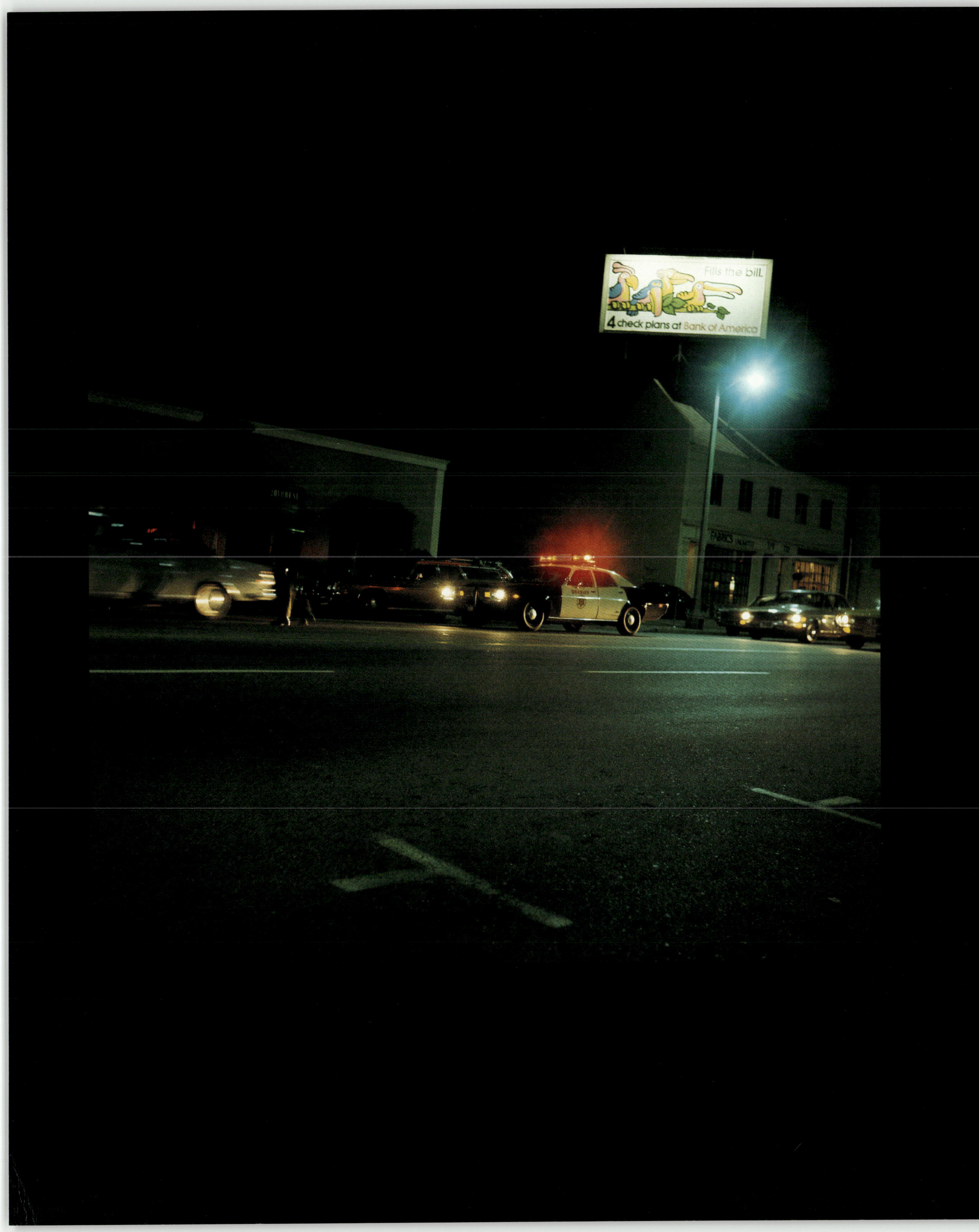
Fills the bill.
4 check plans at Bank of America

Deadman

Riko Mizuno Gallery, Los Angeles, California: November 12, 1972

At 8 p.m. I lay down on La Cienega Boulevard and was covered completely with a canvas tarpaulin. Two fifteen-minute flares were placed near me to alert cars. Just before the flares extinguished, a police car arrived. I was arrested and booked for causing a false emergency to be reported. Trial took place in Beverly Hills. After three days of deliberation, the jury failed to reach a decision, and the judge dismissed the case.

PREVIOUS TWO SPREADS
Chris Burden, *Deadman*, 1972
Riko Mizuno Gallery, Los Angeles, California: November 12, 1972

RIGHT
Chris Burden, *Deadman*, 1972
Relic: Canvas tarpaulin

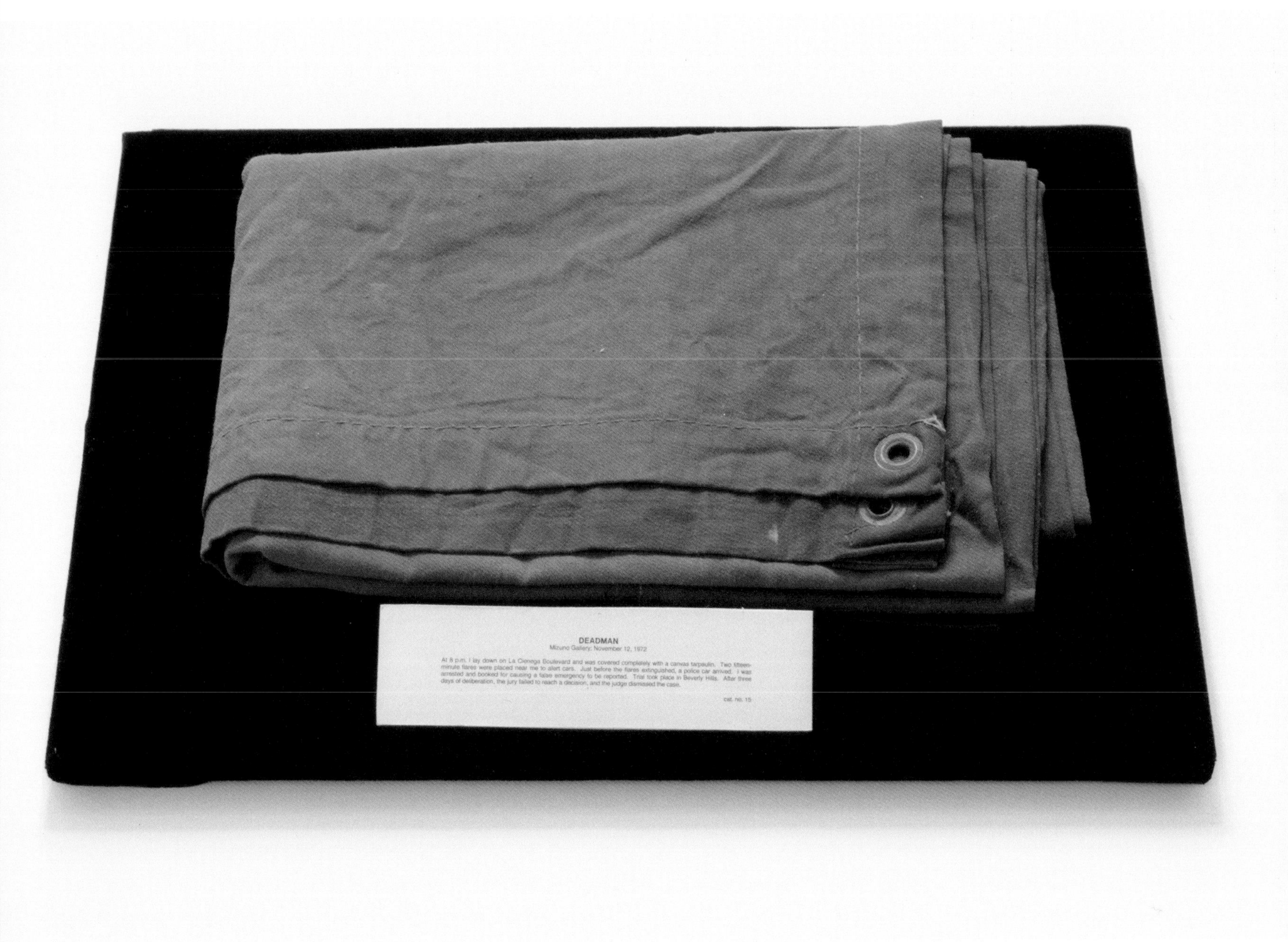
DEADMAN
Mizuno Gallery, November 12, 1972
At 8 p.m. I lay down on La Cienega Boulevard and was covered completely with a canvas tarpaulin. Two fifteen-minute flares were placed near me to alert cars. Just before the flares extinguished, a police car arrived. I was arrested and booked for causing a false emergency to be reported. Trial took place in Beverly Hills. After three days of deliberation, the jury failed to reach a decision, and the judge dismissed the case.
cat. no. 15

Poster for Jack Goldstein's performance *Burial Piece*, California Institute of the Arts, Valencia, June 9, 1972

JACK GOLDSTEIN PERFORMANCE JUNE 9 8 PM

GALLERY A-402
HOURS 12-5 PM TUES-FRI
California Institute of the Arts
24700 McBean Parkway
Valencia California 91355

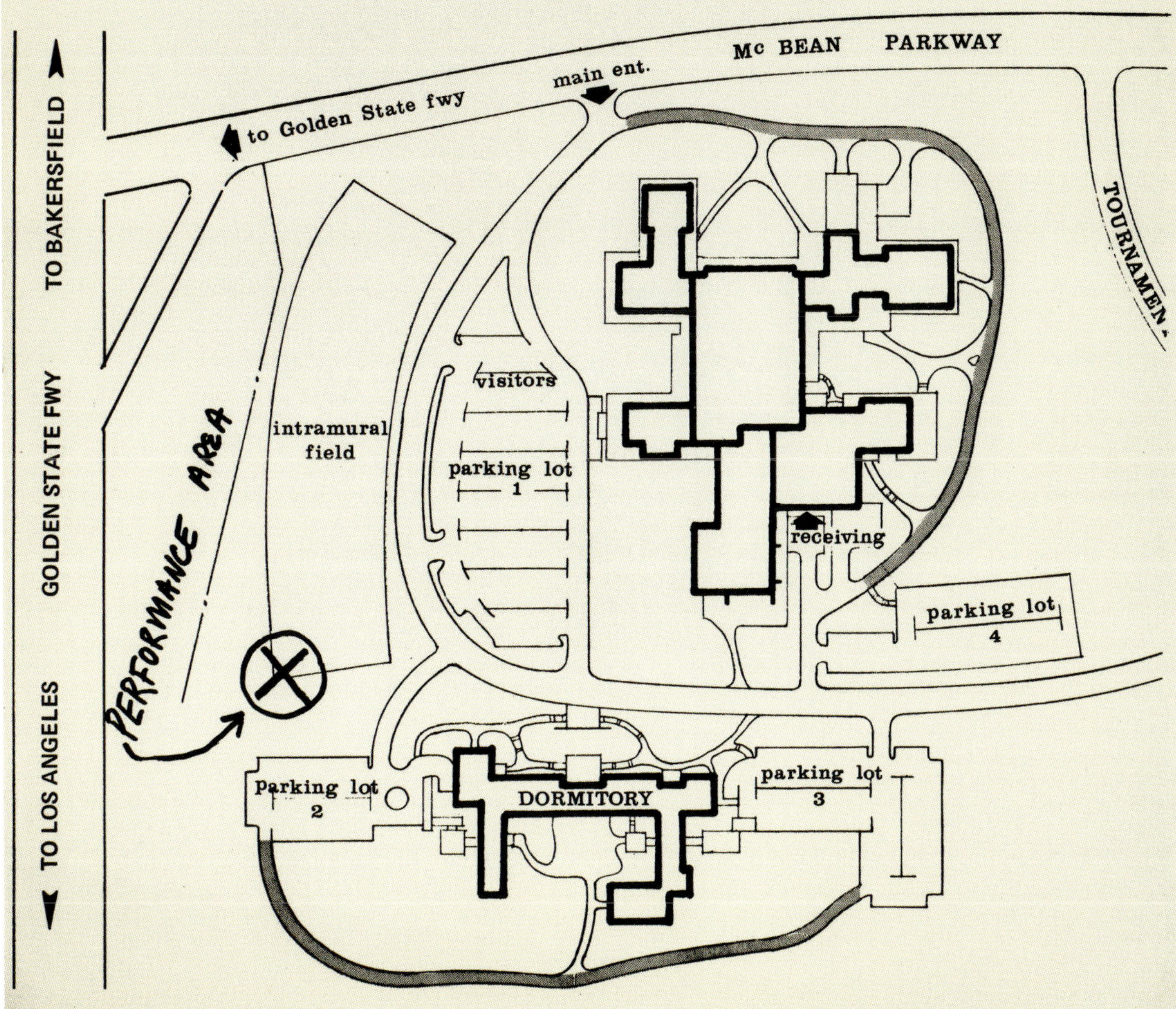

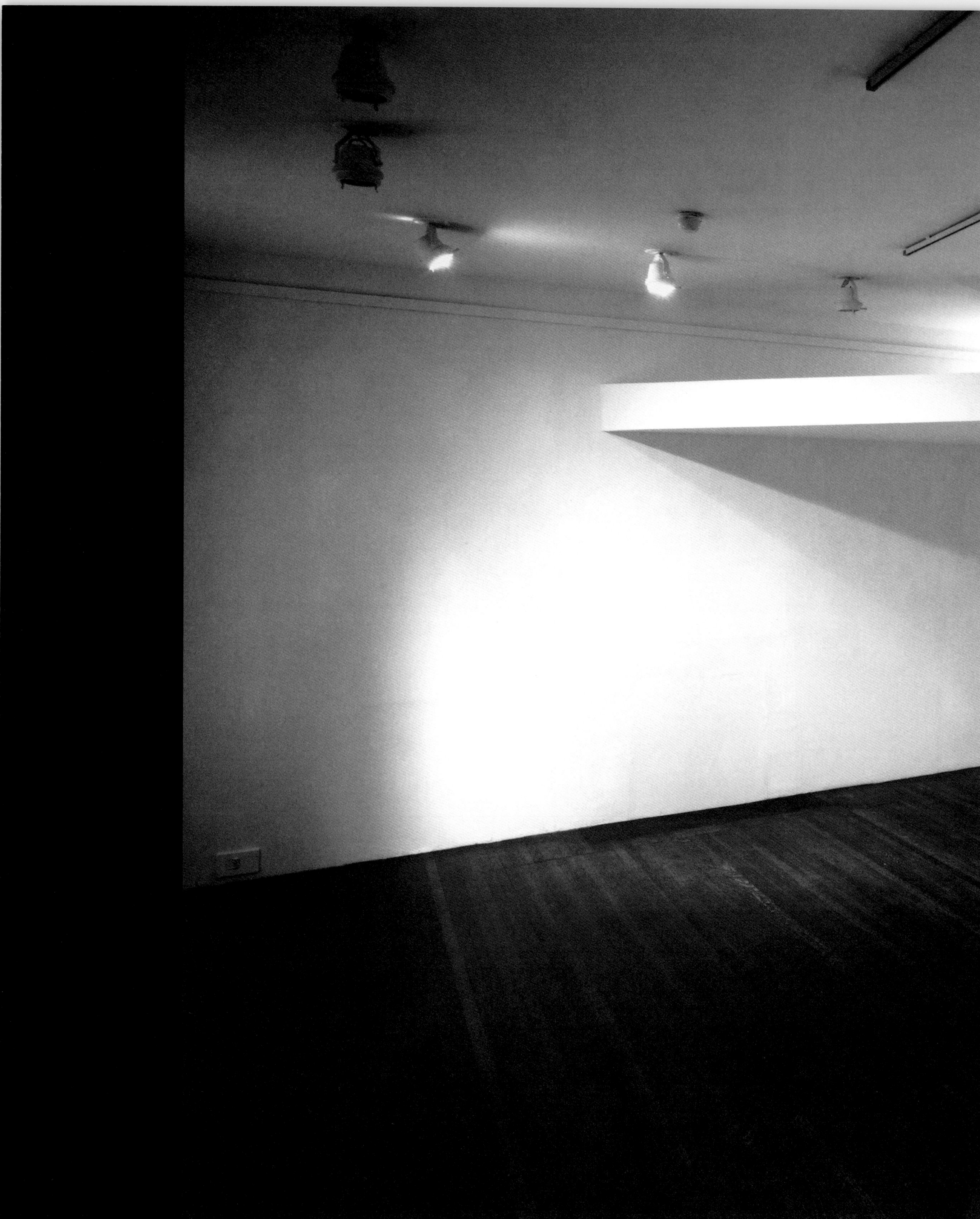

White Light/White Heat

Ronald Feldman Fine Arts, New York, New York:
February 8–March 1, 1975

For my one-man show at Ronald Feldman, I requested that a large triangular platform be constructed in the southeast corner of the gallery. The platform was ten feet above the floor and two feet below the ceiling; the outer edge measured eighteen feet across. The size and height of the platform were determined by the requirement that I be able to lie flat without being visible from any point in the gallery. For twenty-two days, the duration of the show, I lay on the platform. During the entire piece, I did not eat, talk, or come down. I did not see anyone, and no one saw me.

PREVIOUS SPREAD
Chris Burden, *White Light/White Heat*, 1975
Ronald Feldman Fine Arts, New York, New York: February 8–March 1, 1975

RIGHT
Chris Burden, *White Light/White Heat*, 1975
Relic: Section of board

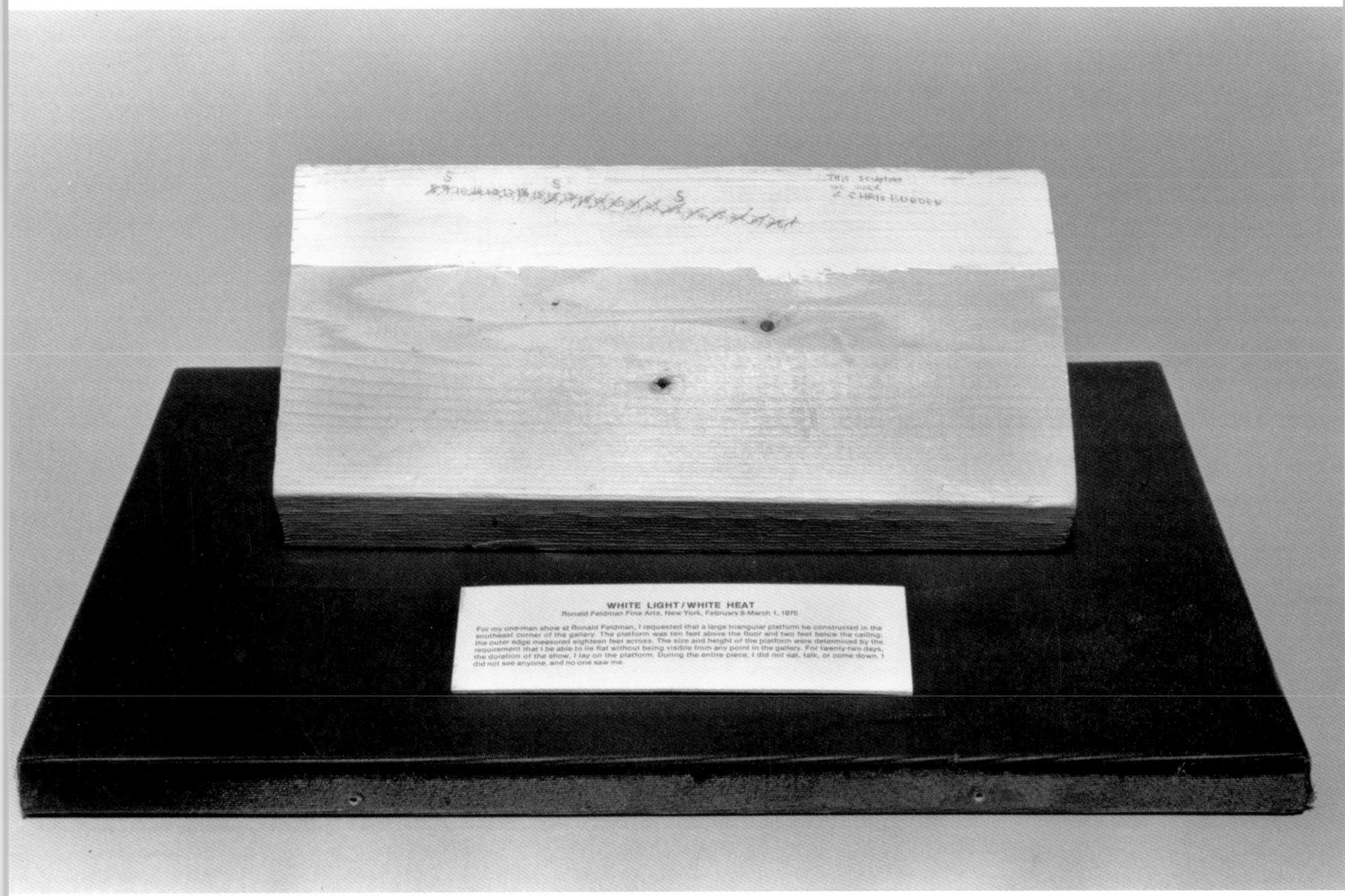
WHITE LIGHT / WHITE HEAT
Ronald Feldman Fine Arts, New York, February 8–March 1, 1975
For my one-man show at Ronald Feldman, I requested that a large triangular platform be constructed in the southeast corner of the gallery. The platform was ten feet above the floor and two feet below the ceiling; the outer edge measured eighteen feet across. The size and height of the platform were determined by the requirement that I be able to lie flat without being visible from any point in the gallery. For twenty-two days, the duration of the show, I lay on the platform. During the entire piece, I did not eat, talk, or come down. I did not see anyone, and no one saw me.

Chris Burden, *B.C. Mexico*, 1973
Newspace, Newport Beach, California: May 25–June 10, 1973

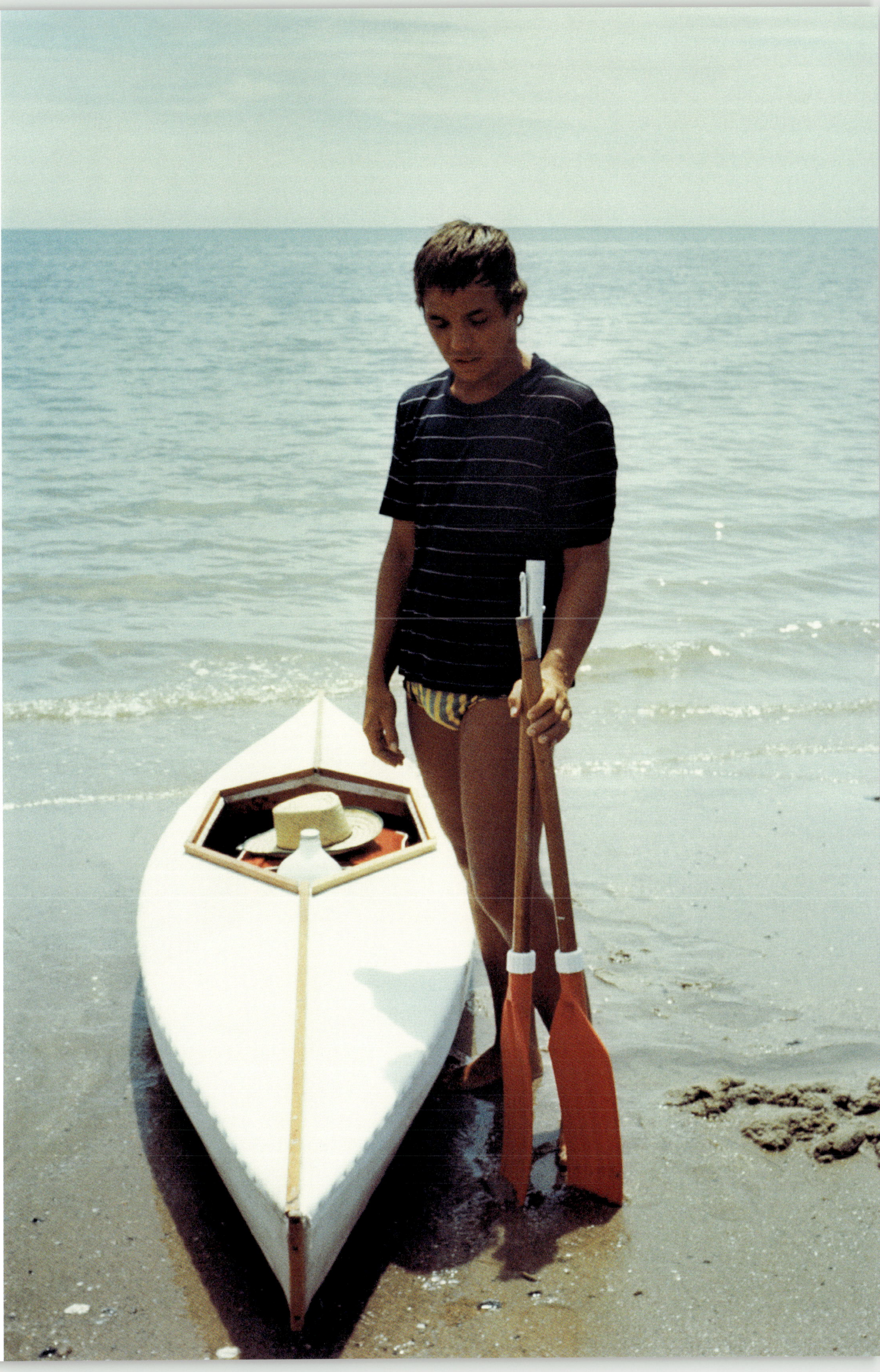

B.C. Mexico

Newspace, Newport Beach, California: May 25–June 10, 1973

I was dropped off in San Felipe, Mexico, on the Sea of Cortez. In a small canvas kayak I paddled southward to a remote beach, carrying some water with me. I survived there for 11 days; the average daily temperature was 120 degrees. On June 7, I paddled back to San Felipe and was driven to Los Angeles. The piece was announced as a show by Newspace, and during my stay in Mexico a notice in the gallery informed visitors of my absence. On June 10 at Newspace, I showed a short movie of my departure and read a diary I had kept.

Chris Burden, *B.C. Mexico*, 1973
Relic: Diary, seashell, stone

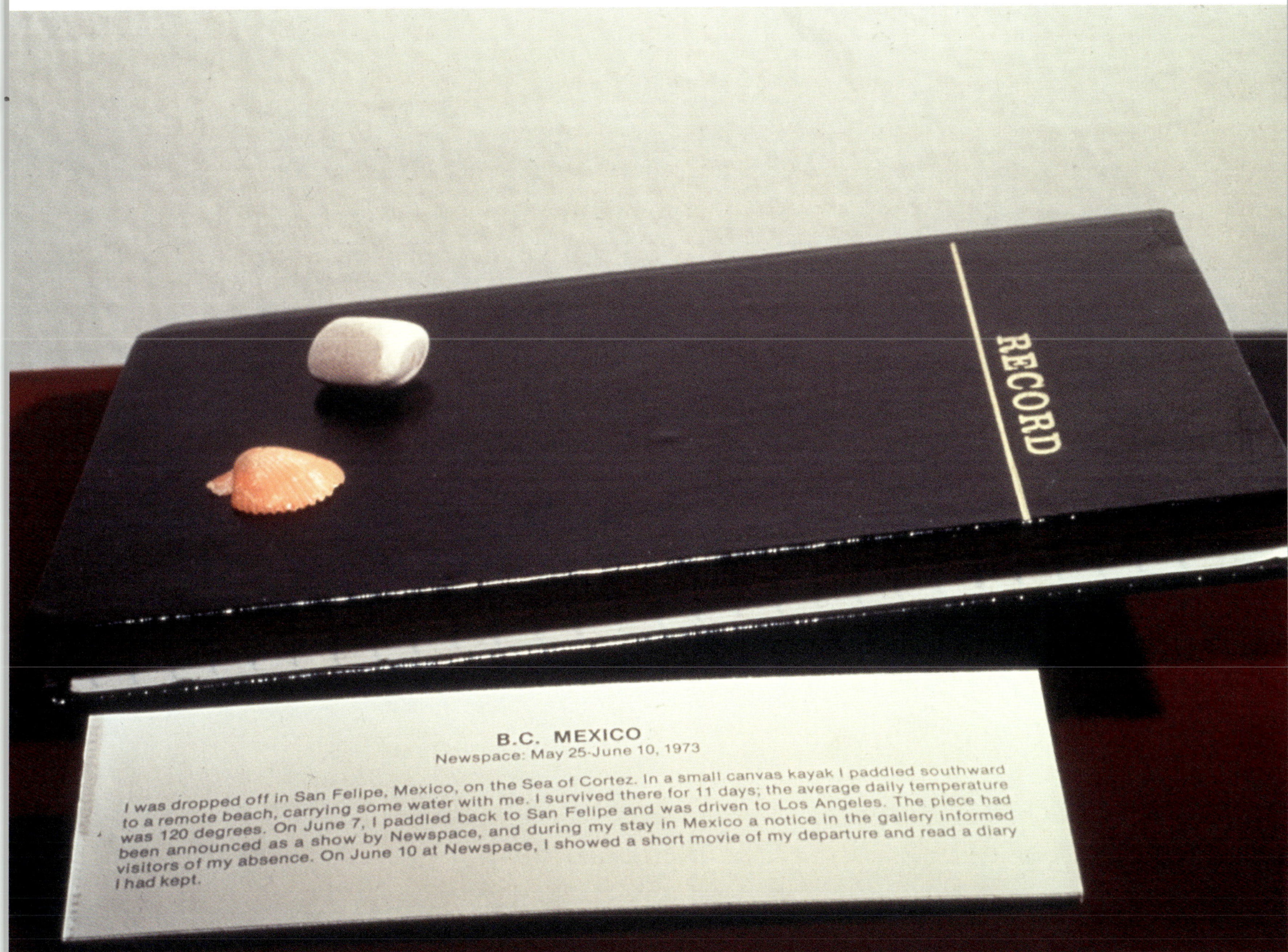
RECORD
B.C. MEXICO
Newspace: May 25-June 10, 1973
I was dropped off in San Felipe, Mexico, on the Sea of Cortez. In a small canvas kayak I paddled southward to a remote beach, carrying some water with me. I survived there for 11 days; the average daily temperature was 120 degrees. On June 7, I paddled back to San Felipe and was driven to Los Angeles. The piece had been announced as a show by Newspace, and during my stay in Mexico a notice in the gallery informed visitors of my absence. On June 10 at Newspace, I showed a short movie of my departure and read a diary I had kept.

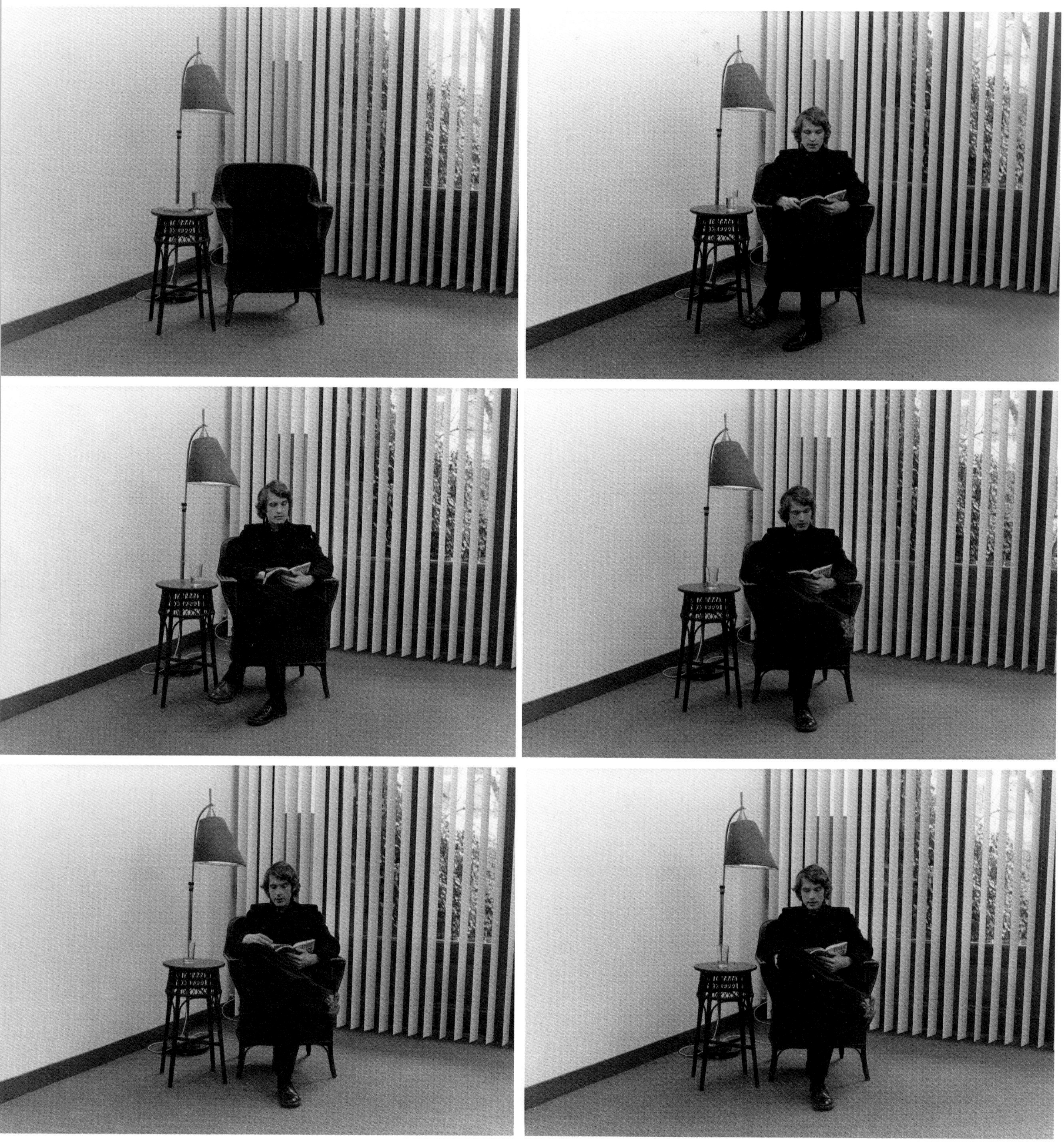

Bas Jan Ader, *The boy who fell over Niagara Falls*, 1972
Performance at Art & Project, Amsterdam

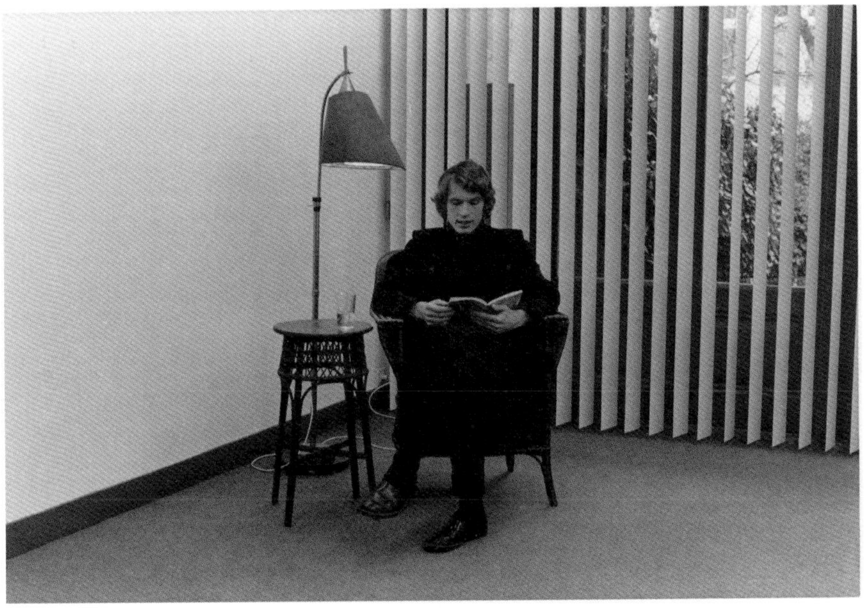
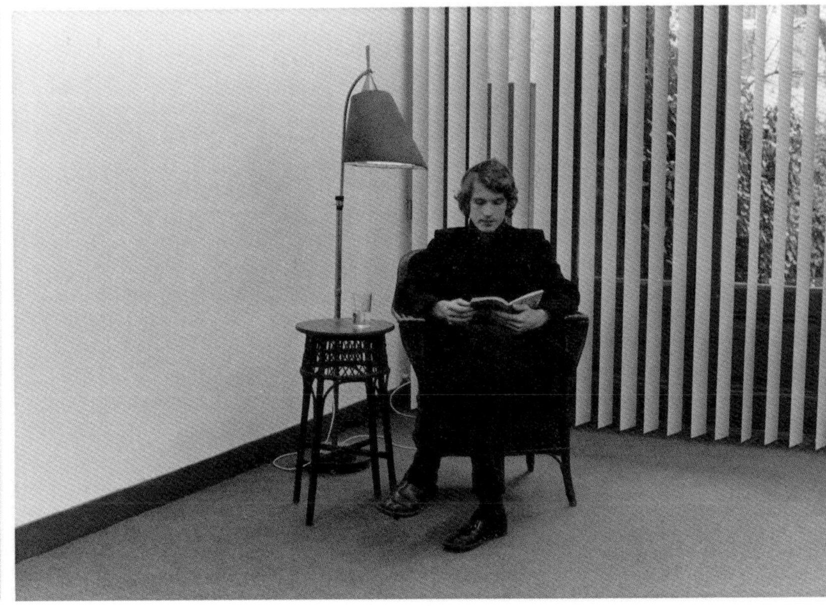
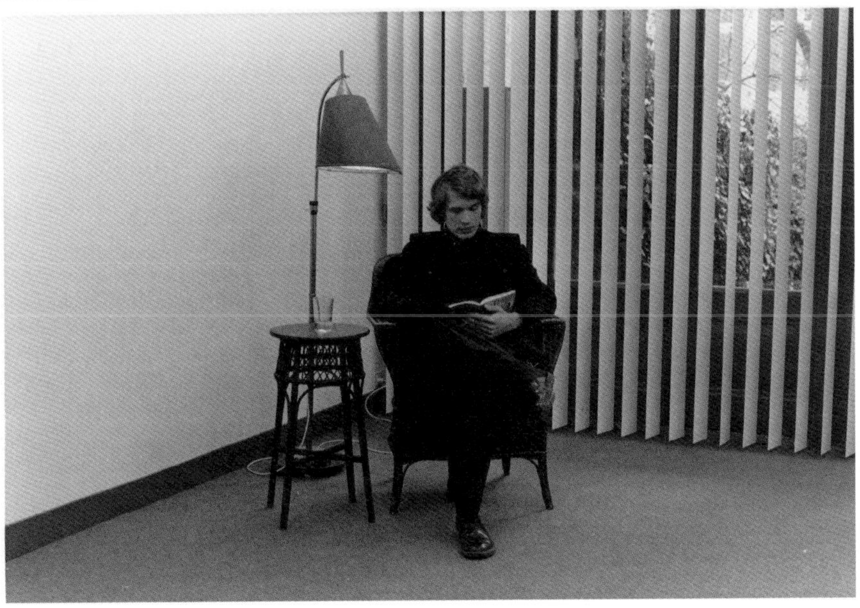
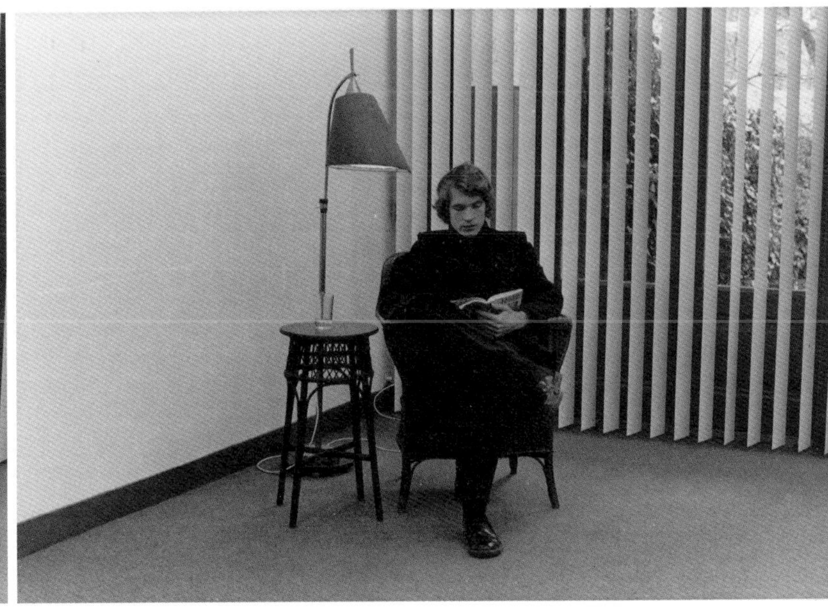
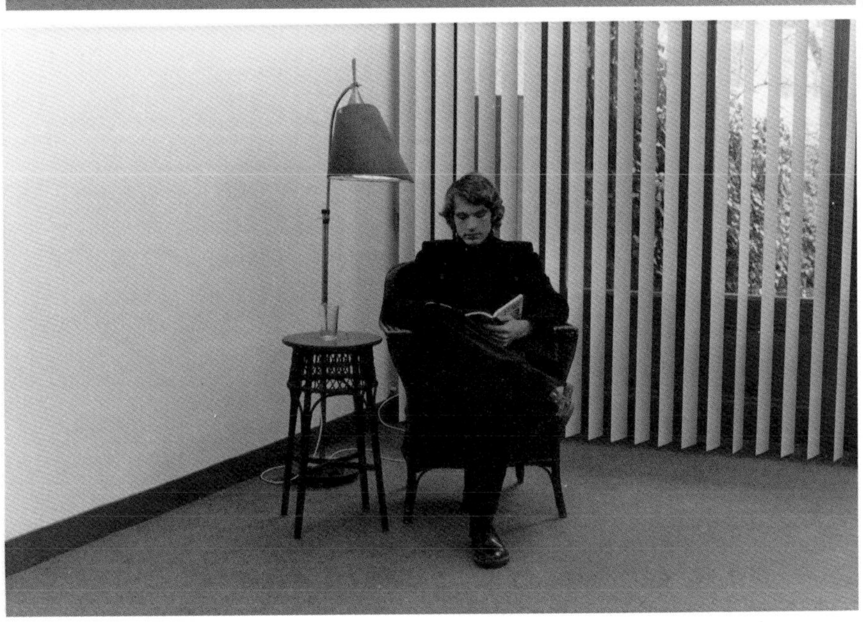
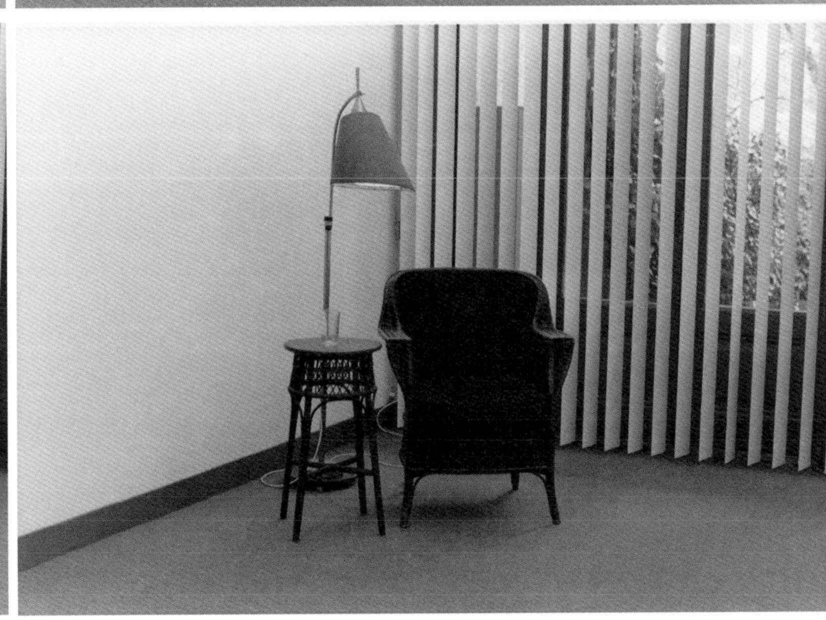

II

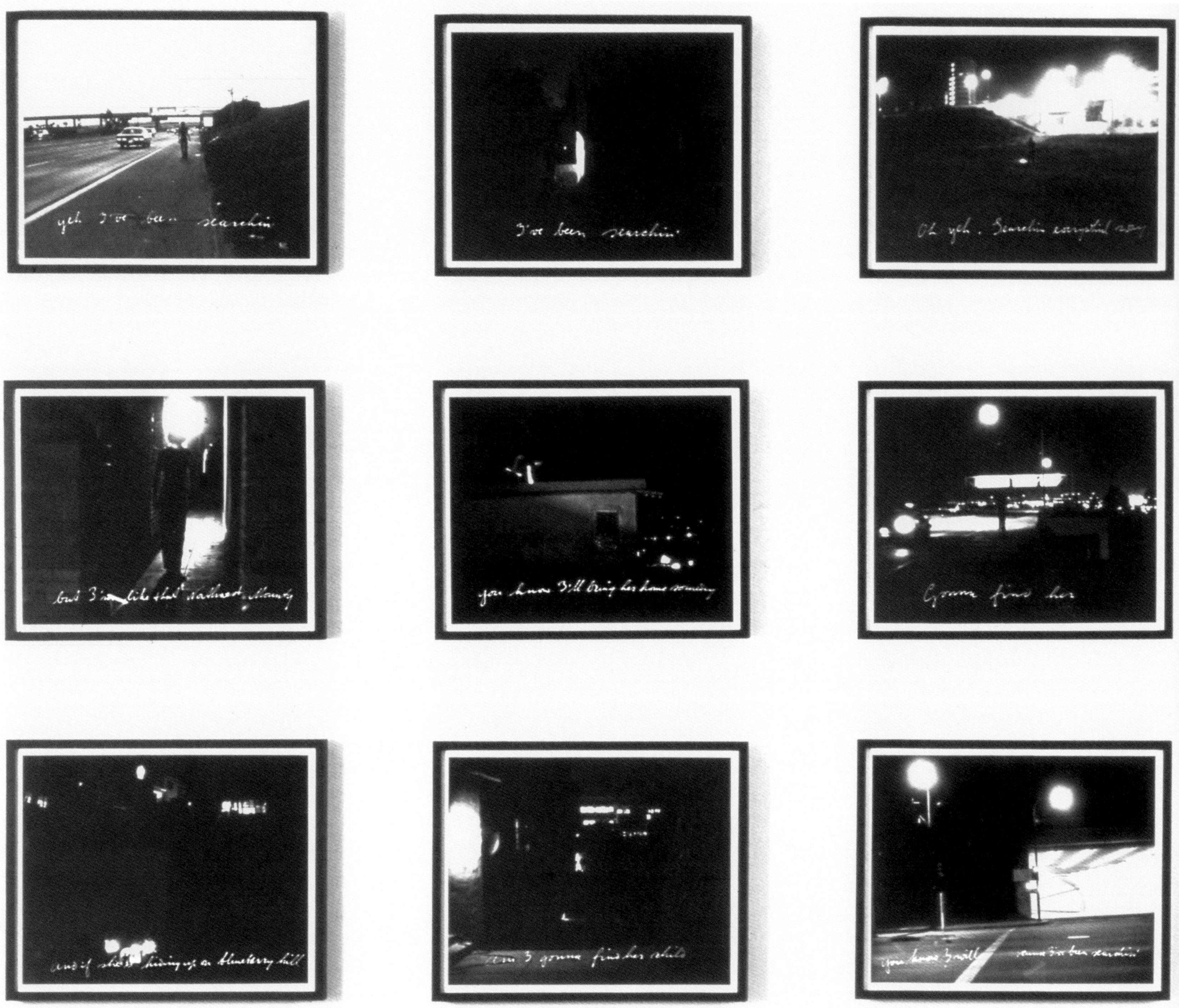

Bas Jan Ader, *In search of the miraculous (One night in Los Angeles)*, 1973

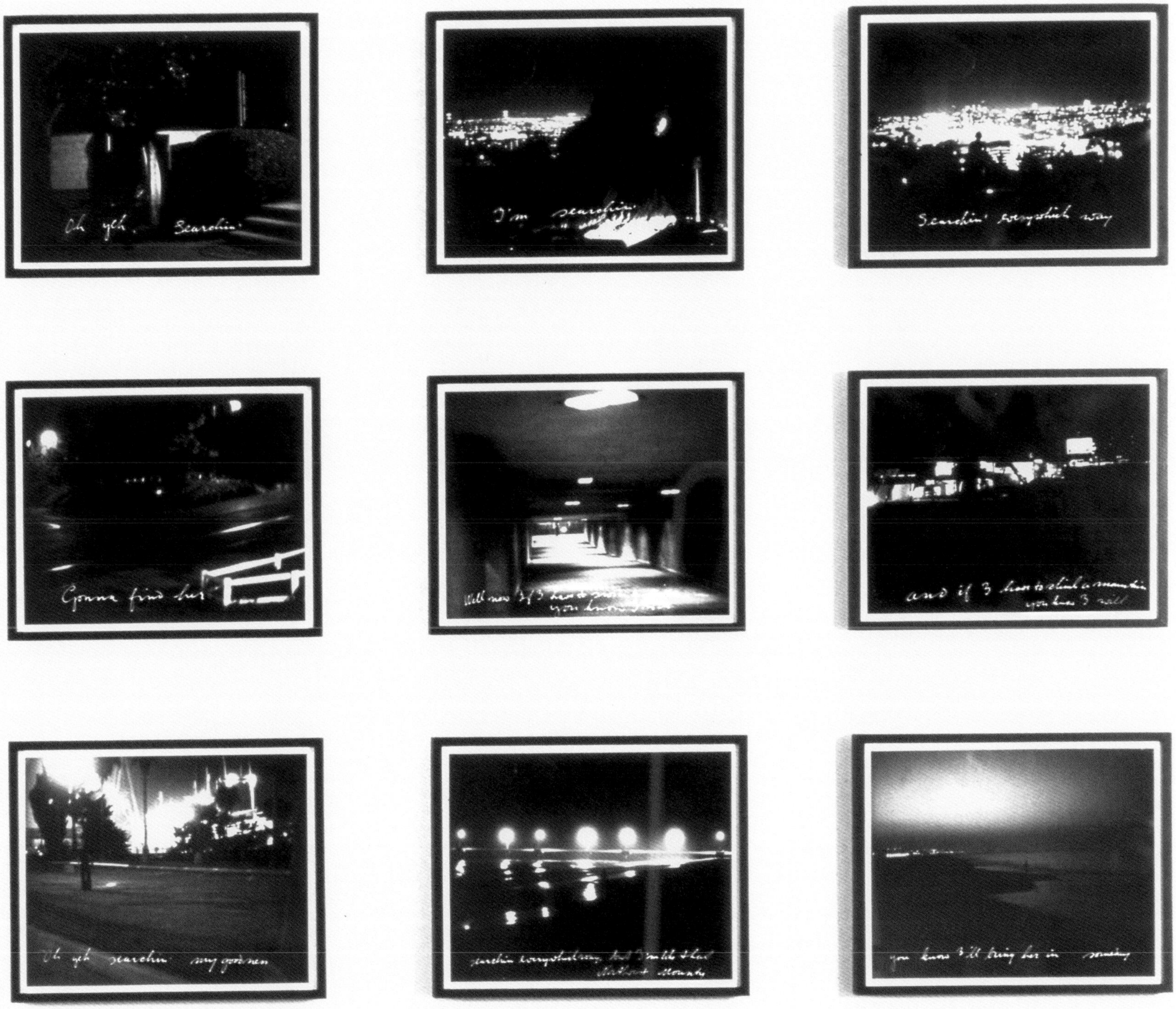
Oh yeh, Searchin'
I'm searchin'
Searchin' everywhich way
Gonna find her
Oh yeh searchin' my goodness
you know I'll bring her in someday

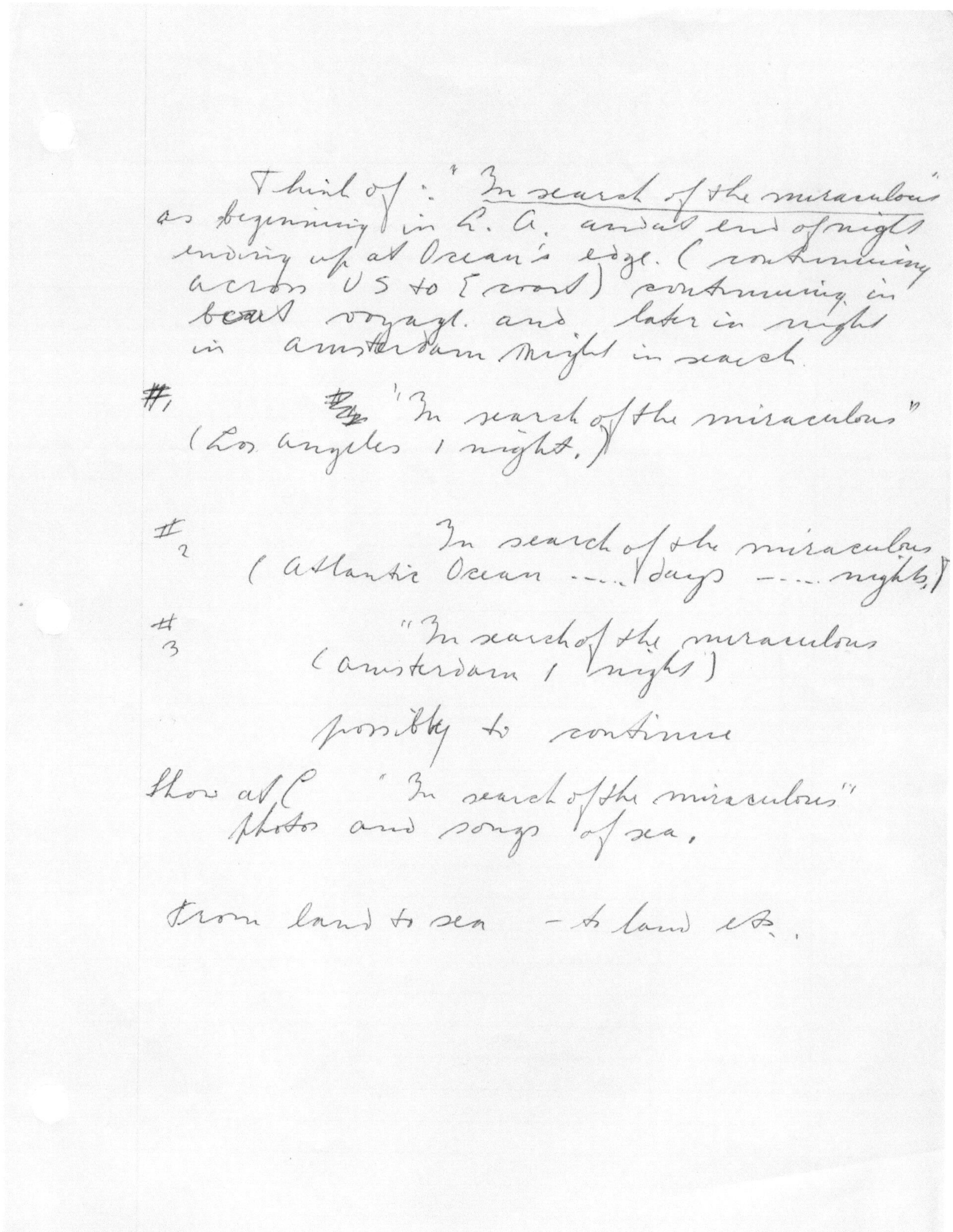

Think of: "In search of the miraculous"
as beginning in L.A. and at end of night
ending up at Ocean's edge. (continuing
across US to [coast]) continuing in
boat voyage. and later in night
in Amsterdam night in search.

#1 "In search of the miraculous"
(Los Angeles 1 night.)

#2 In search of the miraculous
(Atlantic Ocean ..... days ..... nights)

#3 "In search of the miraculous
(Amsterdam 1 night)

possibly to continue

Show at C "In search of the miraculous"
photos and songs of sea.

From land to sea – to land etc.

Bas Jan Ader, *In search of the miraculous*, 1975

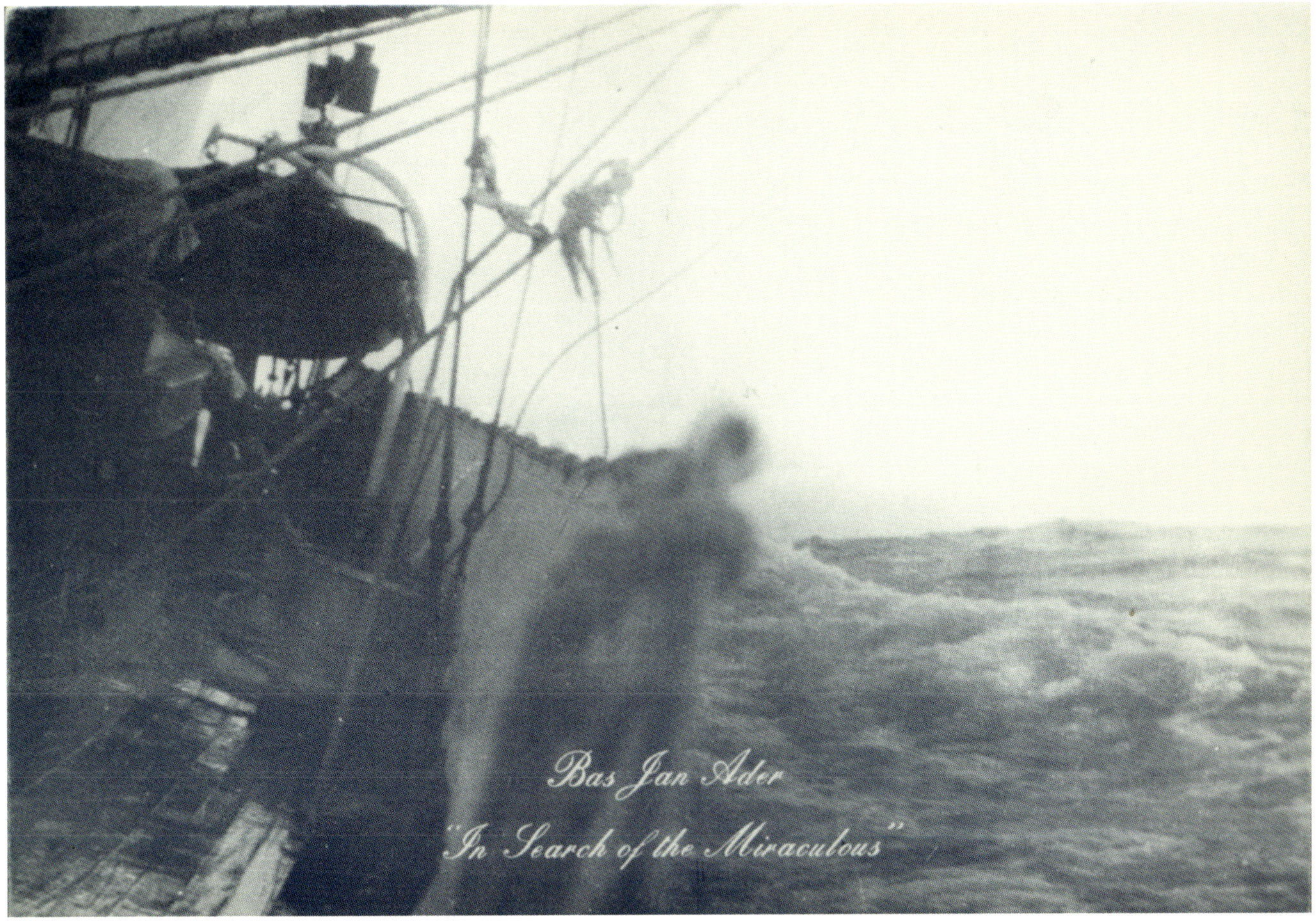

Tuesday Evening

April 22, 8–10 p.m.

Claire S. Copley Gallery

918 N. La Cienega Blvd.

Los Angeles, California 90069

April 22 – May 17, 1975

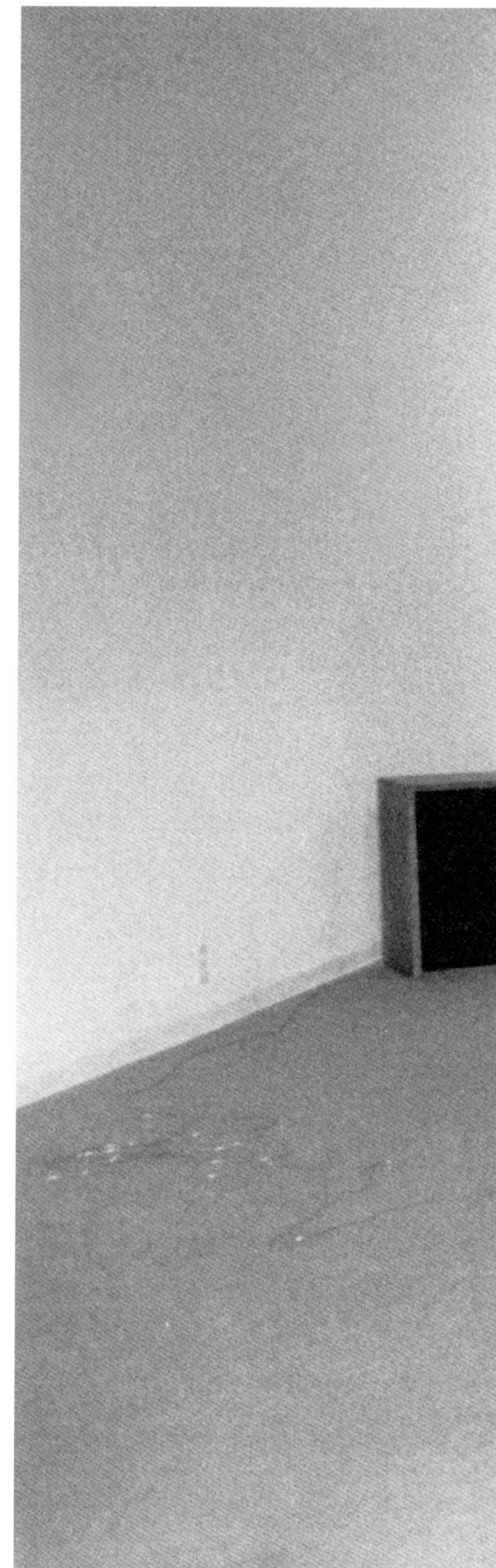

RIGHT AND FOLLOWING SPREAD
Bas Jan Ader, ***In search of the miraculous*****, 1975**

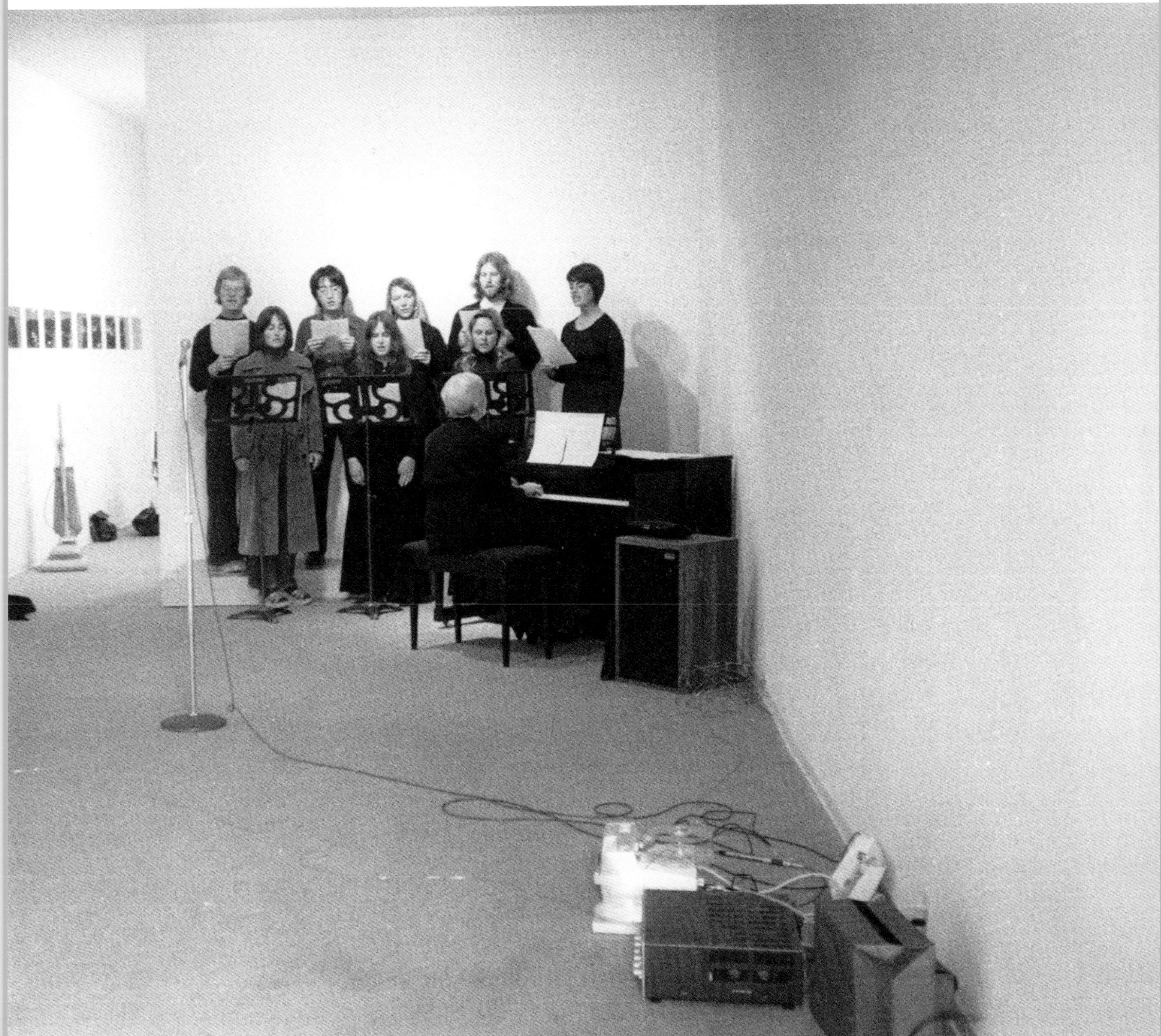

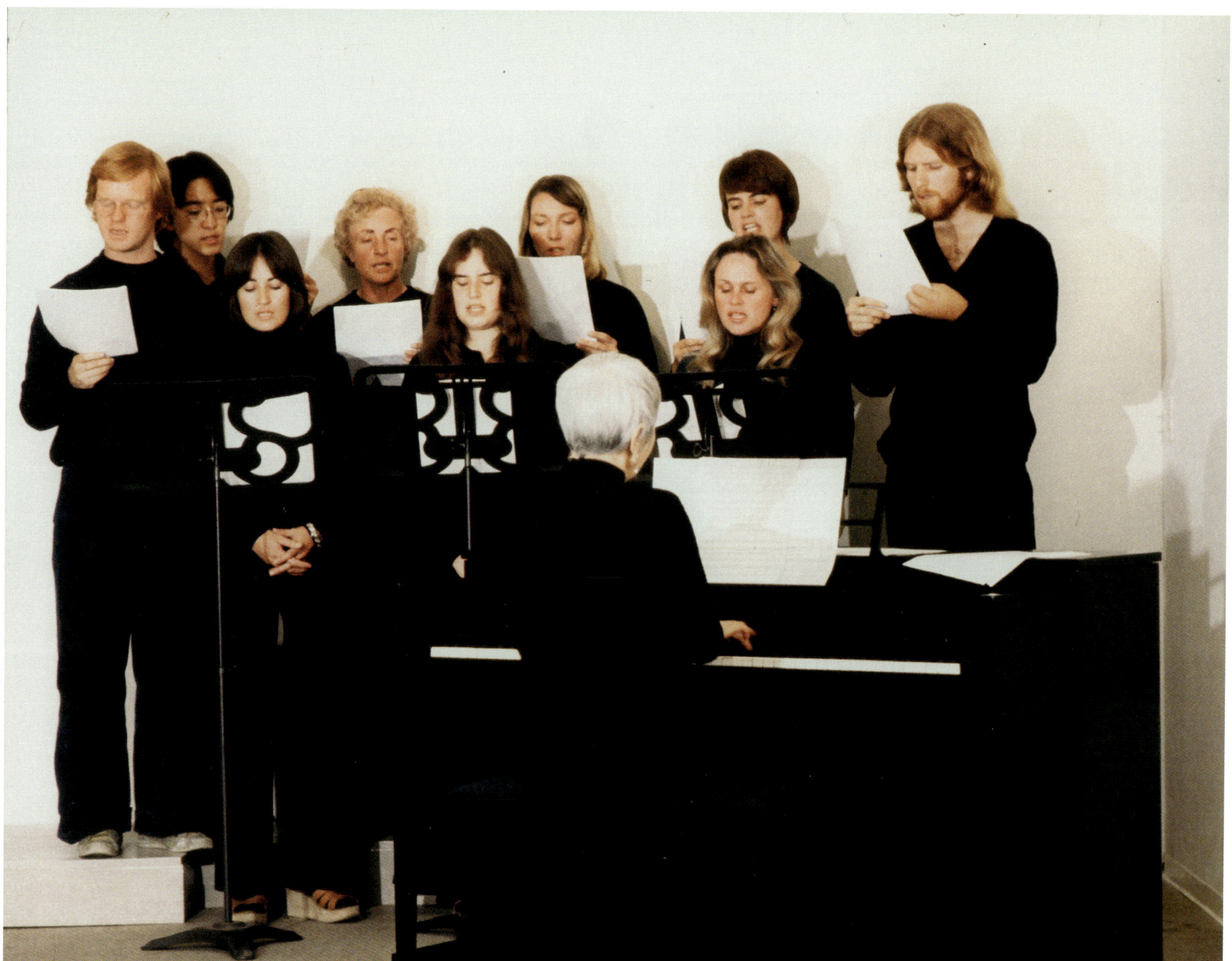

art & project

bulletin 89

1007 amsterdam
willemsparkweg 36
(020) 713991

drukwerk aan
printed matter to

bas jan ader

"in search of the miraculous"
(songs for the north atlantic; july 1975 -   )

in cooperation with the claire s. copley gallery, los angeles, usa, and the groninger museum, groningen, holland

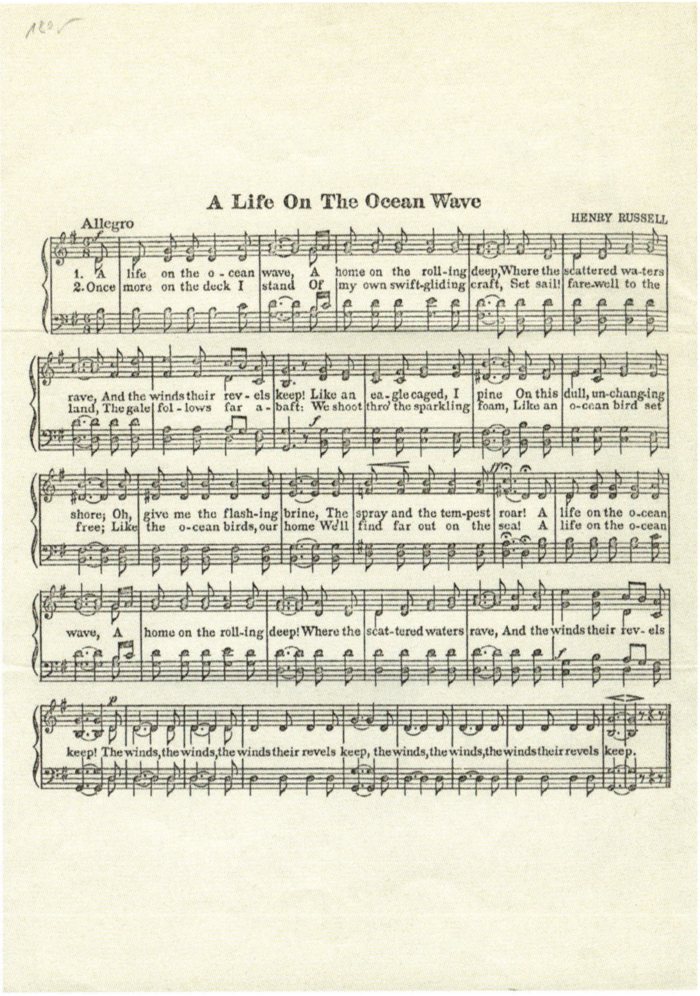

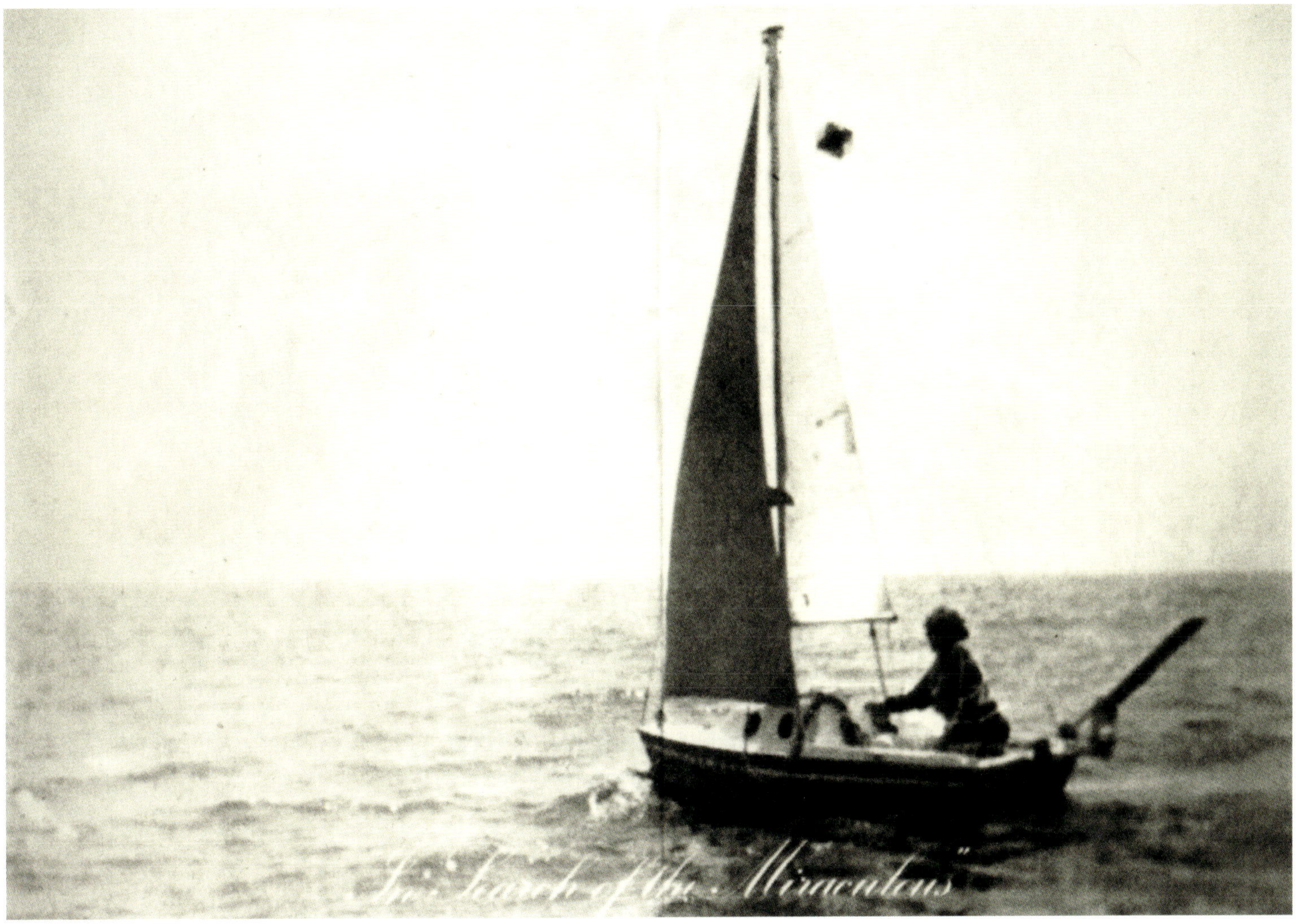

RIGHT AND FOLLOWING SPREAD
Jack Goldstein, *Suite of 9 Records with Sound Effects*, 1976

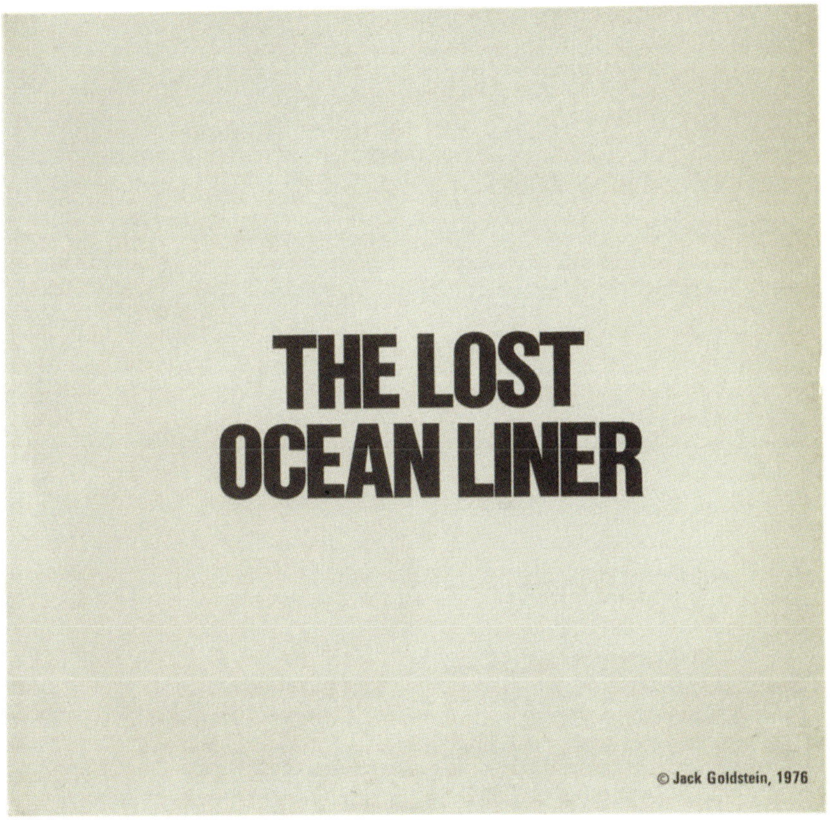
THE LOST
OCEAN LINER
© Jack Goldstein, 1976

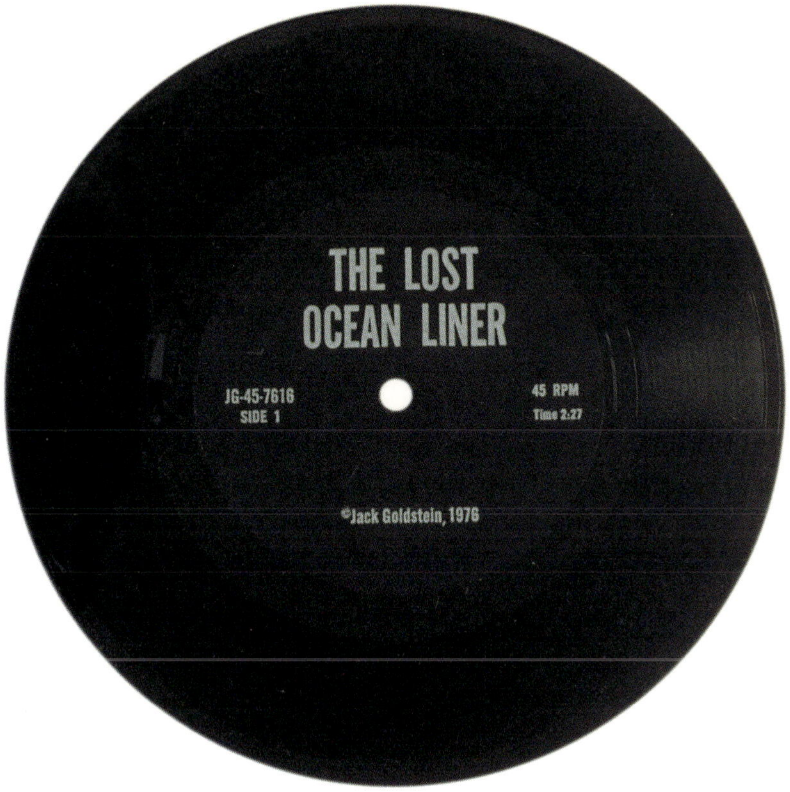
THE LOST
OCEAN LINER
JG-45-7616
SIDE 1
45 RPM
Time 2:27
©Jack Goldstein, 1976

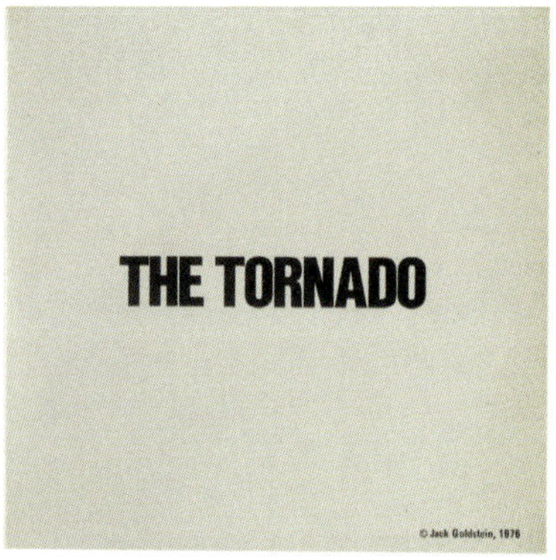
THE TORNADO
© Jack Goldstein, 1976
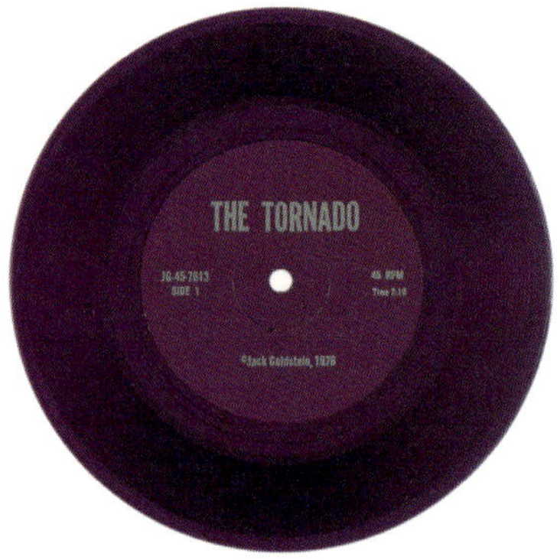
THE TORNADO
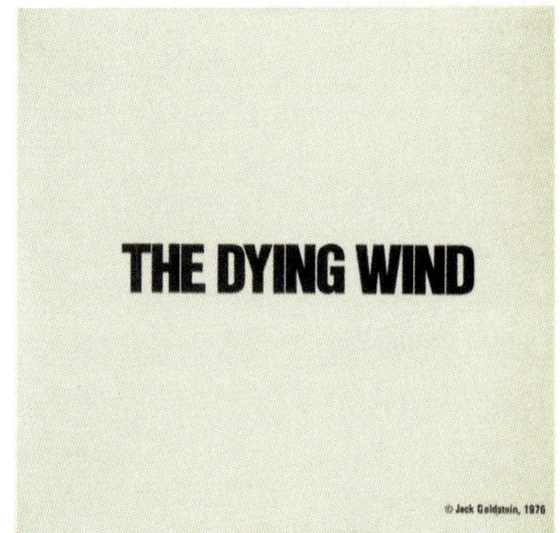
THE DYING WIND
© Jack Goldstein, 1976
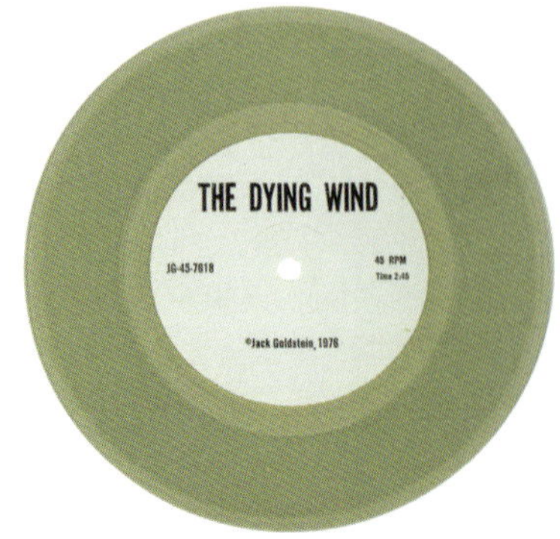
THE DYING WIND
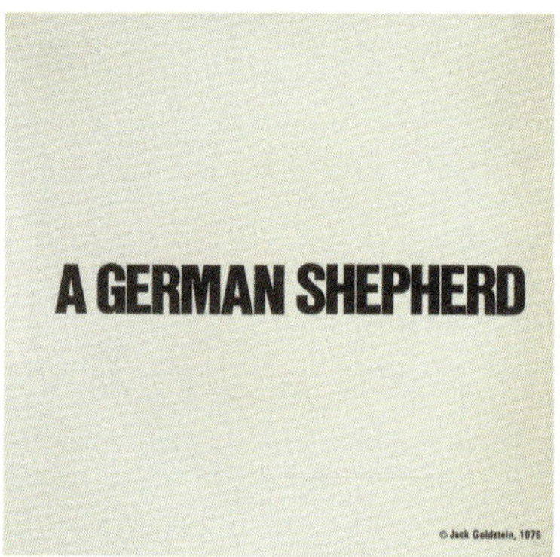
A GERMAN SHEPHERD
© Jack Goldstein, 1976
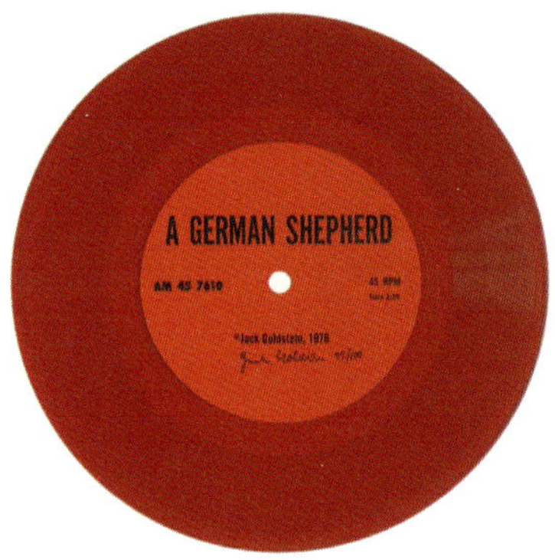
A GERMAN SHEPHERD
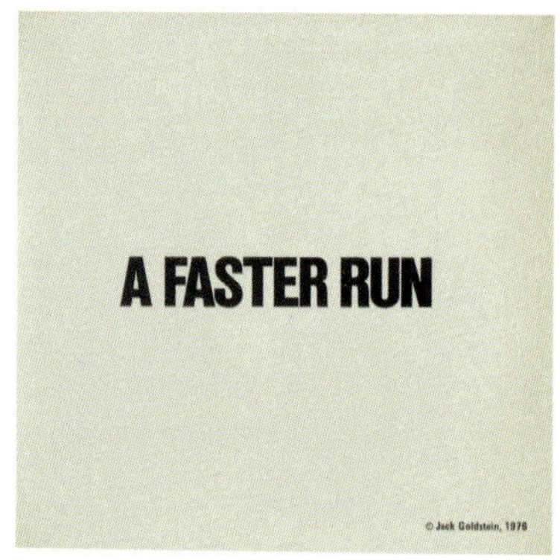
A FASTER RUN
© Jack Goldstein, 1976
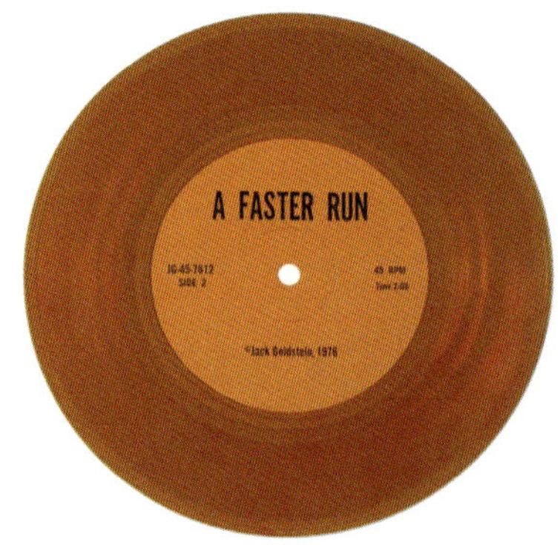
A FASTER RUN

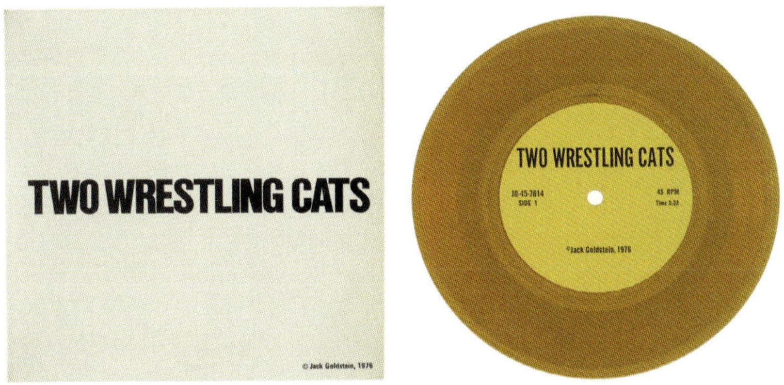
TWO WRESTLING CATS
© Jack Goldstein, 1976
TWO WRESTLING CATS

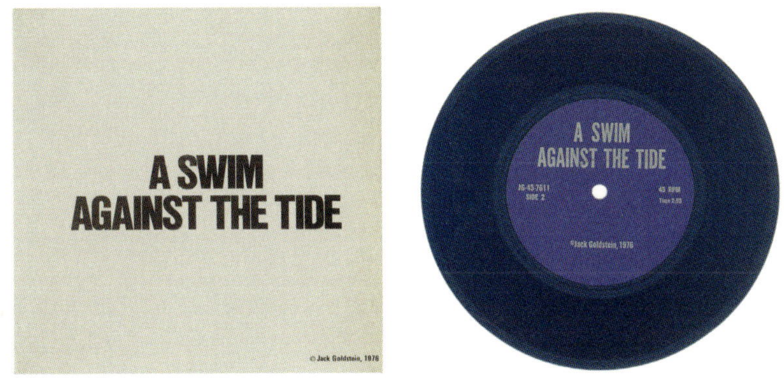
A SWIM
AGAINST THE TIDE
© Jack Goldstein, 1976
A SWIM
AGAINST THE TIDE

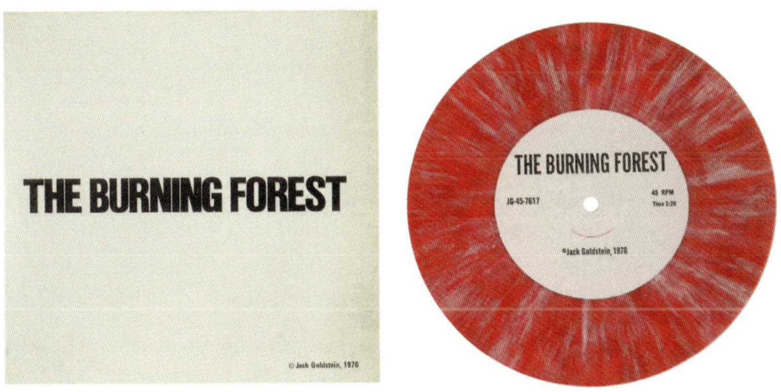
THE BURNING FOREST
© Jack Goldstein, 1976
THE BURNING FOREST

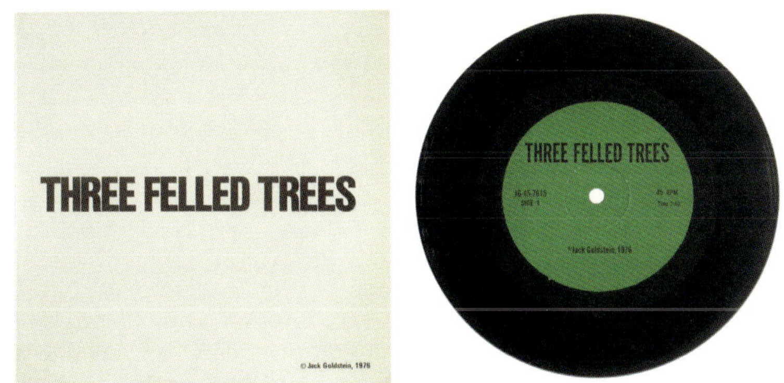
THREE FELLED TREES
© Jack Goldstein, 1976
THREE FELLED TREES

Jack Goldstein, *The Pull*, 1976

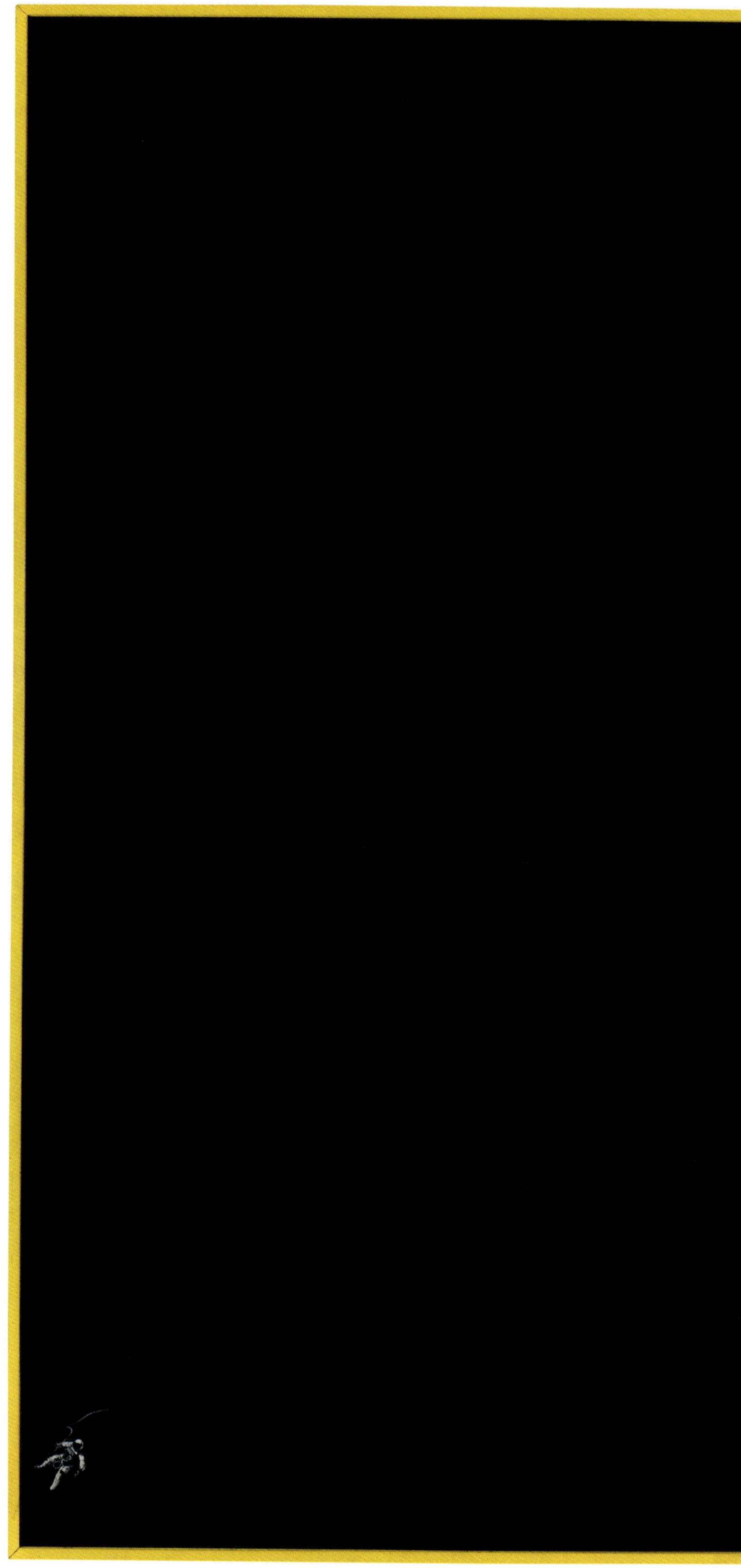

Jack Goldstein, *Untitled*, 1979

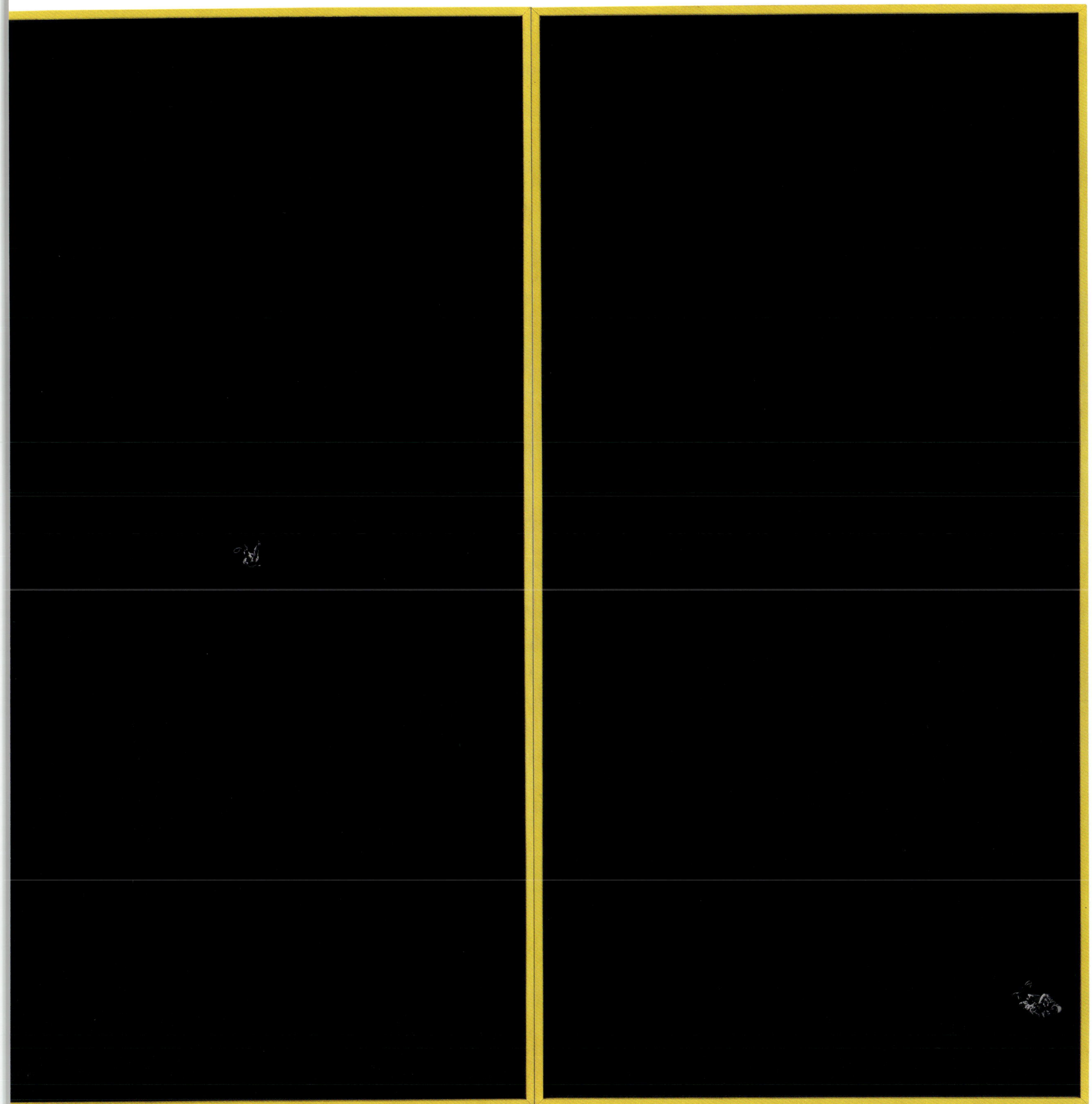

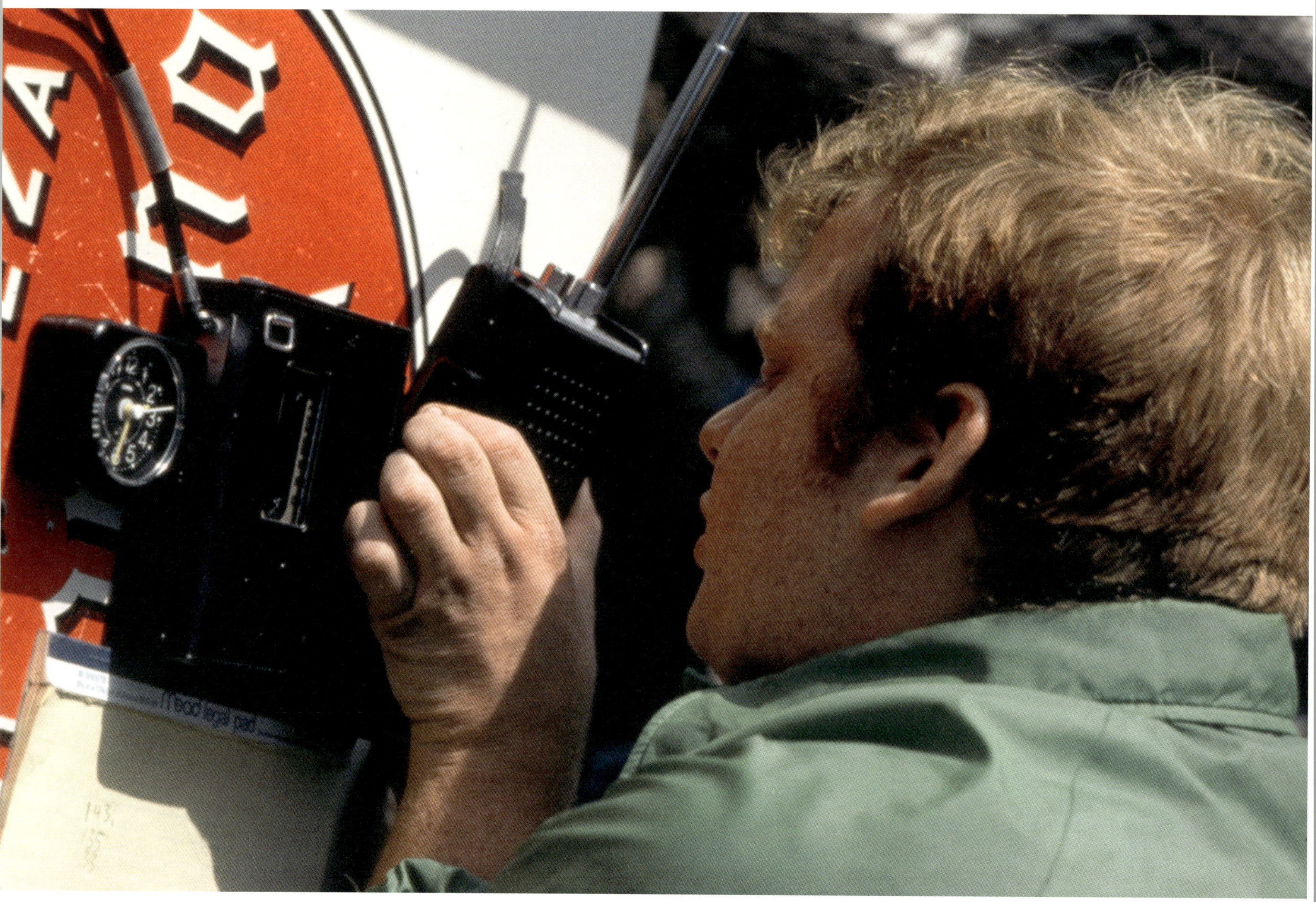

Chris Burden, *Solaris*, 1980
Pacific Ocean, Santa Monica, California: October 23, 1980

SOLARIS

CB TO MISSION CONTROL, HOUSTON

I AM OUT HERE

I AM ON THE EDGE

I AM AN ASTRONUT

ROTATION. 12 over 30, 39 over 52, 14 over 23

VECTOR .027

HULL TEMPERATURE 273

OVER AND OUT.

MISSION CONTROL, HOUSTON, TO CB

YOU'RE LOOKING GOOD

1, 47, 58 UNTIL SPLASHDOWN

PROCEED ALPHA (CODE: ALPHA - towards shore

(OR) BETA BETA - away from shore

(OR) RED RED - Mexico, South

(OR) GREEN GREEN - Canada, North)

OVER AND OUT.

Solaris script, 1980

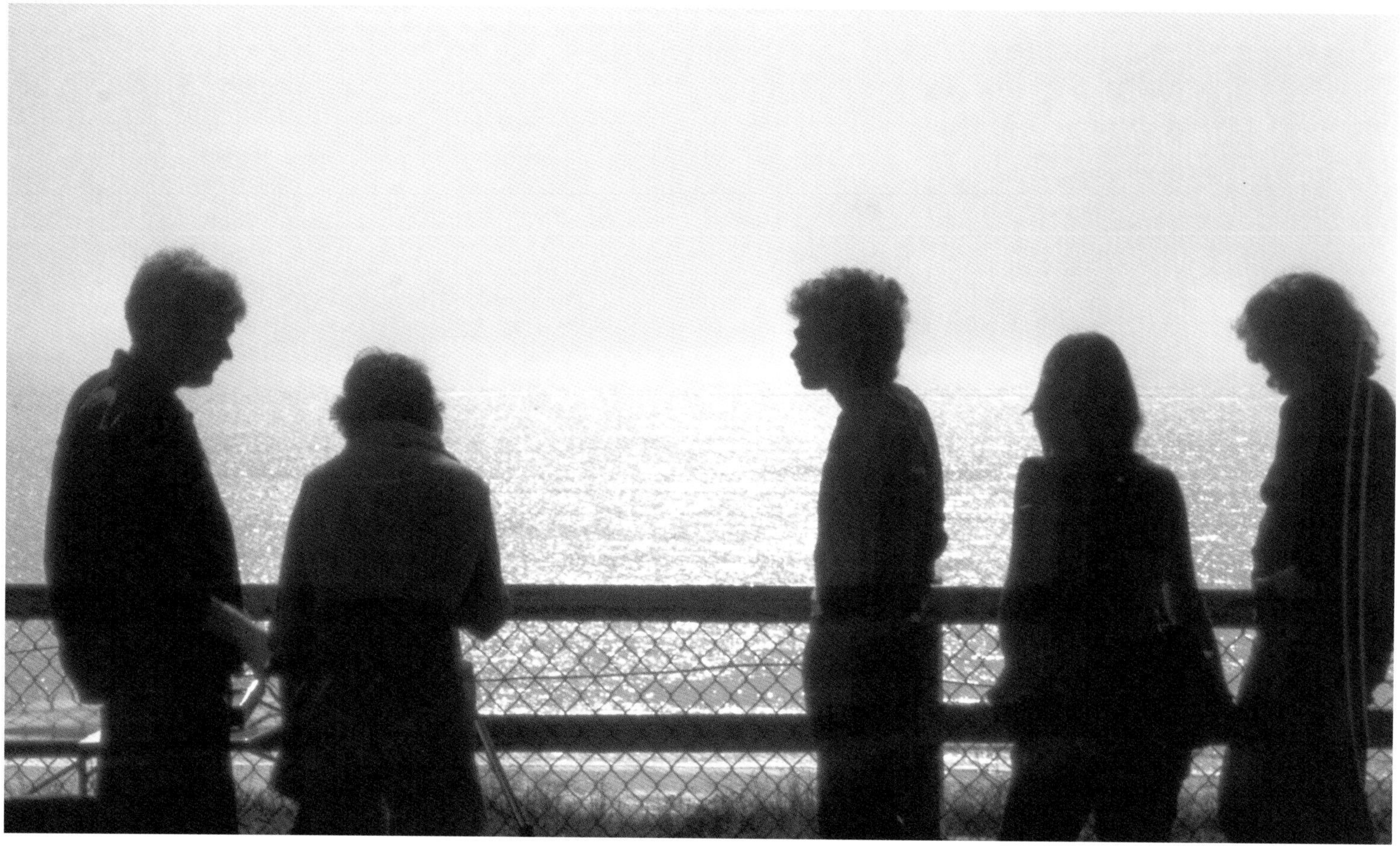

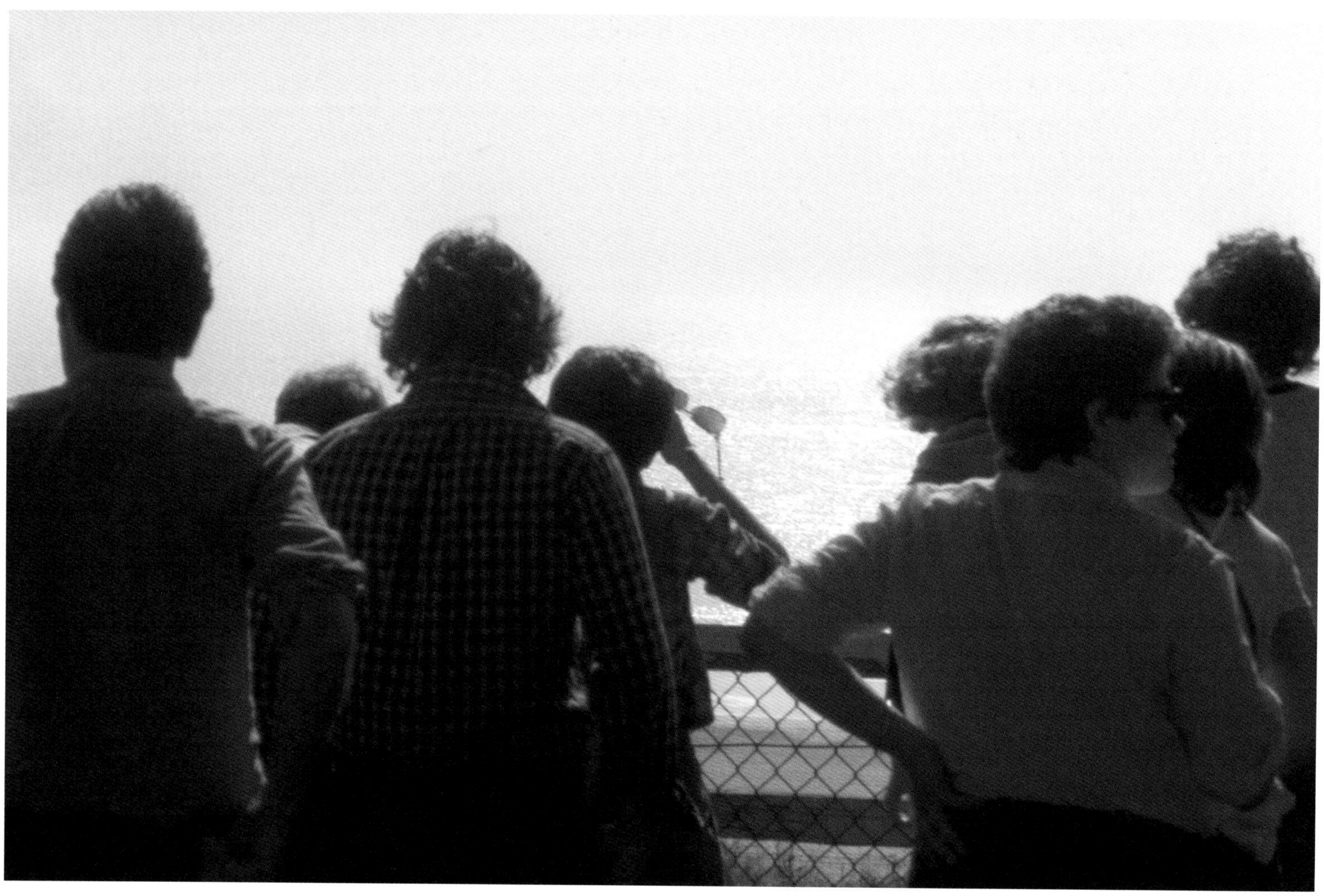

Chris Burden, *Solaris*, 1980
Pacific Ocean, Santa Monica, California: October 23, 1980

Solaris

Pacific Ocean, Santa Monica, California: October 23, 1980

Visitors were requested to come to a specific location on the Santa Monica bluffs overlooking the Pacific Ocean between the hours of 2 pm and 4 pm. Equipped with a walkie-talkie, I was floating in a small canvas kayak two to three miles out in the ocean, directly in the glare of the setting sun. I was invisible to the naked eye and visitors could only view me by looking through a powerful telescope. The foreshortening and glare provided the illusion that I was floating through some highly volatile gaseous substance. On shore near the telescope, a small metal table equipped with a black clock, a walkie-talkie and a small tape recorder provided the symbolic materials for Houston “Mission Control.” Using the walkie-talkies I could communicate with Mission Control.
A typical transmission would consist of:

C.B. to Mission Control, Houston.
I am out here.
I am on the edge.
I am an Astronut.
Rotation 12 over 30, 39 over 52,
14 over 23.
Vector .027.
Hull temperature 273
Over and out.

At four o’clock, splashdown was announced and the telescope was removed.

Chris Burden, *Solaris*, 1980
Relic: Card table, walkie-talkie

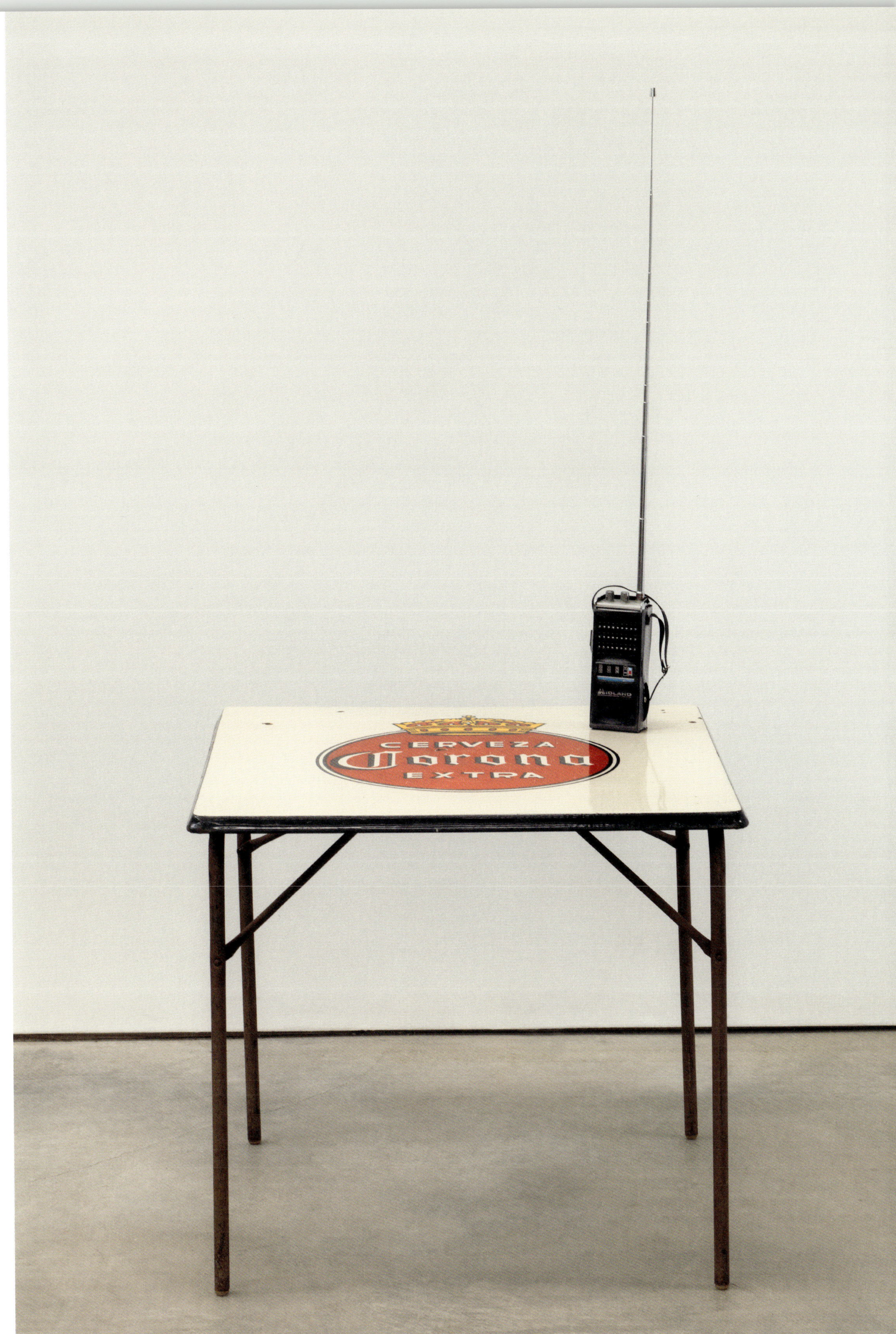
CERVEZA
Corona
EXTRA

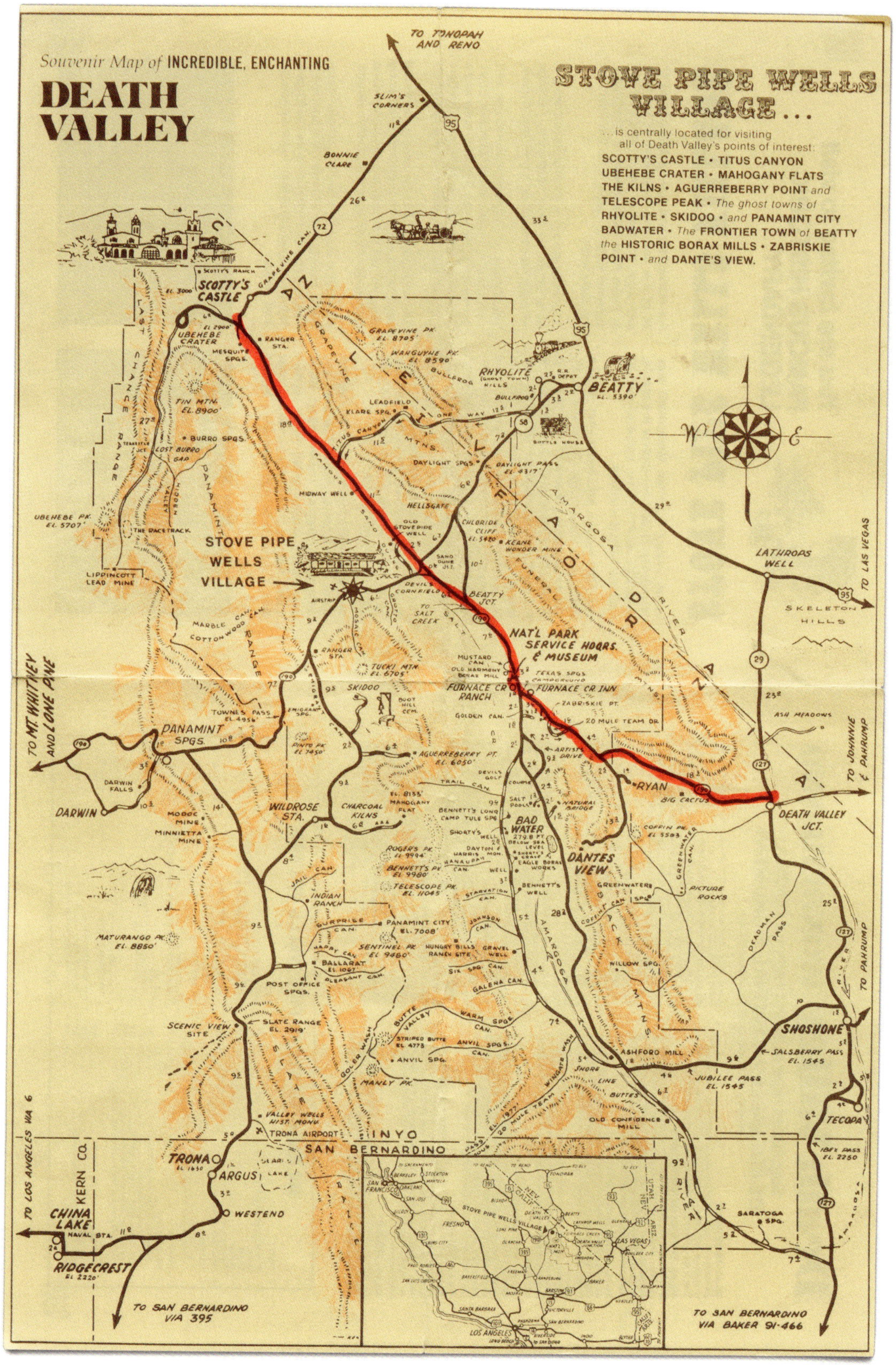

ABOVE
Death Valley Run map, 1976

RIGHT
Chris Burden, *Death Valley Run*, 1976
Death Valley, California: October 14, 1976

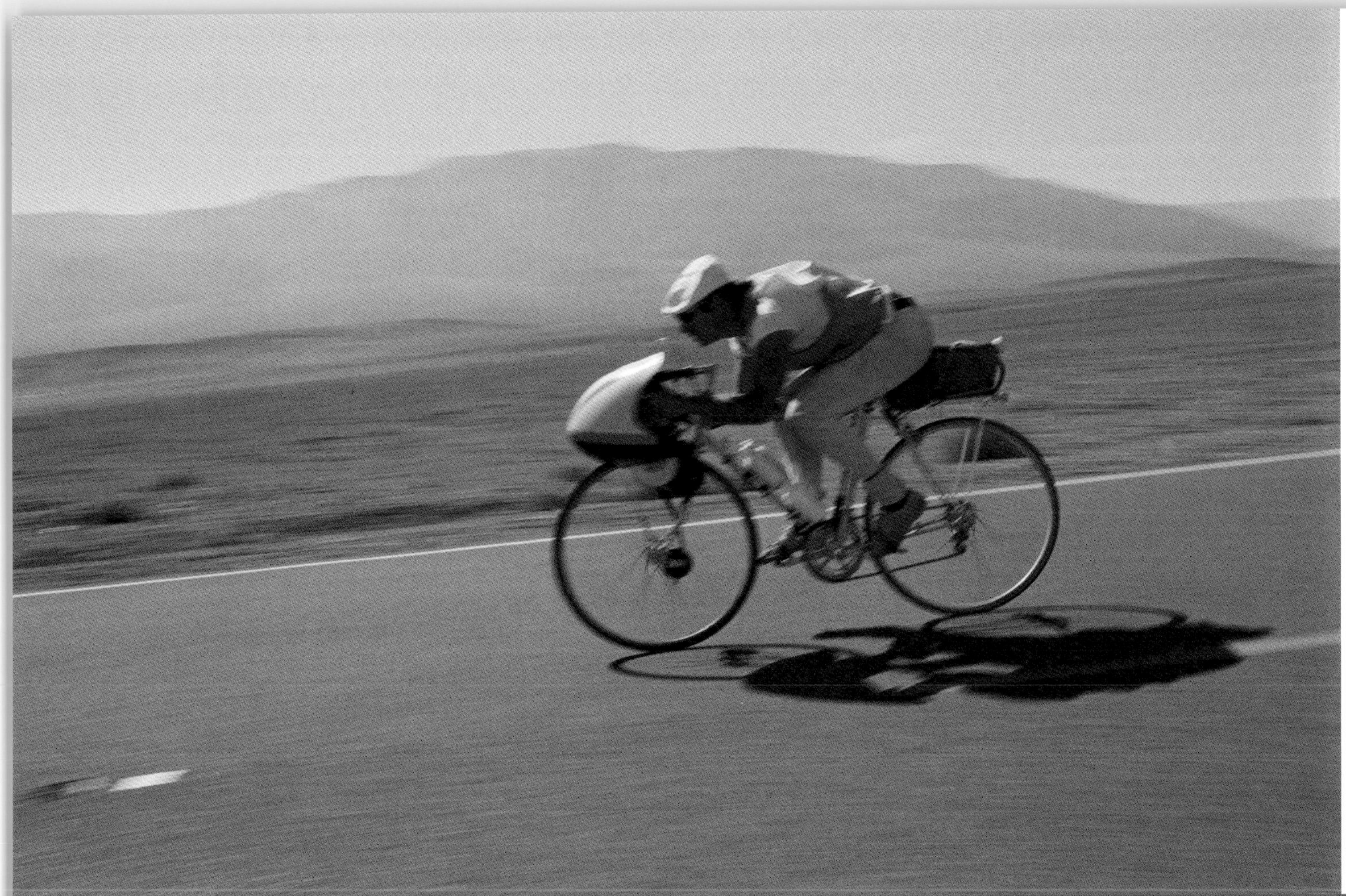

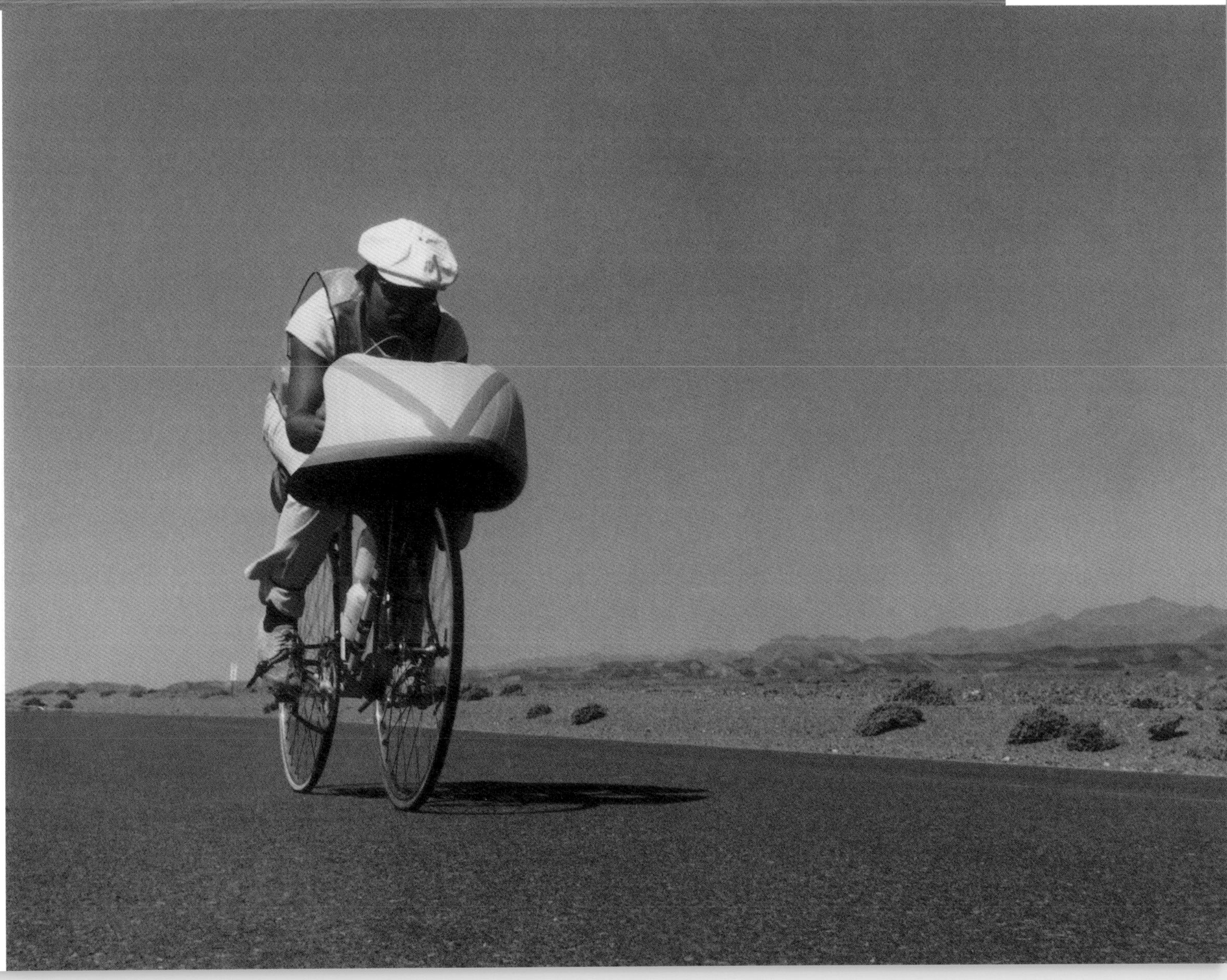

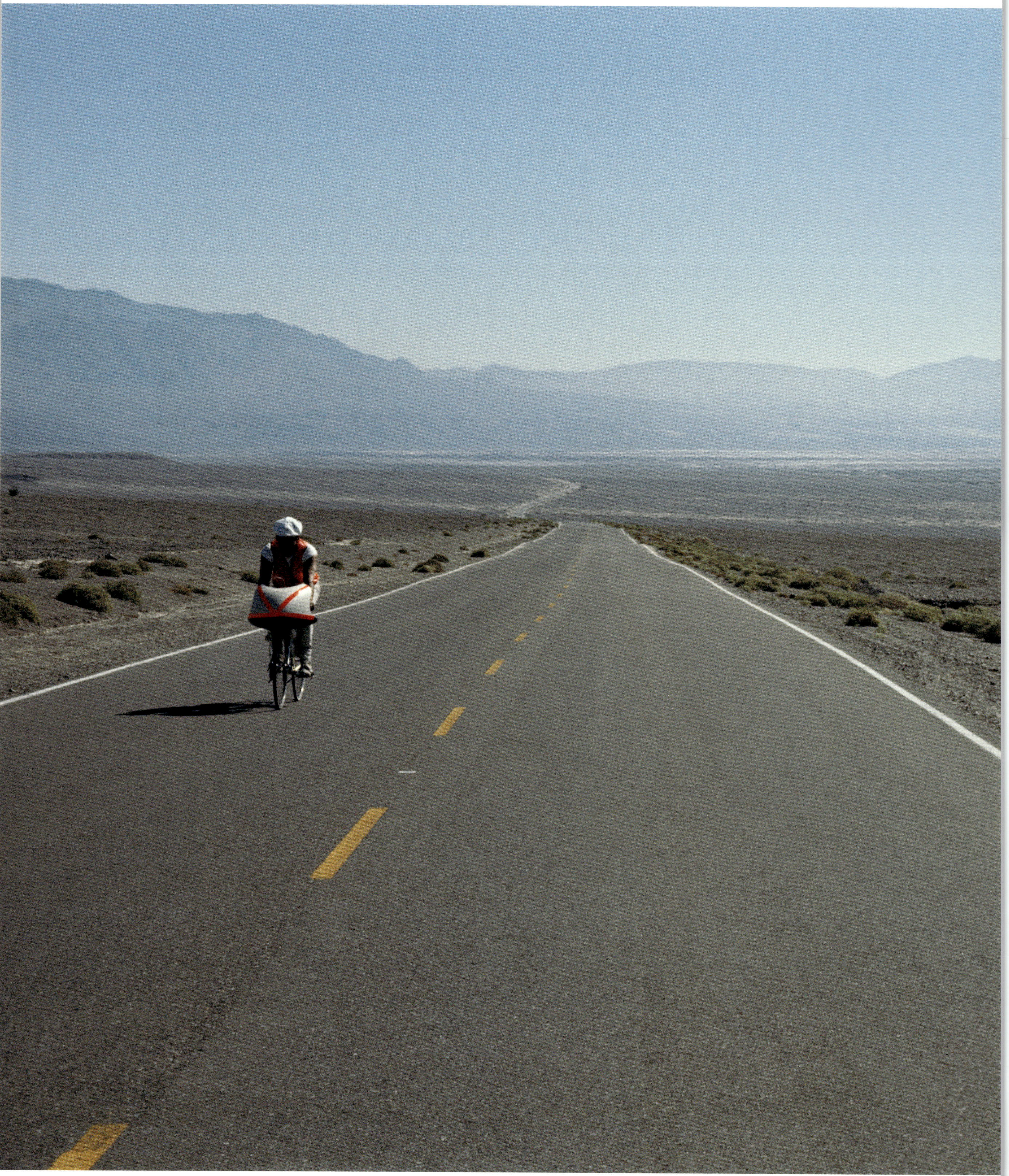

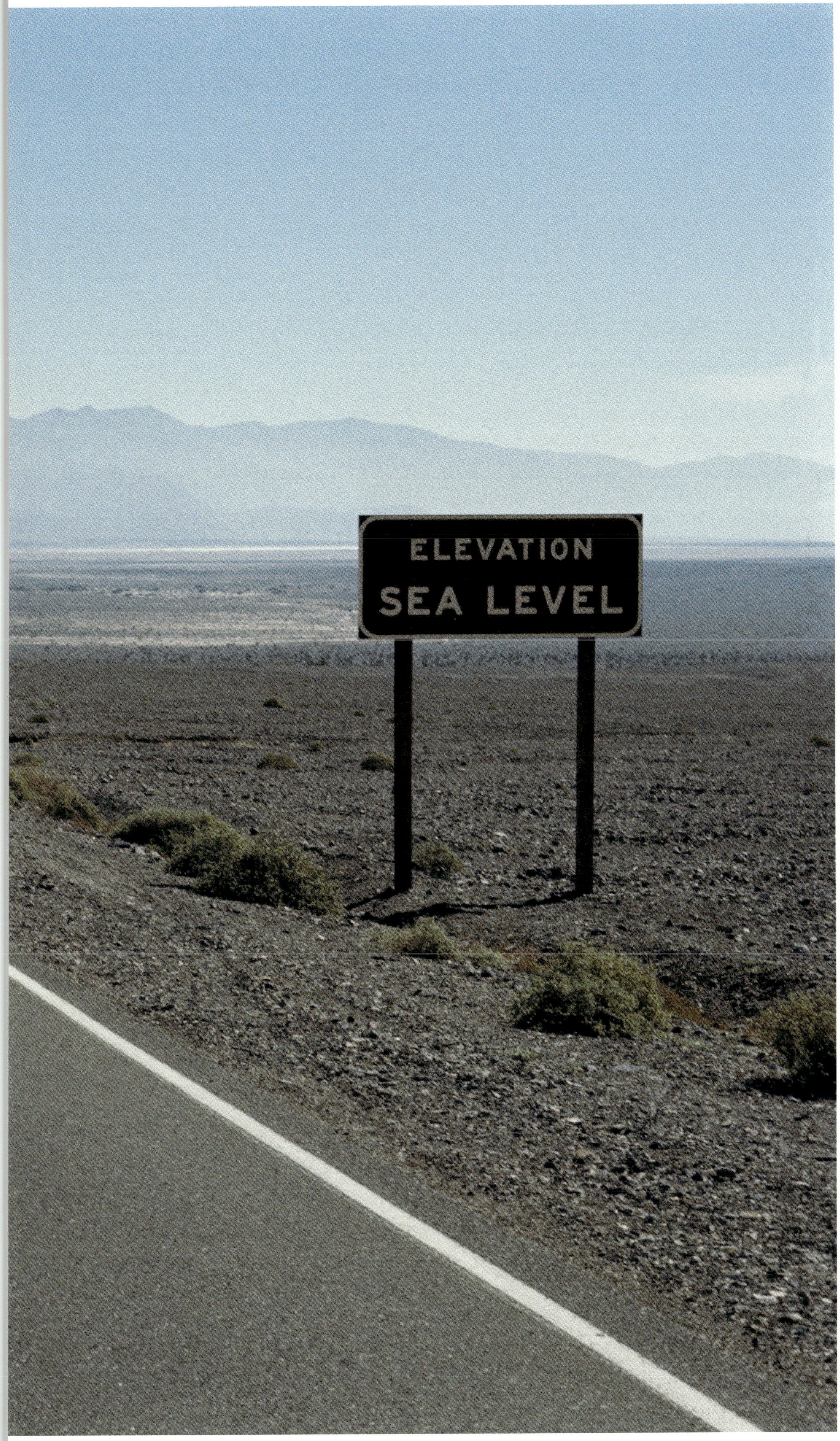
ELEVATION
SEA LEVEL

Death Valley Run

Death Valley, California: October 14, 1976

On October 14, 1976, I made the smallest motorized crossing of Death Valley on record. An ultra-light racing bicycle with fragile "sew up" tires was equipped with a quality miniature bicycle motor. The 20cc. (approximately ½ cu. inch) Japanese TAS motor weighed 11 pounds, and was air cooled by a small fan. The engine and bicycle were streamlined with a special fairing. The whole motorized bike with extra tires, gasoline, water and tools weighed 40 pounds.

Because of the heat, the distance, and the mirage effect, I wore white clothes and a luminescent orange vest for safety reasons. My speed along the 84 mile route from Scotty's Castle to Death Valley Junction ranged from a low of 16 mph to a high of 27 mph. The total trip including refueling stops took about 7 hours.

PREVIOUS SPREAD
Chris Burden, *Death Valley Run*, 1976
Death Valley, California: October 14, 1976

RIGHT
Chris Burden, *Death Valley Run*, 1976
Relic: Customized bicycle

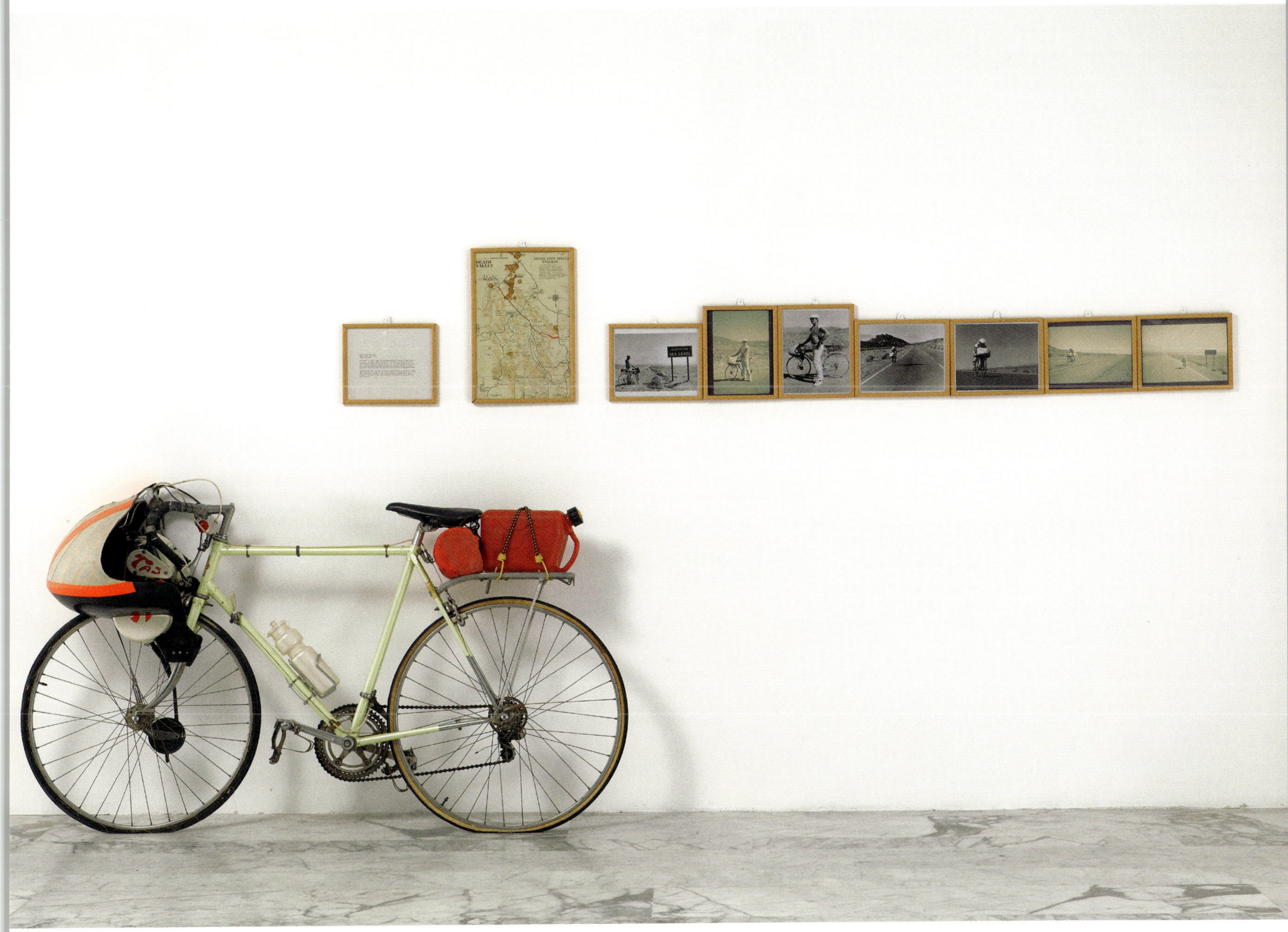

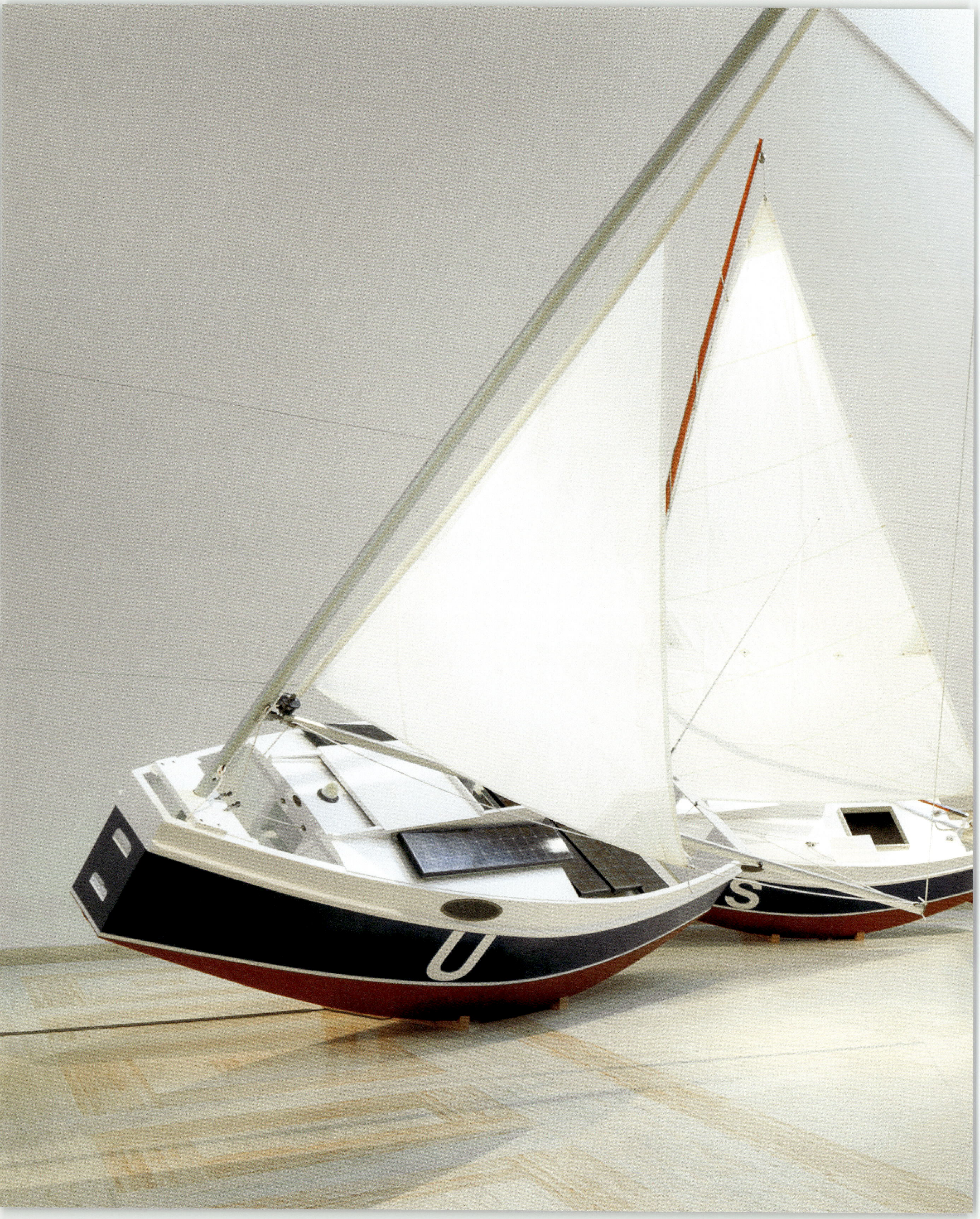
U
S

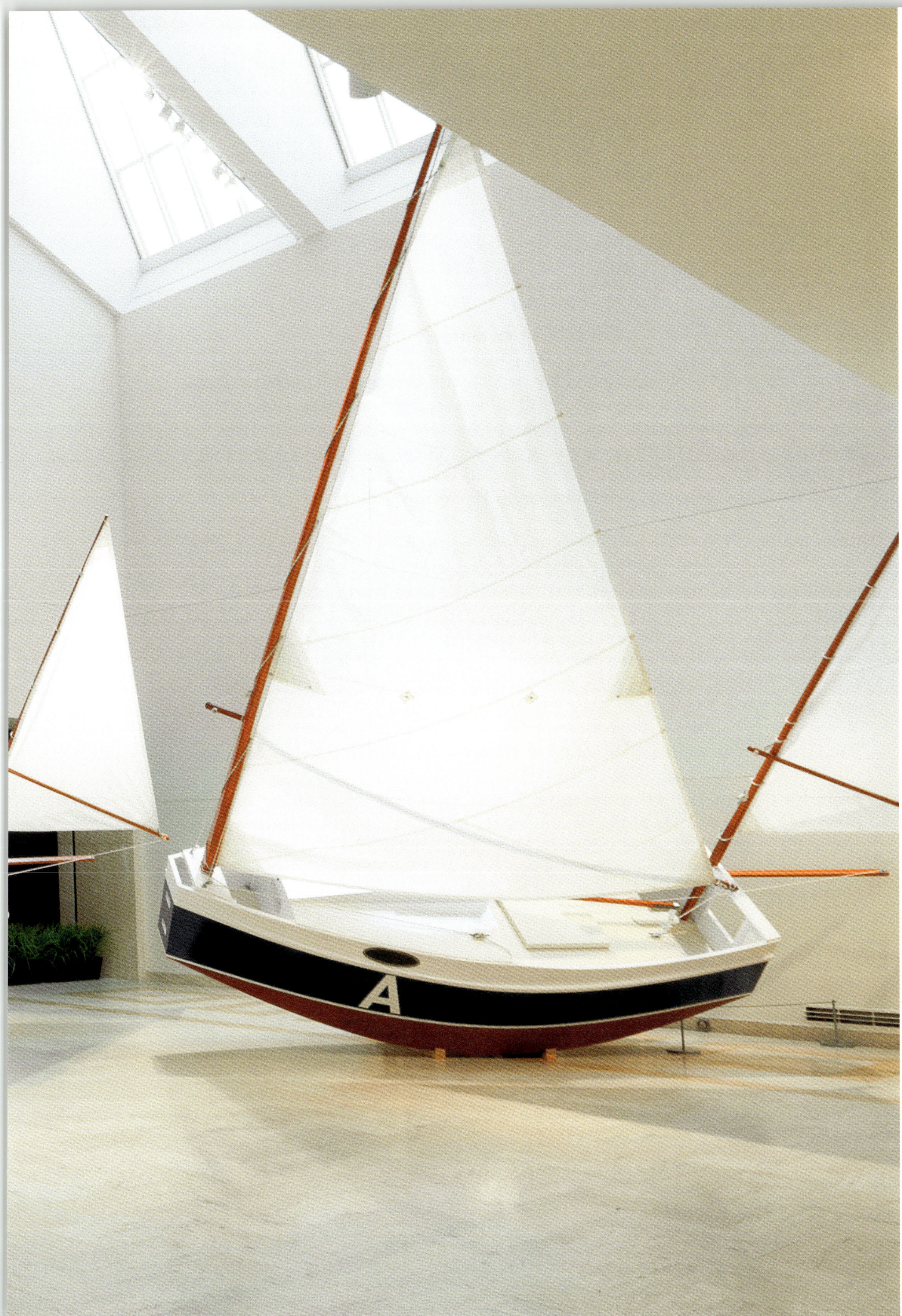
A

Three Ghost Ships

These three small sailboats, called Micro 16's, are designed by yacht designer Phil Bolger. He is known for his common sense, but extremely seaworthy "instant type" construction that is inexpensive and simple to build. One Micro 16 is modified with electronic and mechanical gear to make it totally automatic. They were originally conceived to be launched from Charleston, South Carolina, and travel unmanned to Plymouth, England.

While on view here, the boat outfitted with equipment simulates its motion at sea. The electrical systems, solar charging, and global positioning satellite systems are complete as shown on the lead boat (labeled "U"); these allow it to be set on course for a programmed latitude and longitude. However, the sail-handling equipment shown here is for demonstration only and will require further development to withstand the rigors of the sea. This project, a work-in-progress, will culminate with a transatlantic voyage at some future date.

The crossing will represent a salute to the rich heritage that exists between the U.S.A. and Britain. Both Charleston and Plymouth (a departure point for the Mayflower) were and still are important naval cities, and played significant roles in the development of their respective nations. These three small ships identified as U, S, and A also allude to the crossing of the Nina, the Pinta and the Santa Maria. A small amount of tea could be carried in each boat.

—Chris Burden, 1991

PREVIOUS SPREAD
Chris Burden, *Three Ghost Ships*, 1991

RIGHT
Chris Burden, *Three Ghost Ships I*, 1990

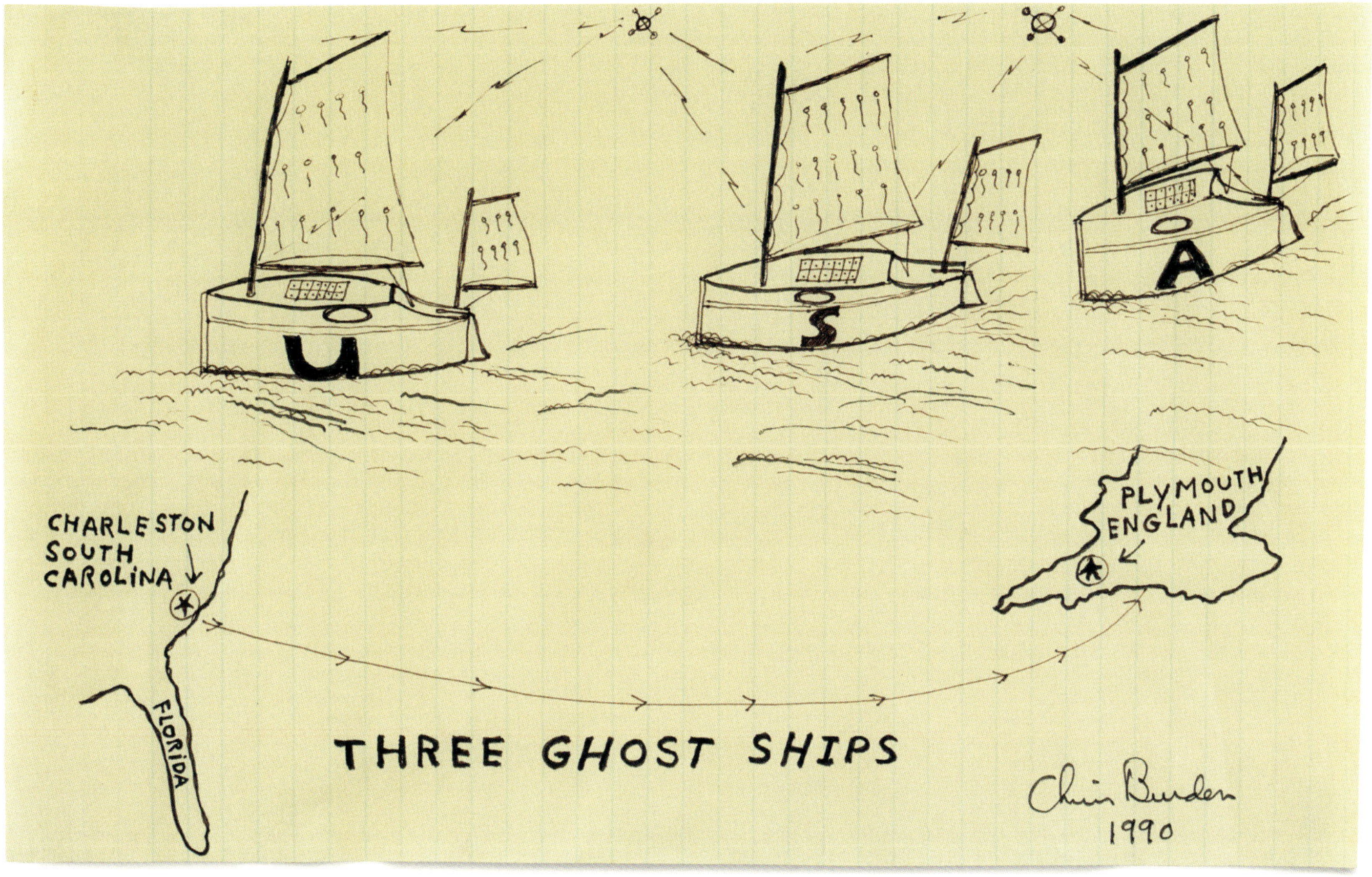
CHARLESTON
SOUTH
CAROLINA
FLORIDA
PLYMOUTH
ENGLAND
THREE GHOST SHIPS
Chris Burden
1990

III

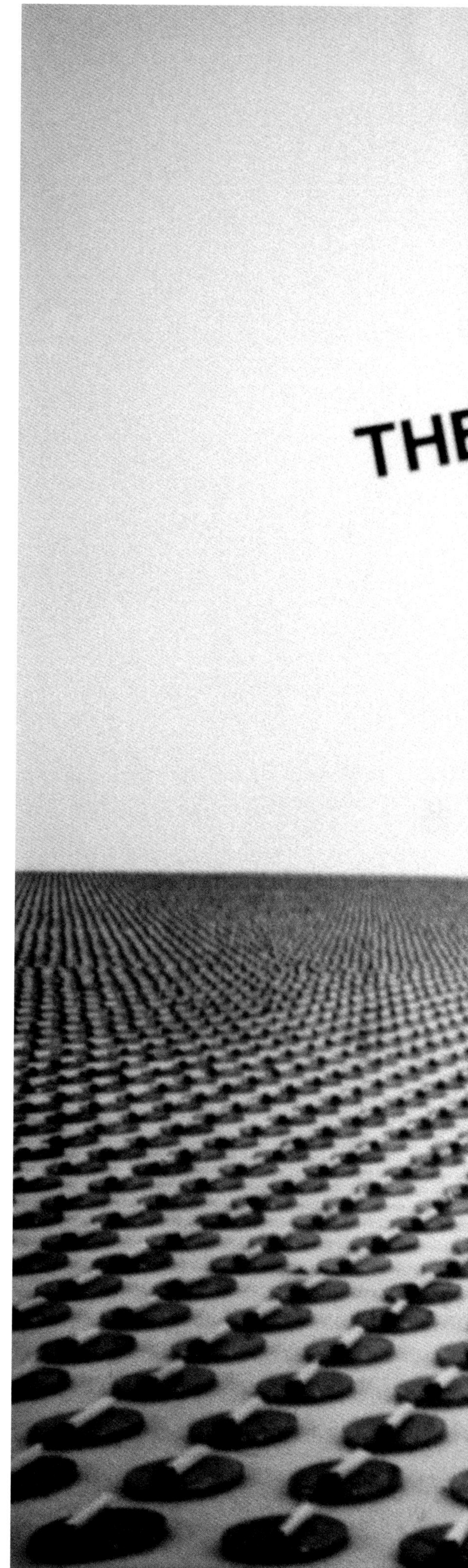

Chris Burden, *The Reason for the Neutron Bomb*, 1979

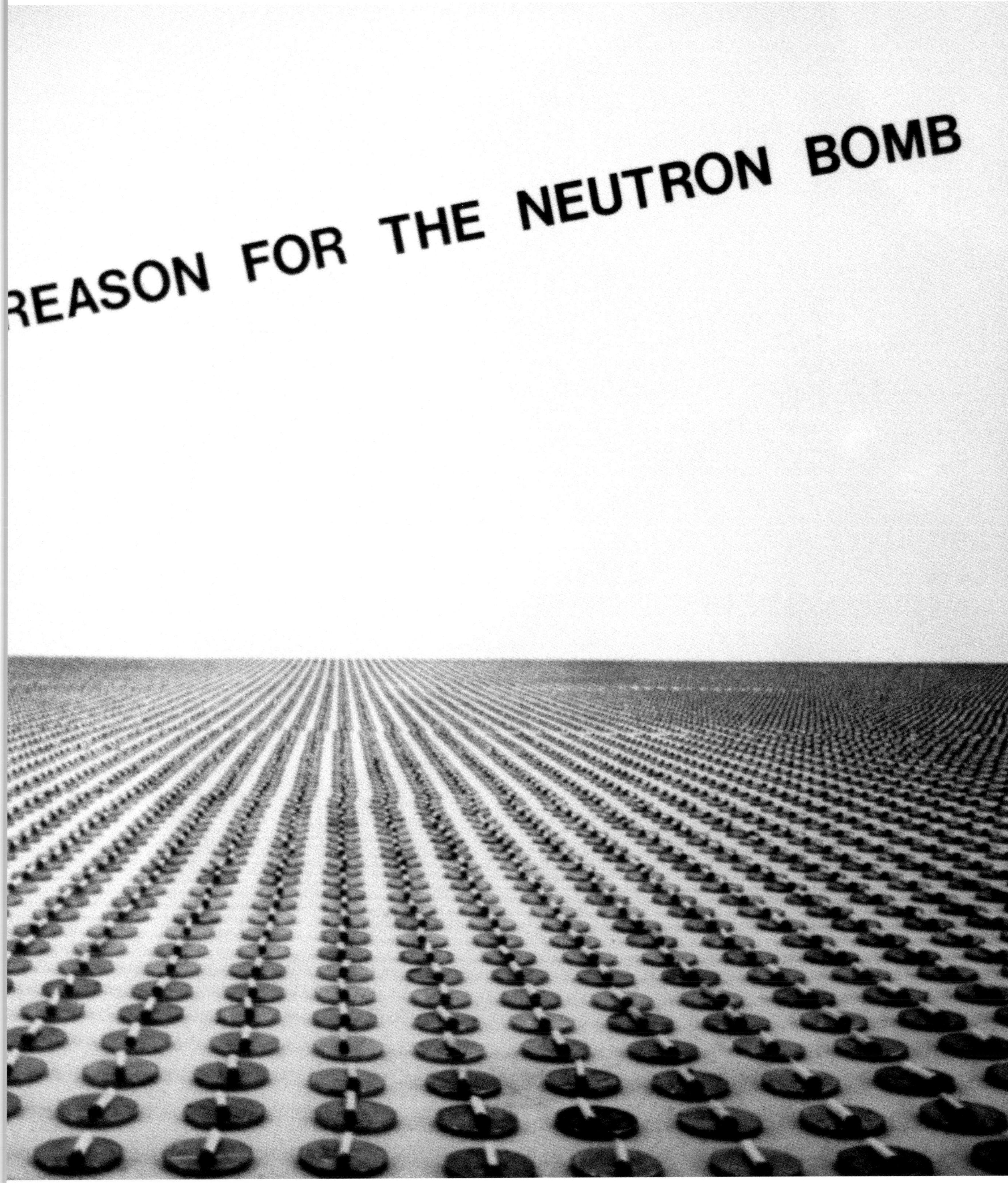
REASON FOR THE NEUTRON BOMB

The Reason for the Neutron Bomb

Behind the Iron Curtain, along the border between Eastern and Western Europe, the Soviet Union maintains an army of 50,000 highly sophisticated tanks. The United States possesses only 10,000 tanks and the combined strength of all the Western European nations, including the NATO forces, is estimated to be no more than 20,000 tanks. The Western European forces are outnumbered by more than two to one. This numerical imbalance is the reason given by our military for the existence of the neutron bomb. Each nickel-and-matchstick combination here represents one Russian tank.

—Chris Burden, 1979

Chris Burden, *The Reason for the Neutron Bomb* (detail), 1979

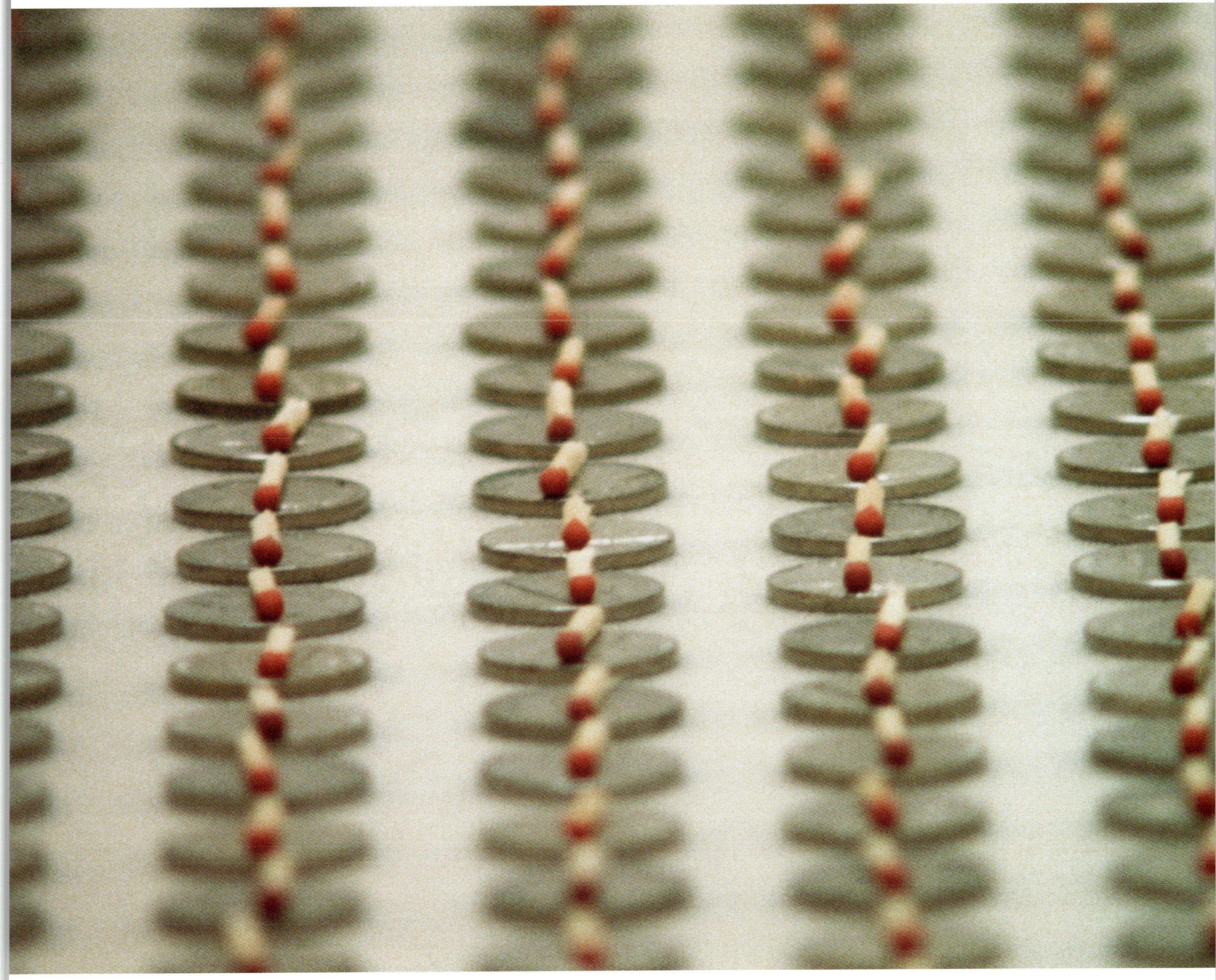

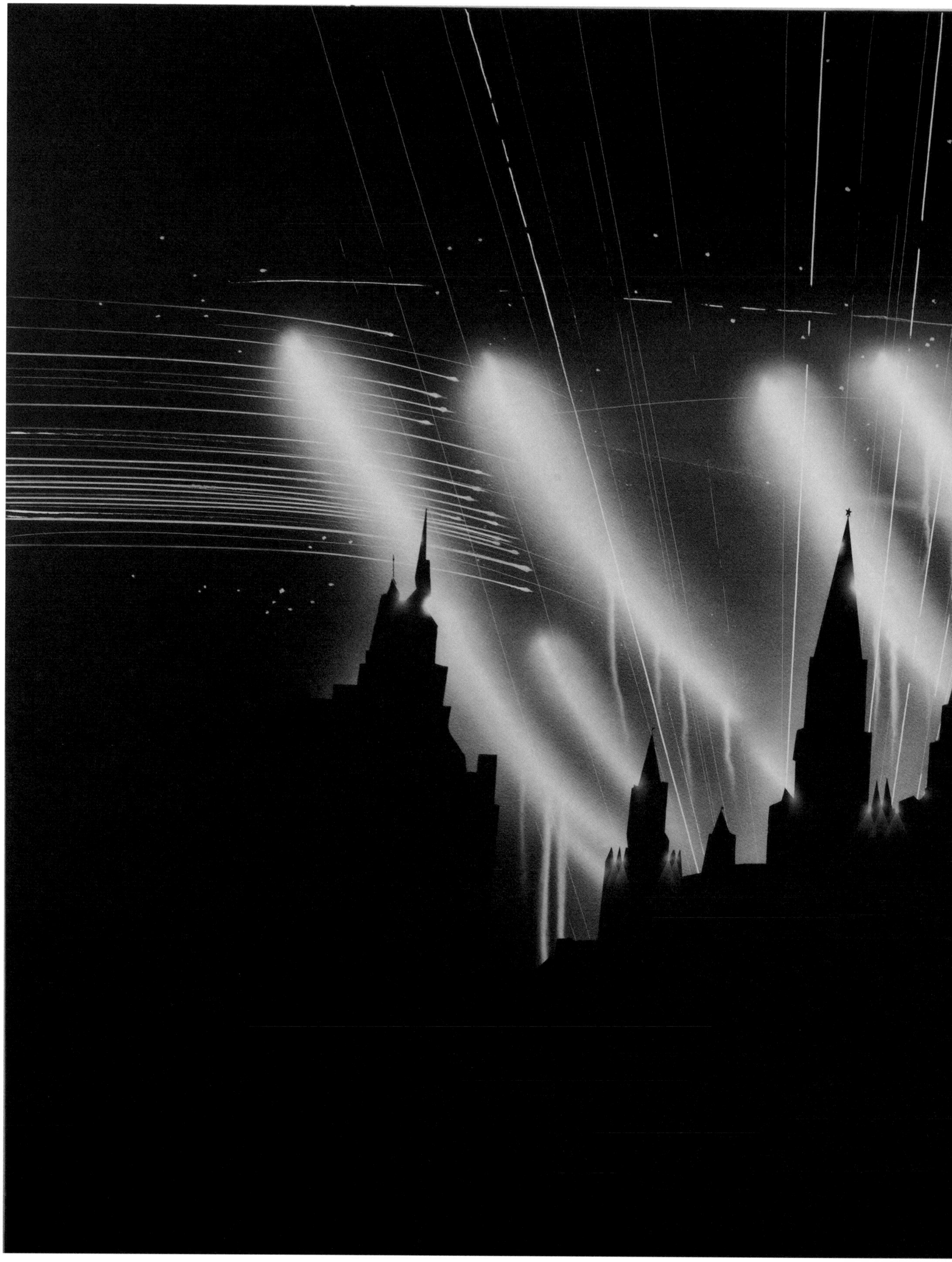

Jack Goldstein, *Untitled*, 1981

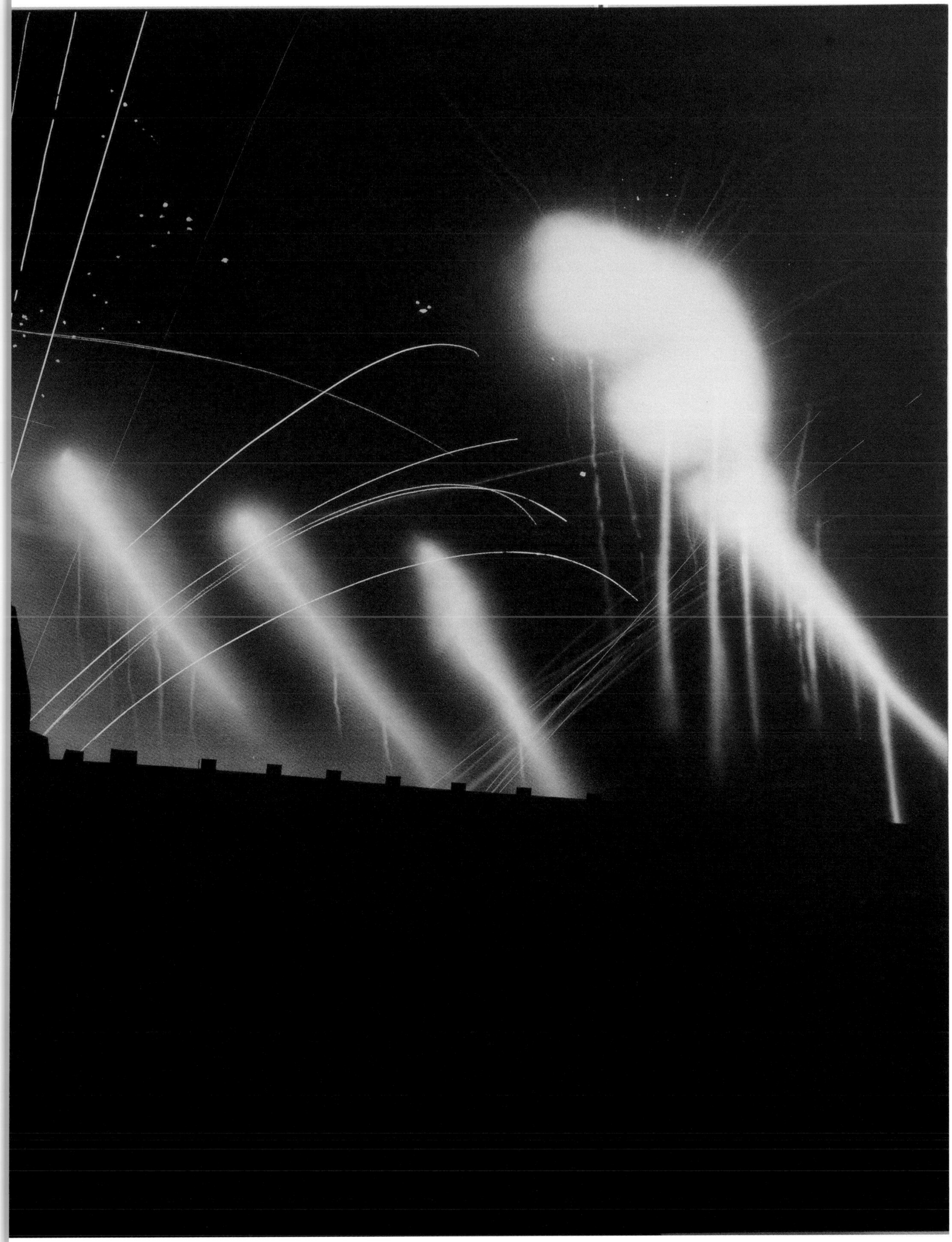

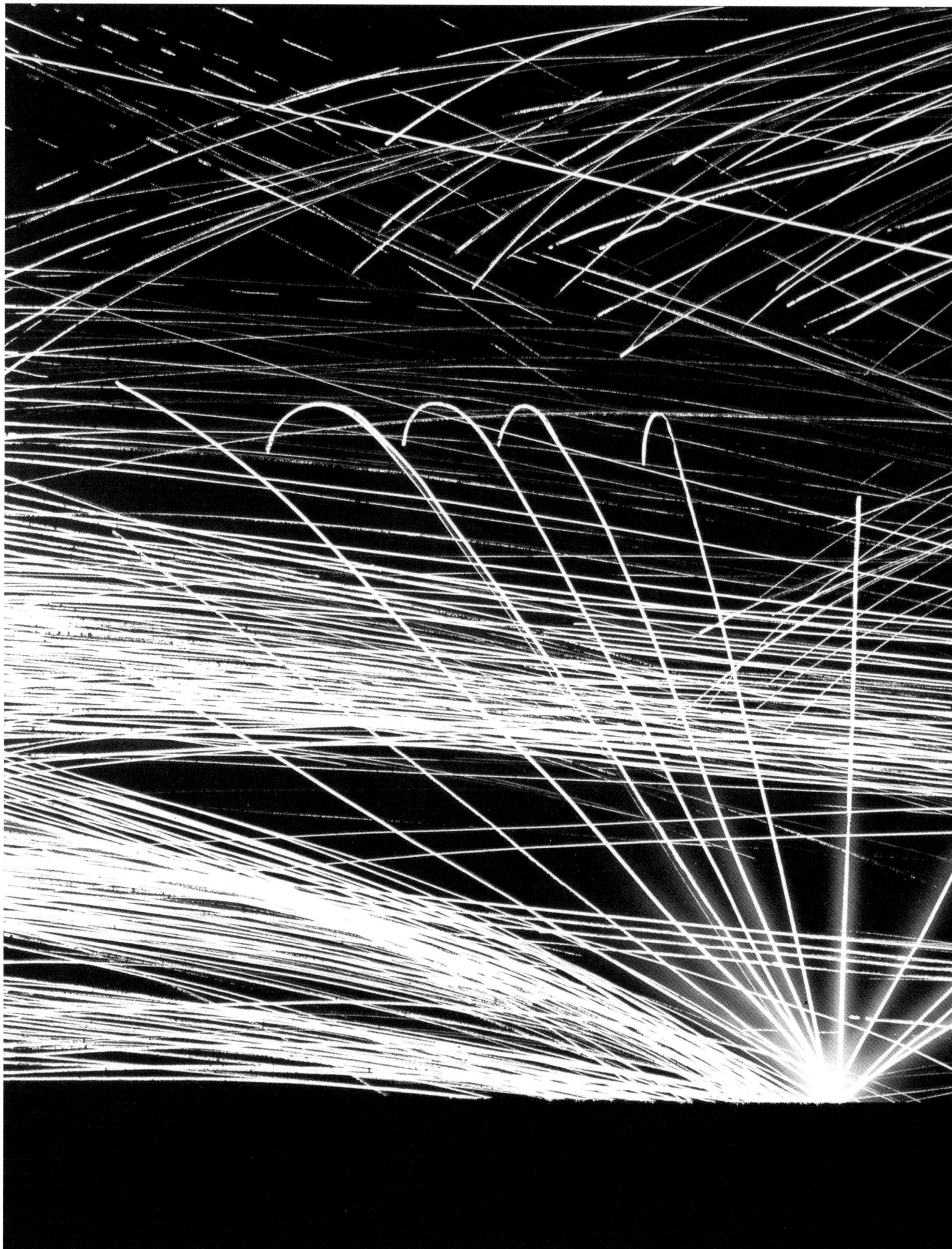

Jack Goldstein, *Untitled (#61 Burning City)*, 1981

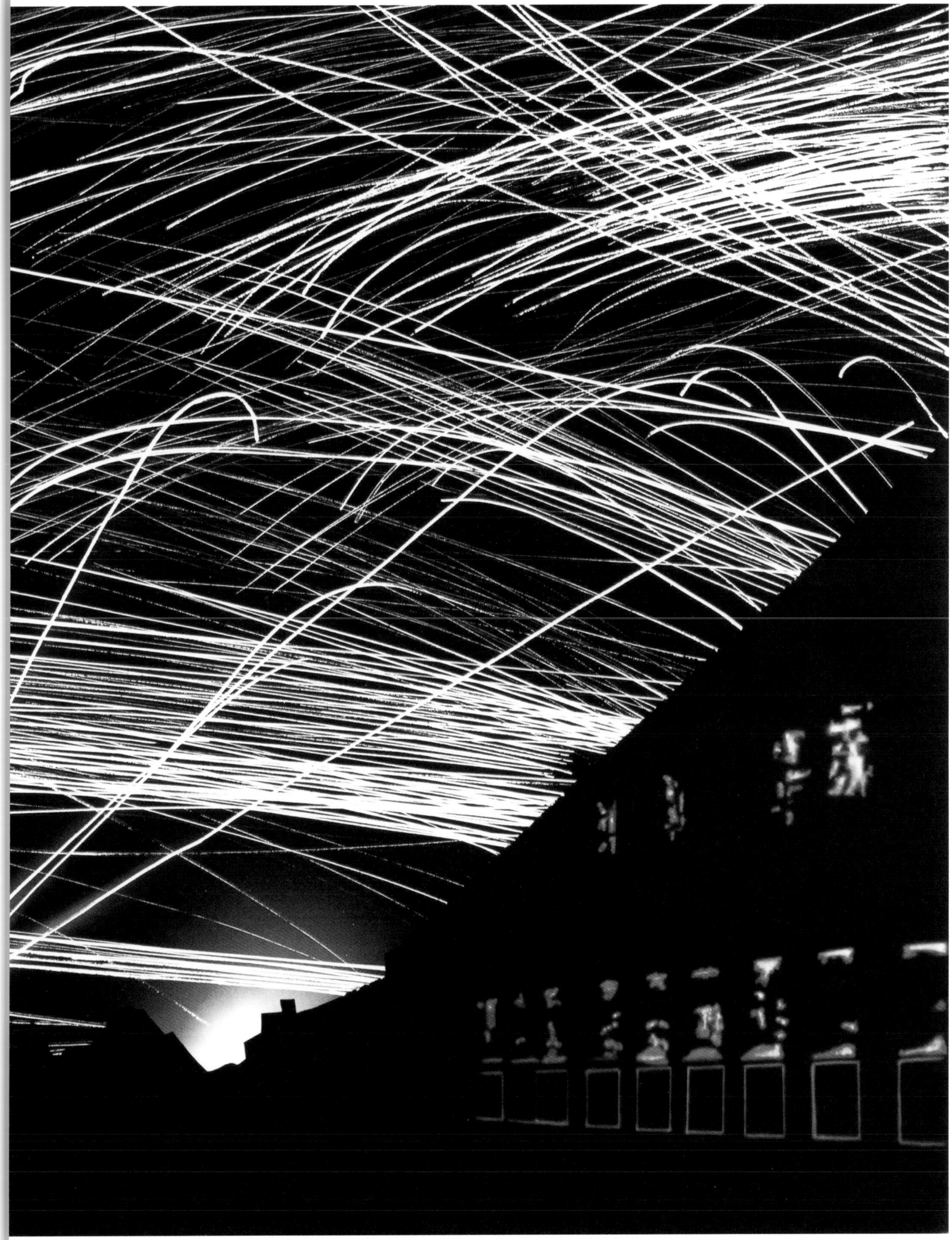

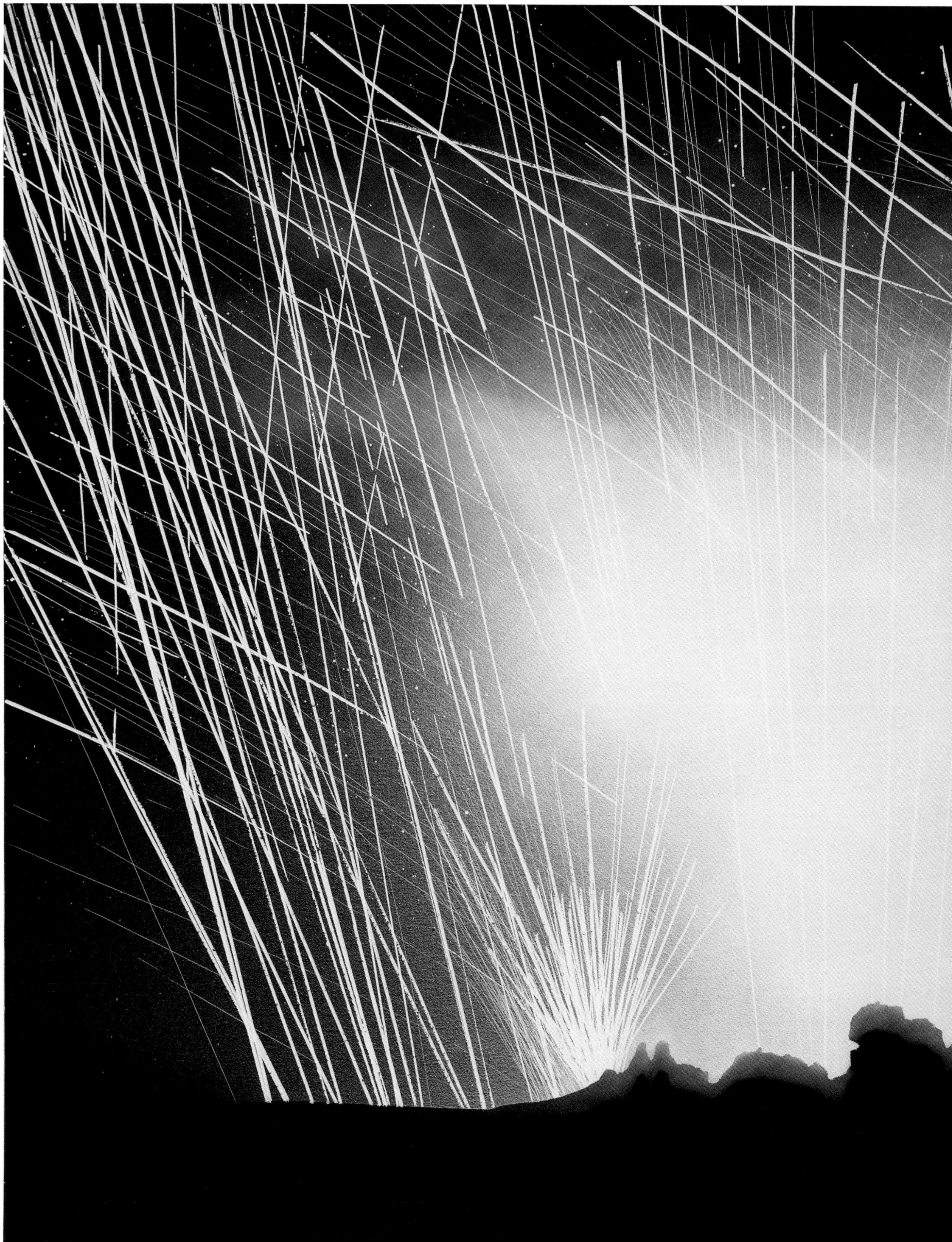

Jack Goldstein, *Untitled*, 1981

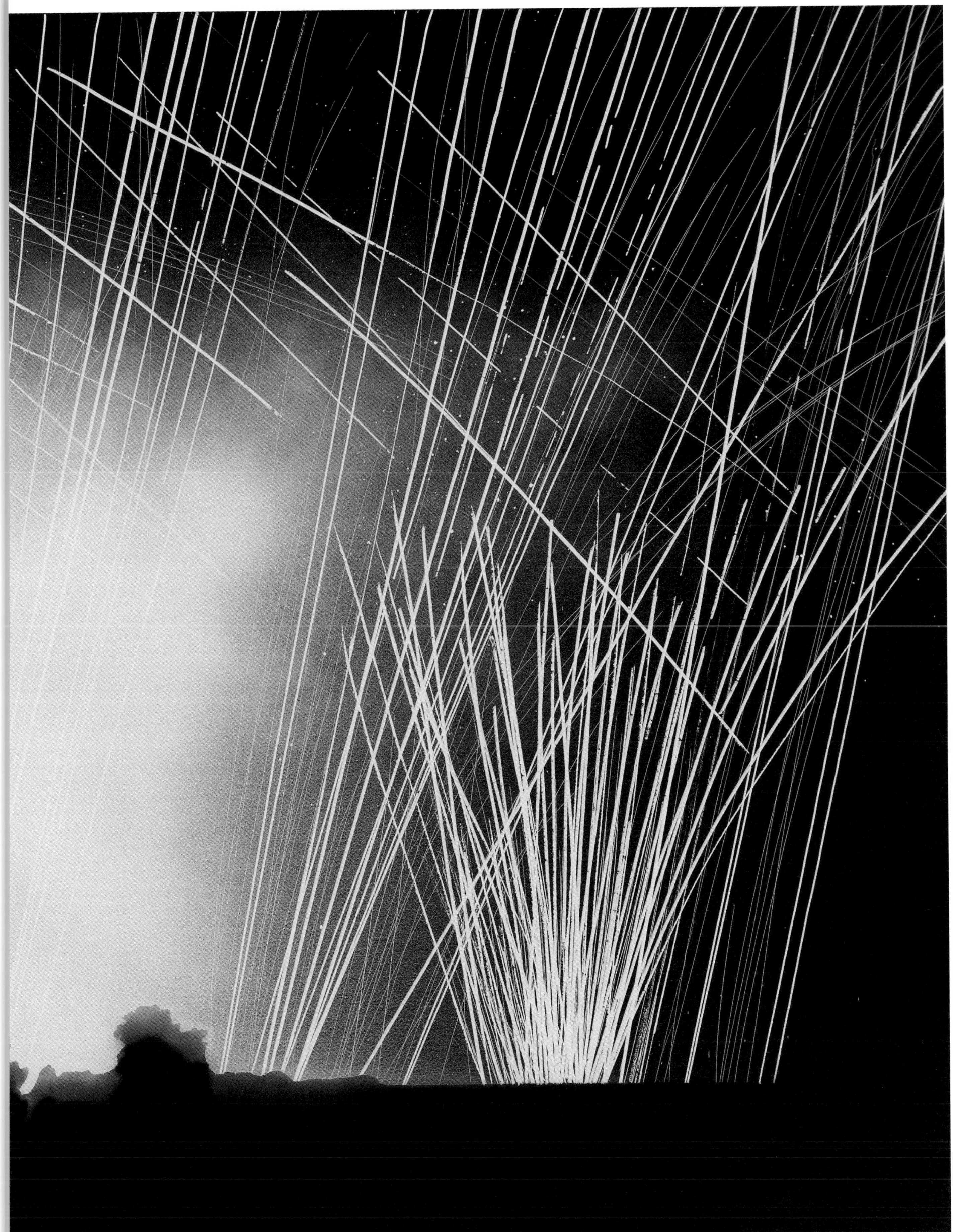

Jack Goldstein, *Untitled*, 1981

Jack Goldstein, *Burning Window*, 1977/2012

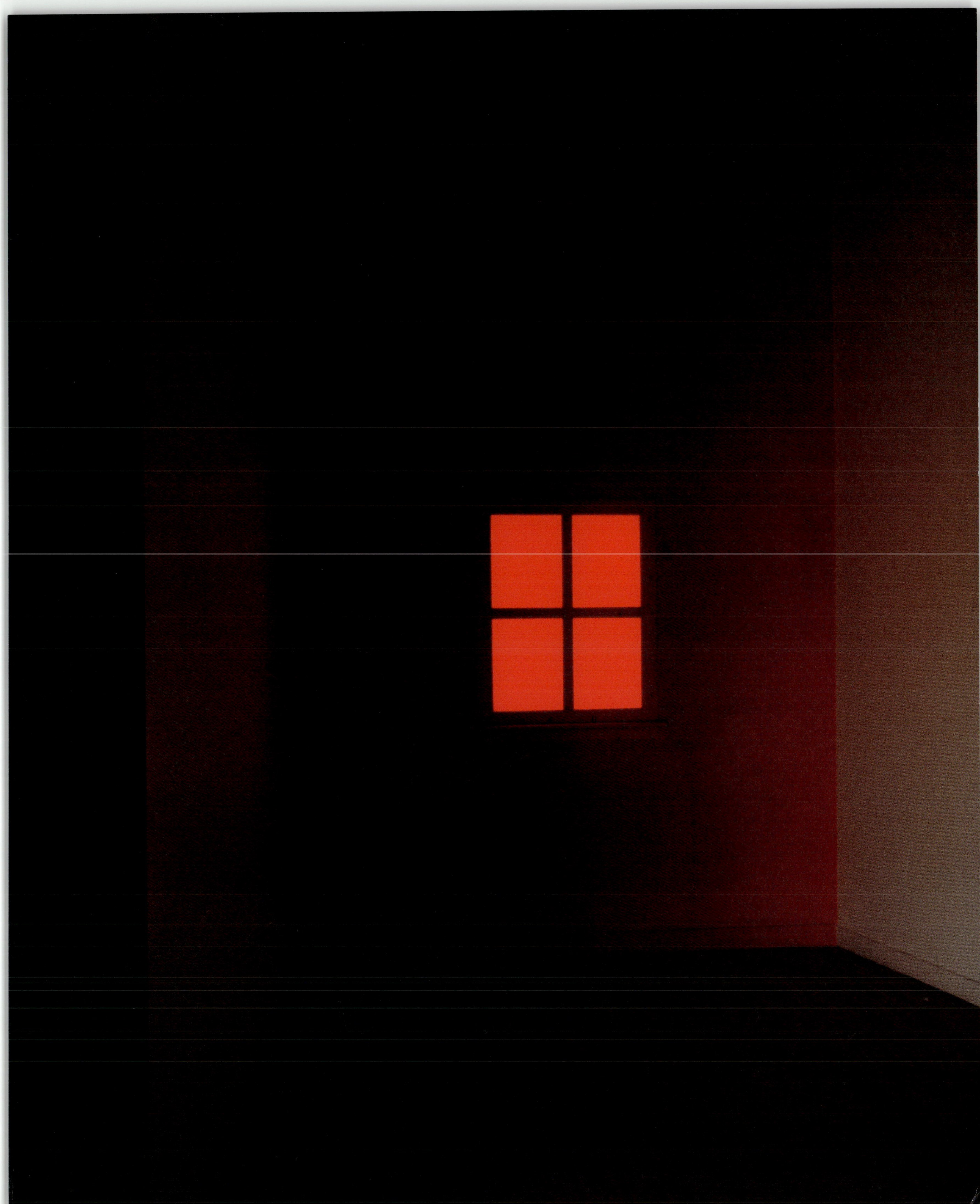

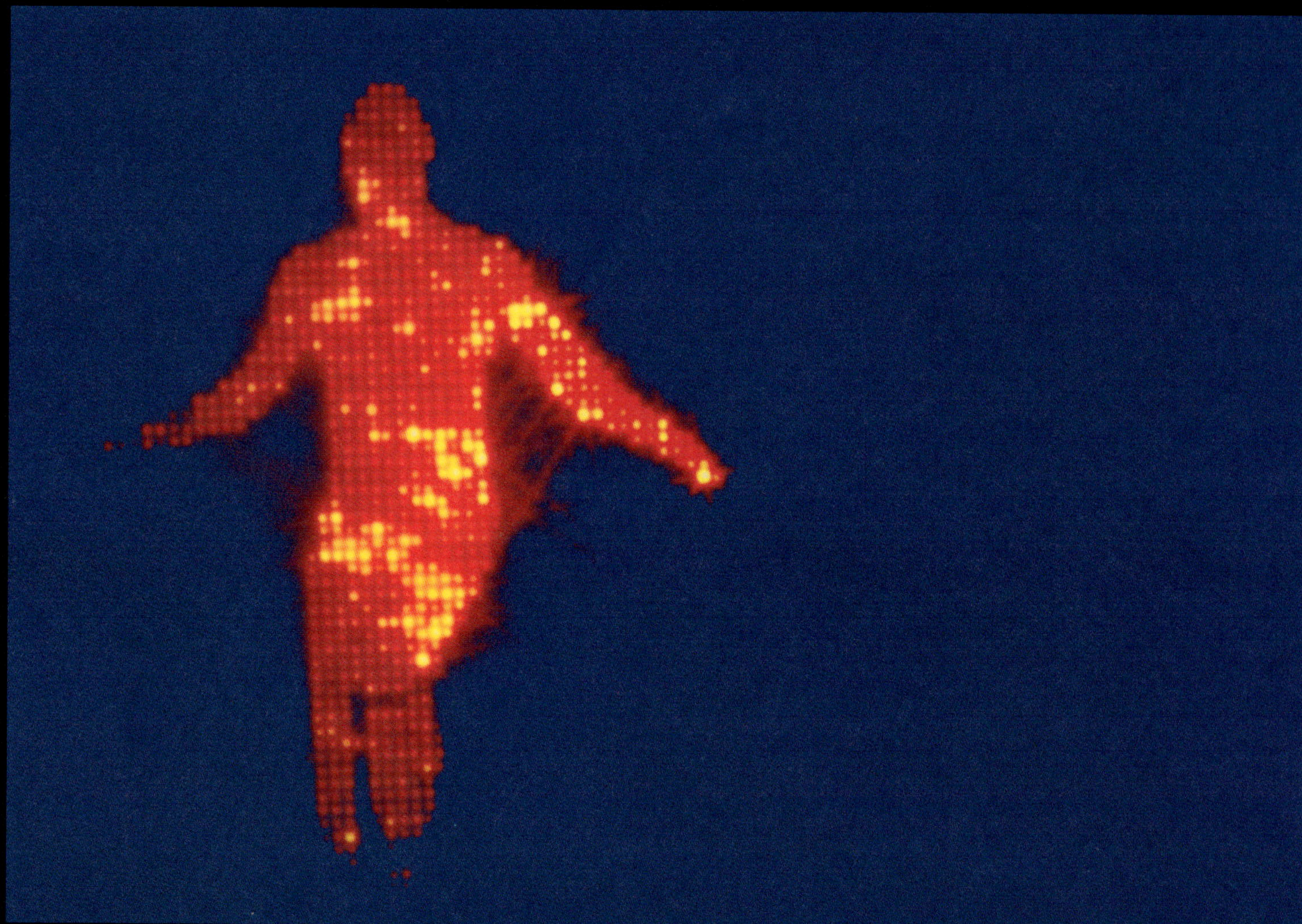

Stills from Jack Goldstein, *The Jump*, 1978

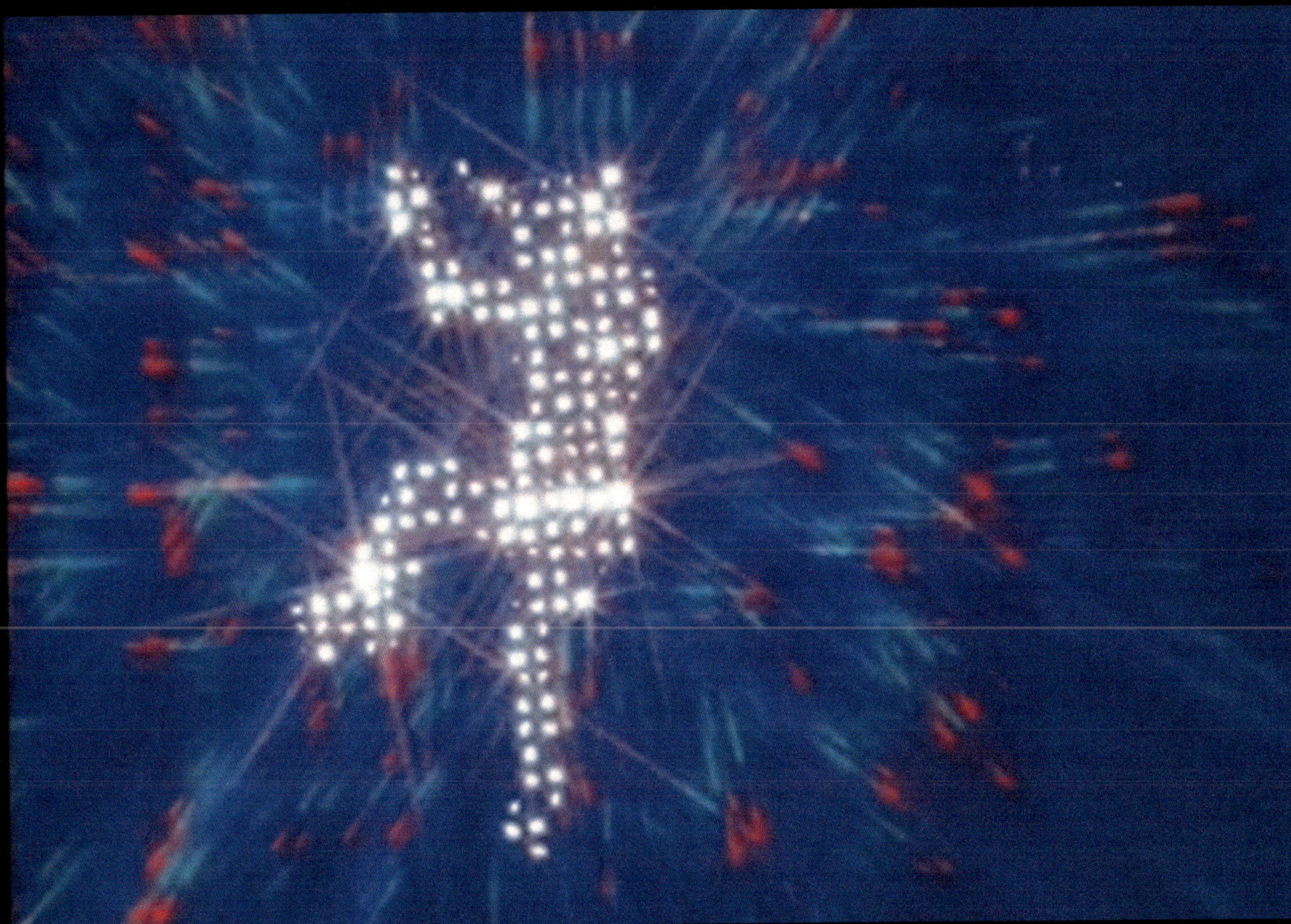

EPILOGUE

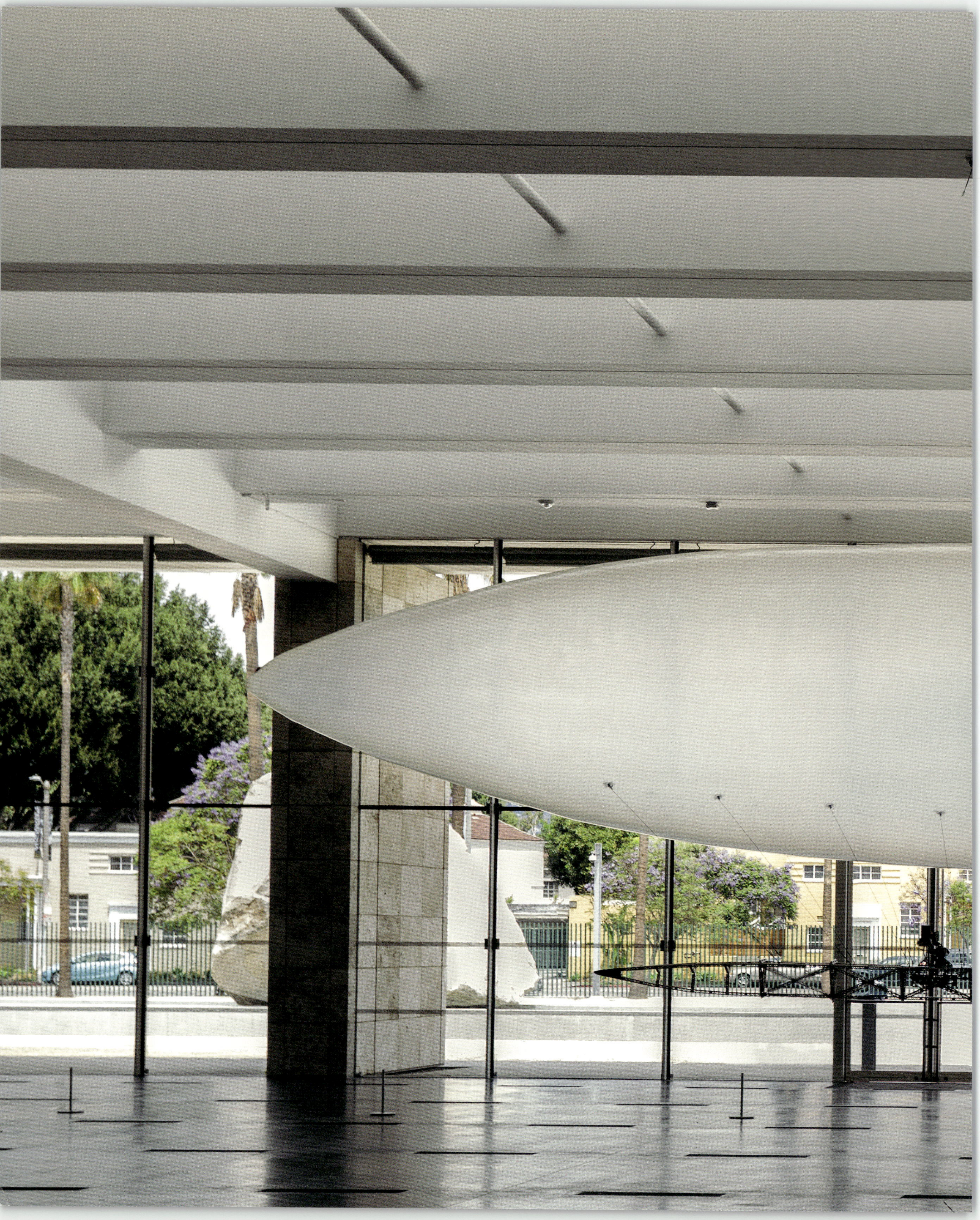

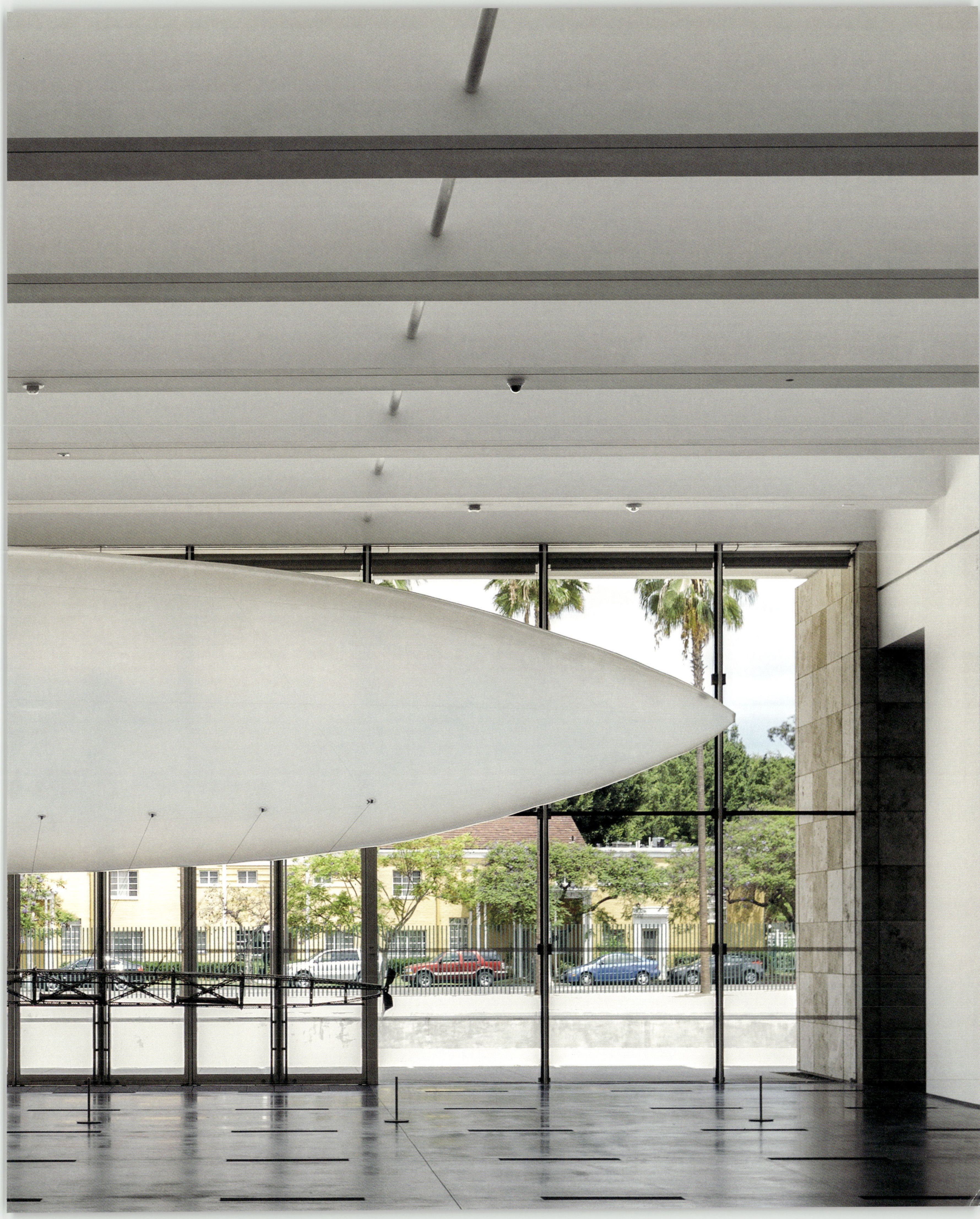

PREVIOUS SPREAD AND RIGHT
Chris Burden, *Ode to Santos Dumont*, 2015

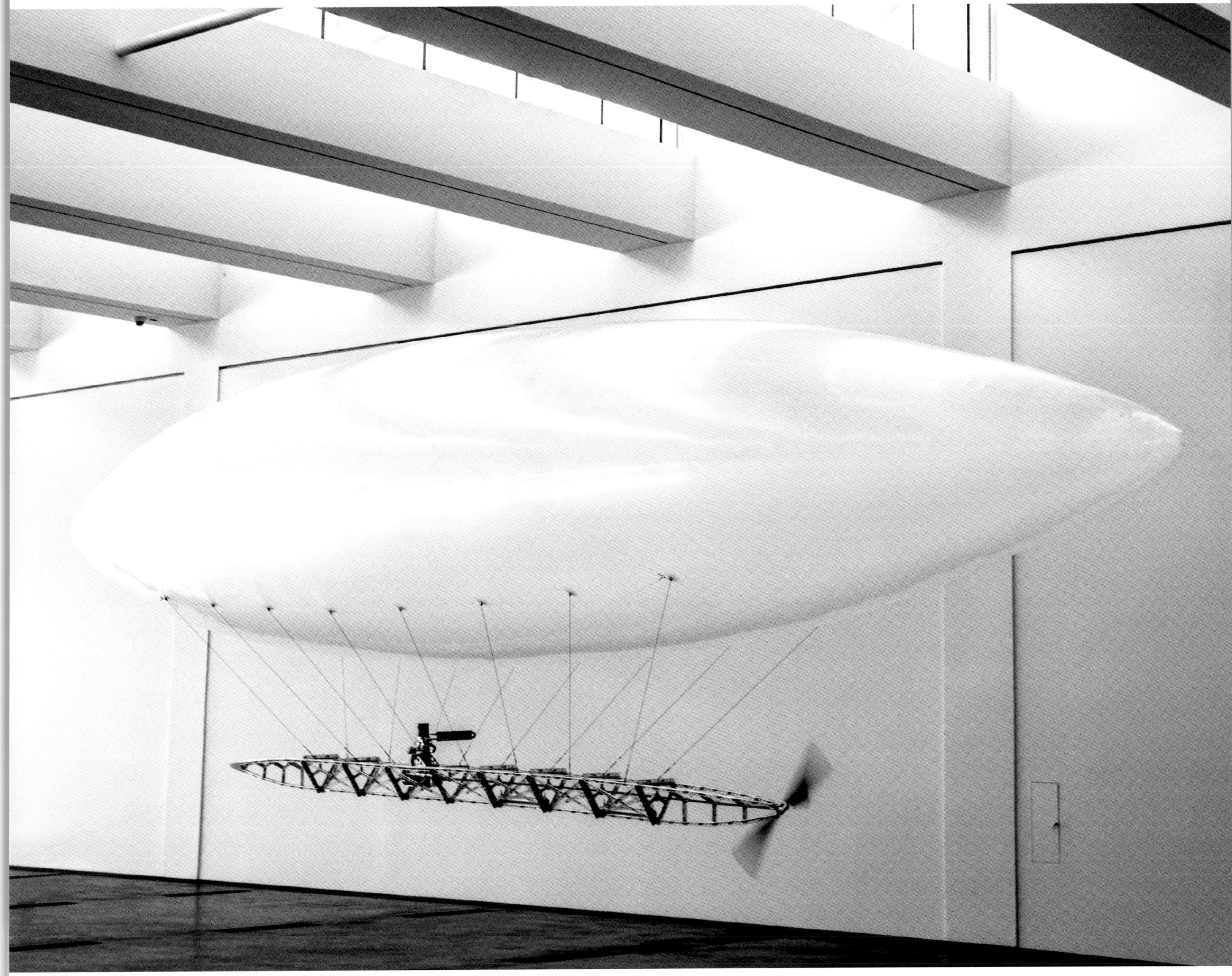

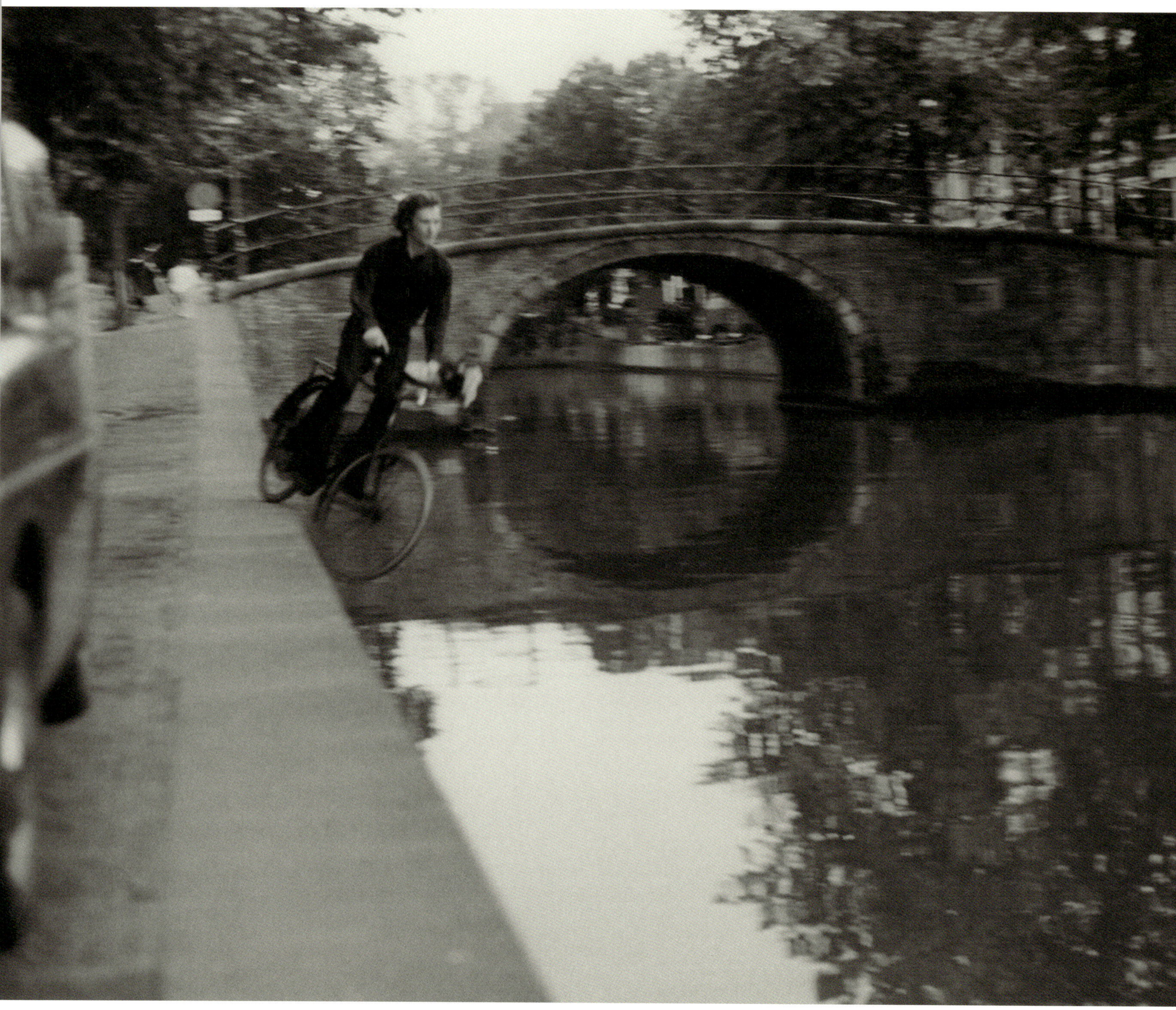

Bas Jan Ader, *Fall 2, Amsterdam*, 1970

SELECTED TIMELINE

Compiled by Jamin An

BAS JAN ADER

1942–1975
b. Winschoten, Netherlands

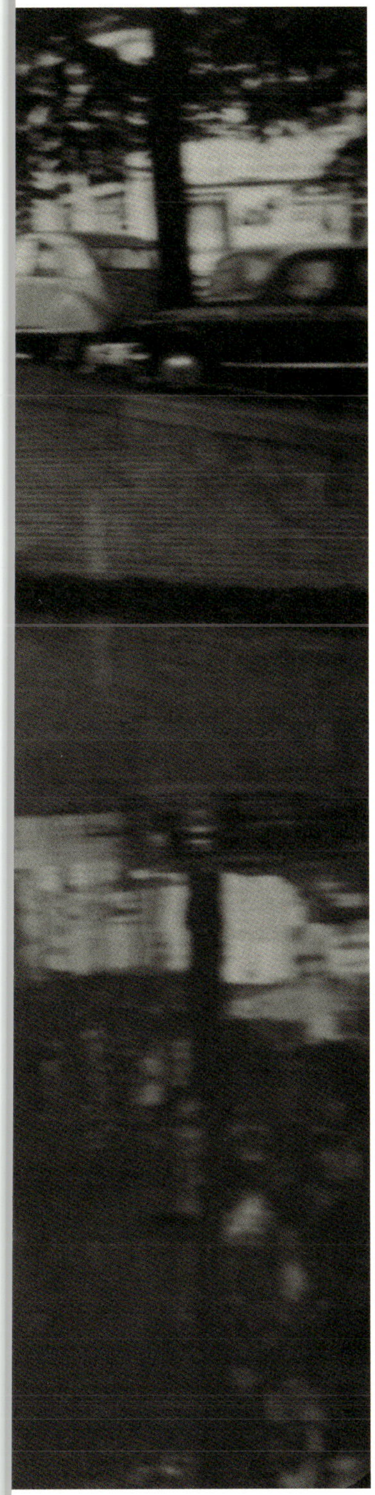

CHRIS BURDEN

1946–2015
b. Boston, MA; d. Topanga, CA

JACK GOLDSTEIN

1945–2003
b. Montreal, Canada; d. San Bernardino, CA

This timeline tracks major biographical and artistic events in the lives of the exhibition's three artists circa 1970. A selection of other artists, artworks, and art historical events is interwoven, offering a sketch of the broader engagement with disappearance in and around Southern California.

1963

Bas Jan Ader connects with fellow Dutch artist and former classmate Ger van Elk in Los Angeles after serving as a crew member on the yacht *Felicidad* for an eleven-month voyage from Morocco to California via the Panama Canal.

1965

Ader earns his BFA from Otis Art Institute in Los Angeles. While at Otis, he meets his future wife, Mary Sue Andersen. Ader and Andersen marry in Las Vegas in June. He then attends Claremont Graduate School in Claremont, California, for his MFA.

1967

Ader mounts his thesis exhibition, *Implosion, Bas Jan Ader*, at Claremont Graduate School (Feb. 4–12).

1969

FEBRUARY

Ader and the artist William Leavitt begin publishing the art journal *Landslide.* Billed as "A quarterly journal of underground art," *Landslide* caricatures the art world with farcically named contributors and fake interviews, among other parodic elements. Seven issues are produced between 1969 and 1970, distributed to a mailing list of approximately forty artists, curators, and critics.

Jack Goldstein completes his BFA at Chouinard Art Institute in Los Angeles.

Chris Burden completes his BA at Pomona College in Claremont.

MAY

The exhibition *The Appearing/Disappearing Image/Object* opens at Newport Harbor Art Museum in Newport Beach, California, and includes works by Michael Asher, John Baldessari, Ron Cooper, Doug Edge, Barry Le Va, Tim Rudnick, and Allen Ruppersberg (May 11–June 28).

AUTUMN

Burden attends University of California, Irvine (UCI) as part of the university's inaugural class of MFA students. The program's faculty includes artists Tony DeLap and Robert Irwin, with whom Burden studies.

1970

APRIL

Ader, with help from Mary Sue Andersen Ader and William Leavitt, films *Fall 1, Los Angeles* (pages 46–47).

JUNE

Ader holds a one-week exhibition at Chouinard Art Institute featuring a single installation and performance work, *Light vulnerable objects threatened by eight cement bricks* (June 1–7).

JULY

John Baldessari, with help from friends and students at the University of California, San Diego, takes his paintings from 1953 to 1966 in his possession and burns them in a crematorium (July 24). *Cremation Project*, a mixed media work, documents the process and results of Baldessari's creative destruction (fig. 1).

SUMMER

Ader visits Amsterdam, where, with help from Ger van Elk and Mary Sue Andersen Ader, he films *Fall 2, Amsterdam* in the city's center, near the intersection of Reguliersgracht and Kerkstraat (pages 48–49).

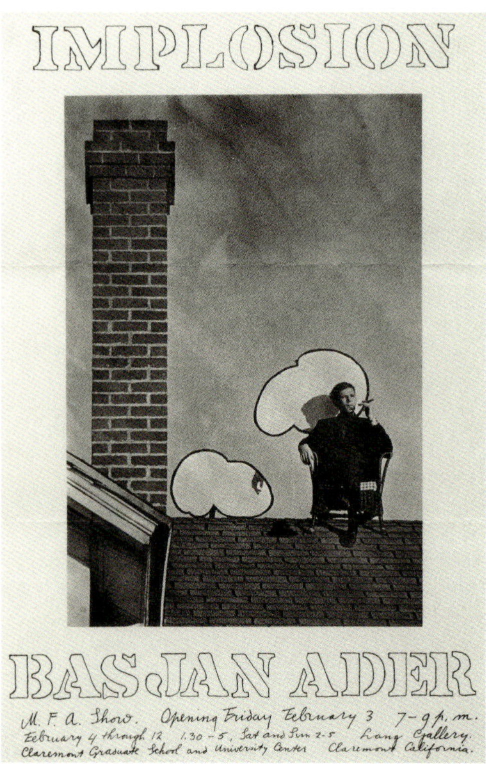

Bas Jan Ader, *Implosion/The artist contemplating the forces of nature*, 1967

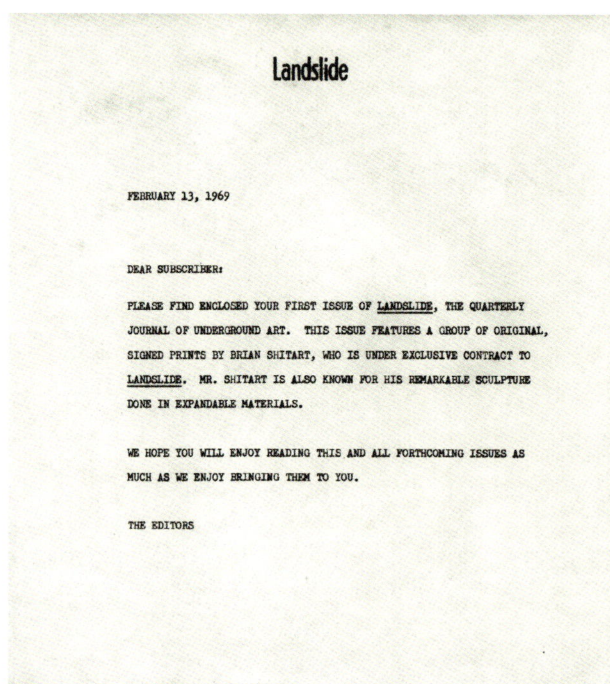

Landslide

FEBRUARY 13, 1969

DEAR SUBSCRIBER:

PLEASE FIND ENCLOSED YOUR FIRST ISSUE OF LANDSLIDE, THE QUARTERLY JOURNAL OF UNDERGROUND ART. THIS ISSUE FEATURES A GROUP OF ORIGINAL, SIGNED PRINTS BY BRIAN SHITART, WHO IS UNDER EXCLUSIVE CONTRACT TO LANDSLIDE. MR. SHITART IS ALSO KNOWN FOR HIS REMARKABLE SCULPTURE DONE IN EXPANDABLE MATERIALS.

WE HOPE YOU WILL ENJOY READING THIS AND ALL FORTHCOMING ISSUES AS MUCH AS WE ENJOY BRINGING THEM TO YOU.

THE EDITORS

Bas Jan Ader, *Landslide: A quarterly journal of underground art*, 1969

AUTUMN

Judy Chicago establishes the Feminist Art Program at California State University, Fresno.

Pomona College appoints Helene Winer Gallery Director and Assistant Professor of Art. Winer moves back to her hometown of Los Angeles after living in London.

Goldstein attends the MFA program at the California Institute of the Arts (CalArts) in Valencia and is one of the first graduate students working under John Baldessari in his famed Post-Studio class. He completes his degree in 1972.

OCTOBER

Goldstein's works are part of the group exhibition *Temple Street Artists* at the Long Beach Museum of Art (Oct. 4–Nov. 1). Here, Helene Winer sees Goldstein's work for the first time and subsequently meets Goldstein and other artists she would go on to present at Pomona College, including William Leavitt and Ader.

1971

JANUARY

UCI MFA students, including Burden, Nancy Buchanan, and Barbara T. Smith, open F Space in Santa Ana, California. The alternative, cooperative gallery becomes an important venue for these and other artists in and around UCI to realize performances and installations, including Burden's well-known performance *Shoot*, 1971. F Space is active until July 1972.

Goldstein mounts a solo exhibition at Pomona College Art Gallery in Claremont, organized by Helene Winer (Jan. 7–31). The exhibition presents the artist's sculptures from 1969 to 1971.

FEBRUARY

Eleanor Antin begins photographing fifty pairs of black rubber boots arranged in varying ways in different public sites—on the beach, in the forest, and outside a church, to name a few. These black-and-white photographs are sent on postcards to recipients around the world. Antin's *100 Boots* series contains 51 postcards, realized between 1971 and 1973.

APRIL

Goldstein organizes a group show in his studio, a space he shares with friend and fellow artist Hirokazu Kosaka at 1356 South Figueroa St., Los Angeles (Apr. 4–24). Entitled *Studio Show*, the exhibition includes Ader, Paul Drake, Ger van Elk, Goldstein, William Leavitt, Allen Ruppersberg, Stephen Sher, and Wolfgang Stoerchle. At Goldstein's request, Helene Winer is named the show's curator.

Burden performs *Five Day Locker Piece* at UCI for his MFA thesis exhibition (Apr. 26–30) (pages 60–63).

MAY

Maurice Tuchman's *Art and Technology* exhibition opens at the Los Angeles County Museum of Art (LACMA) (May 11–Aug. 29).

Goldstein is included in the LACMA exhibition *24 Young Los Angeles Artists* (May 11–July 4).

JUNE

Ader is included in the international exhibition *Sonsbeek buiten de perken* in Arnhem, Netherlands, and screens *Fall 1, Los Angeles*, 1970, and *Fall 2, Amsterdam*, 1970 (June 19–Aug. 15).

AUTUMN

After visiting Judy Chicago's Feminist Art Program in Fresno, Miriam Schapiro invites Chicago to bring the Feminist Art Program to CalArts. They co-teach, working with students such as Suzanne Lacy and Faith Wilding. Sheila Levrant de Bretteville establishes the affiliated Women's Design Program at CalArts.

OCTOBER

Ader shows *Fall 1, Los Angeles*, 1970, and *Fall 2, Amsterdam*, 1970, in *Prospekt '71: Projektion*, Düsseldorf (Oct. 8–17).

NOVEMBER

Burden performs *You'll Never See My Face in Kansas City* at the Morgan Gallery in Kansas City, Missouri (Nov. 6) (pages 64–65).

DECEMBER

Burden performs *Disappearing* (Dec. 22–24) (pages 30–31).

Goldstein presents his sculptures for the last time in an exhibition at OK Harris Gallery in New York (Dec. 9–30). By this point, Goldstein has begun making films and will do so with greater intensity in the following years, many of them in his studio space (pages 42–45 and 50–53).

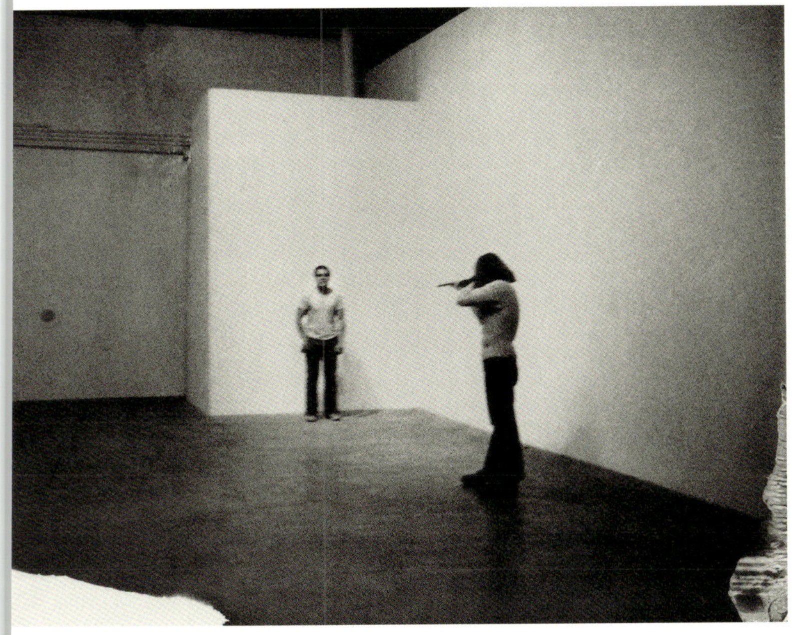

Chris Burden, *Shoot*, 1971. F Space, Santa Ana, California: November 19, 1971

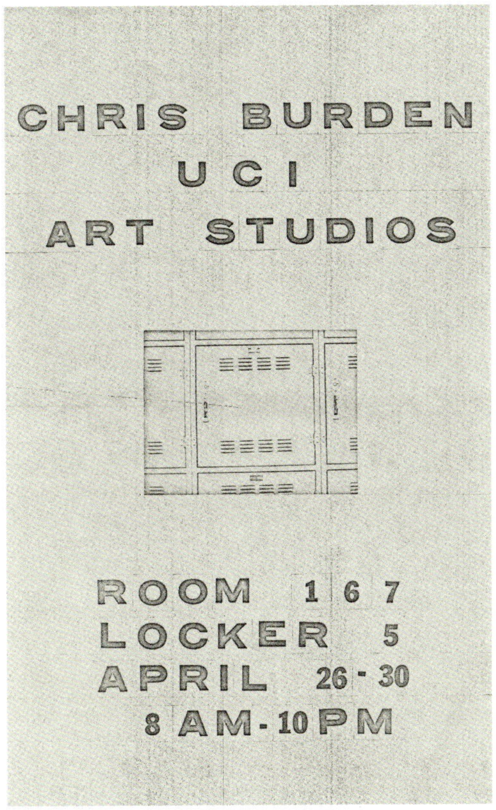

Chris Burden's MFA exhibition announcement, 1971

1972

JANUARY

Helene Winer organizes a three-person group show featuring the work of Ader, Ger van Elk, and William Leavitt at the Pomona College Art Gallery (Jan. 18–Feb. 20). Ader's *Fall 1, Los Angeles*, 1970, *Fall 2, Amsterdam*, 1970, *Nightfall*, 1971, and *Untitled (Sweden)*, 1971, are included in the exhibition (pages 54–57 and 32–35).

Judy Chicago and Miriam Schapiro organize *Womanhouse*, a collaborative installation realized with students from the Feminist Art Program. *Womanhouse* takes place in an old Hollywood mansion at 533 N. Mariposa Street, Los Angeles (Jan. 30–Feb. 28).

MARCH

Helene Winer organizes a three-part "Performance Series" at the Pomona College Art Gallery. The series features Hirokazu Kosaka, Wolfgang Stoerchle, and Burden.

On March 6, Kosaka executes an untitled performance before a gallery audience. Covered by a mound of dirt and an electric blanket, Kosaka lies on the gallery floor for forty minutes, at which point he removes himself from under the dirt and blanket to lie elsewhere on the gallery floor. An assistant sifts the same dirt over Kosaka's body in its new location. After several minutes, Kosaka moves a third and final time, leaving an indexical trace of his lain body.

On March 13, Stoerchle presents a sequence of five performances in a prosceniumlike setting, with the audience on one side of the gallery and Stoerchle on the other. Performing alone with a mirror and rug as props, Stoerchle engages in a series of simple physical acts, from walking with a mirror between his legs to undressing. The series infamously concludes with Stoerchle, having undressed out of his sweatsuit, urinating on the rug in successive spurts of stopping and starting.

On March 20, Burden performs *Match Piece* with his then-wife Barbara Burden. The artist described the piece as follows:

Two-thirds of the gallery floor was covered with white paper. A closed circuit television system was installed in the room. The monitor was placed so that the audience could watch the piece or see it in the monitor, but could not

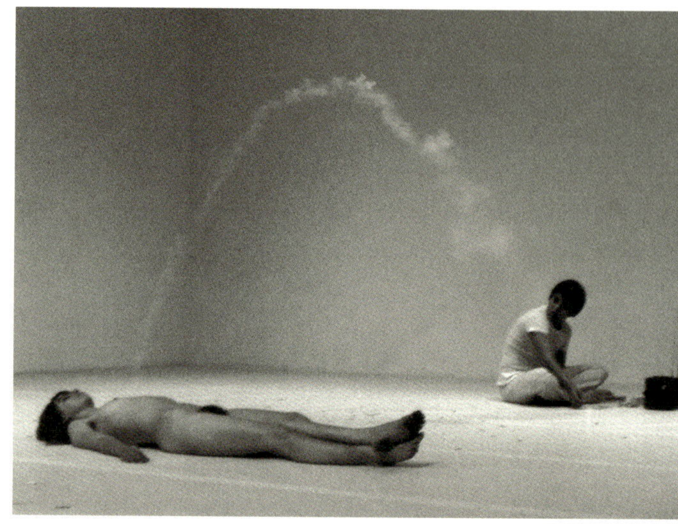

Chris Burden, *Match Piece*, 1972. Pomona College, Claremont, California: March 20, 1972

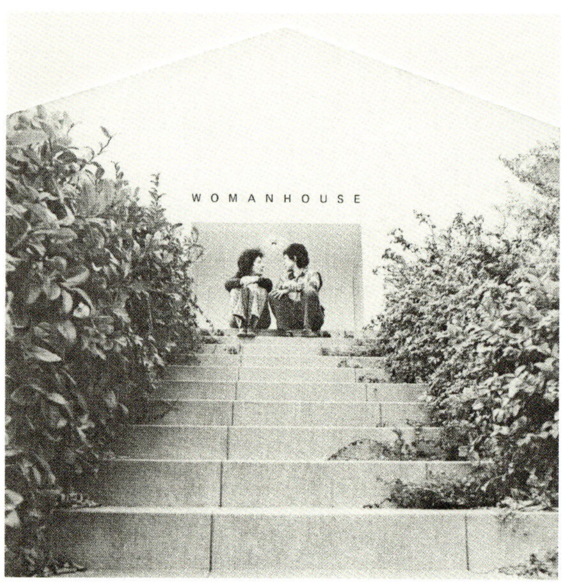

Cover of *Womanhouse* exhibition catalogue, 1972

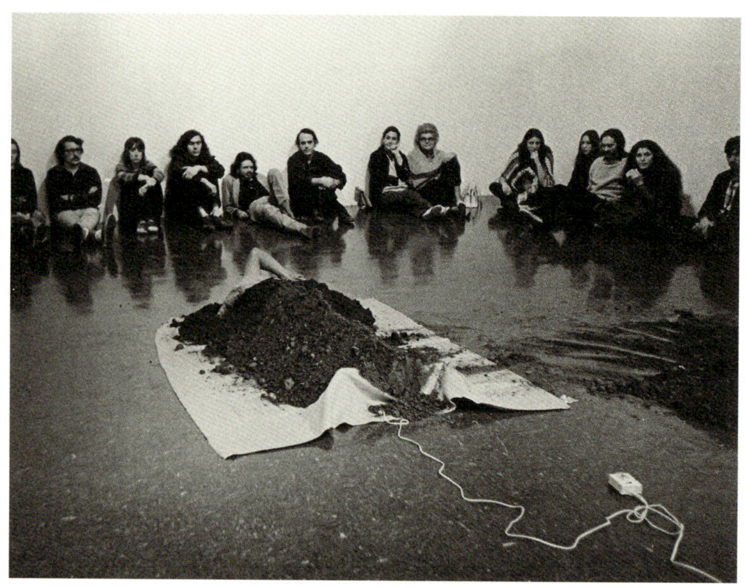

Hirozaku Kosaka, *Untitled*, 1972. Photograph of performance at Pomona College Museum of Art, Claremont, California

do both at once. I sat on the floor at the opposite end of the room. Two miniature TVs were placed so that I could view them while I made match rockets and shot them at a nude woman lying on the floor about fifteen feet from me. The rockets were made by wrapping the match head with foil and igniting it with another match. Range and accuracy were impossible to control. Some of the rockets landed on her body leaving small burns, others landed in the audience. The piece began before the audience arrived and ended when everyone had left, lasting about three hours.

APRIL

Ader mounts his first exhibition with the Amsterdam gallery Art & Project, where he performs *The boy who fell over Niagara Falls* (Apr. 15–21) (pages 82–83).

JUNE

Goldstein performs *Burial Piece*, burying himself underground on the CalArts campus in Valencia (June 9).

Ader has a solo exhibition at the Kabinett für aktuelle Kunst in Bremerhaven, Germany (June 17–July 2). He screens his *Fall* films and again performs *The boy who fell over Niagara Falls* (page 160).

Judy Chicago, Suzanne Lacy, Sandra Orgel, and Aviva Rahmani perform *Ablutions* at Guy Dill's studio in Venice, California, as part of a Feminist Art Program performance art workshop (fig. 5). Hearing a soundtrack of women telling their stories of rape, the audience enters the studio littered with cracked egg shells and encounters multiple performers executing repetitive tasks. A nude woman sits in the center, bound completely by another with gauze bandages. In front of her, three metal tubs are filled with egg, blood, and clay. Two other nude performers bathe in each tub, one after the other, and are then wrapped in a sheet. Another performer nails beef kidneys in an orderly line around the perimeter of the space. *Ablutions* concludes with two clothed women stringing rope over the entire space, tying up the disparate performers and the environment in a single intricate web.

OCTOBER

Helene Winer organizes a solo exhibition of works by Allen Ruppersberg at the Pomona College Art Gallery (Oct. 31–Nov. 22). The exhibition includes Ruppersberg's large-scale photo/text work *Where's Al?*, 1972 (fig. 3). Winer is subsequently forced to leave her position and moves to New York. Goldstein soon follows, splitting his time between Los Angeles and New York.

NOVEMBER

Burden performs *Deadman* at Riko Mizuno Gallery on La Cienega Boulevard in Los Angeles (Nov. 12) (pages 66–71). The artist lies on the street under a canvas tarpaulin, as if a victim at the scene of a traffic accident. Burden is arrested and prosecuted for allegedly causing a false emergency. Barbara T. Smith covers the trial the following January to February 1973 for *Artweek*, and Helene Winer testifies in Burden's defense.

Exhibition announcement for *Chris Burden*, Riko Mizuno Gallery, 1972

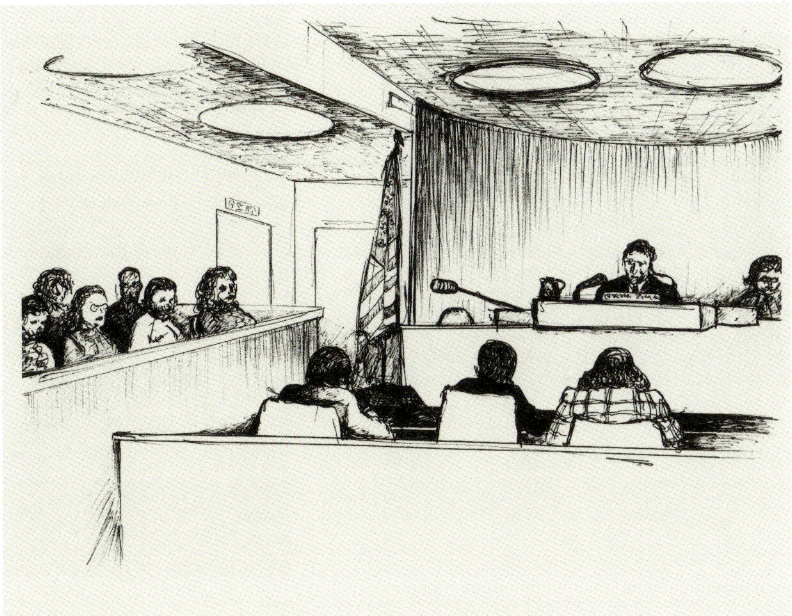

Barbara T. Smith, *Deadman* courtroom sketch, 1973

Goldstein holds a solo exhibition at Riko Mizuno Gallery with a performance and three days of film screenings (Nov. 19–24). For the performance, Goldstein modifies and restages *Burial Piece*.

DECEMBER

Jane Livingston and Marcia Tucker organize Bruce Nauman's solo exhibition at LACMA, *Bruce Nauman: Work from 1965 to 1972* (Dec. 19, 1972–Feb. 18, 1973). The exhibition takes place six years after the artist's first solo show in Los Angeles, at Nicholas Wilder Gallery in May 1966.

In 1972, David Hammons performs *Murder Mystery (Spade Run Over by a Volkswagen)*, in which a cardboard cutout spade is "crushed" under the tire of a Volkswagen Beetle. The work is part of a series of early seventies performances known as the *Spade Mysteries*, where Hammons manipulated—cut, buried, chained—the spade in various ways. The *Spade Mysteries* take place around the same time as his *Spade* series of body prints, an extension of the body prints he began in 1968. All three bodies of work reveal his sustained engagement with tropes of absence, presence, and the black body.

1973

APRIL

Ader performs *The boy who fell over Niagara Falls*, 1972, as part of the exhibition *1, 2, or 4 Day Exhibits and Evening Performances*, Gallery A-402, CalArts (Mar. 28–June 1).

MAY–JUNE

Burden performs *B.C. Mexico* over the course of eleven days, followed by a film screening and reading at Newspace in Newport Beach, California, three days after his return from San Felipe (May 25–June 10) (pages 79–81).

AUTUMN

Ader begins his unfinished triptych *In search of the miraculous*. He completes the first work, *In search of the miraculous (One night in Los Angeles)*, with a single night walk through Los Angeles toward the Pacific Ocean. Mary Sue Andersen Ader takes the photographs of Ader's nighttime walk (pages 86–87).

OCTOBER

Claire S. Copley opens her eponymous gallery in Los Angeles with an inaugural exhibition of works by William Wegman. The gallery is active for five years, from 1973 to 1977.

NOVEMBER

The Woman's Building opens (Nov. 28). Earlier in the year, Judy Chicago, Sheila Levrant de Bretteville, and Arlene Raven had established the Feminist Studio Workshop (FSW) as an independent women's art school. After attracting enough interest, they leased and renovated the former Chouinard Art Institute building near MacArthur Park to house the FSW in the renamed Woman's Building.

1974

SPRING

Ader starts teaching at UCI. The following summer, he prepares for his transatlantic sailing voyage. Borrowing a boat from UCI colleague Tony DeLap, Ader practices on the Los Angeles coast between Marina del Rey and Catalina Island.

In 1974, the art collective Asco stages *Decoy Gang War Victim* multiple times in Los Angeles. The members create fake crime scenes at night, such as in an iconic example where the artist Gronk lies prostrate on the ground in the middle of the road surrounded by burning flares. Asco members photograph the fictive scenes and send the pictures to media outlets, sowing confusion and intervening in the mainstream media's sensationalized, stereotypical attention to gang violence in the city.

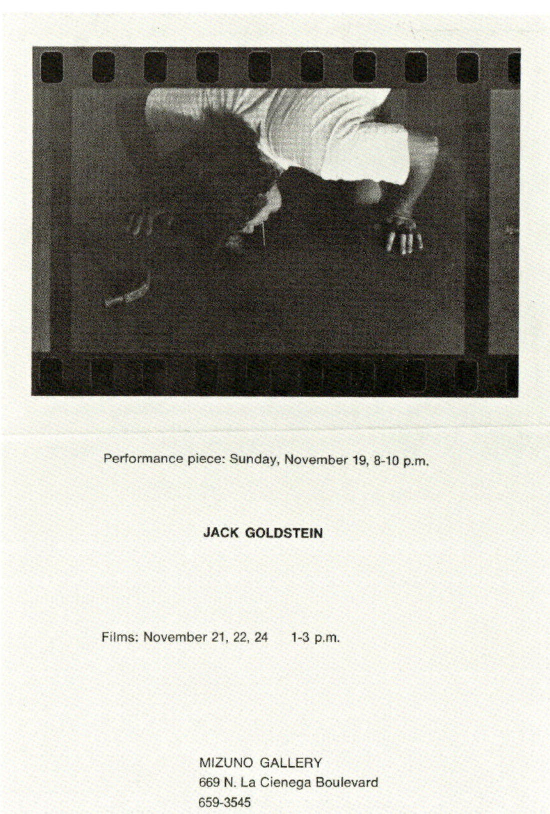

Performance piece: Sunday, November 19, 8-10 p.m.

JACK GOLDSTEIN

Films: November 21, 22, 24 1-3 p.m.

MIZUNO GALLERY
669 N. La Cienega Boulevard
659-3545

Exhibition announcement for *Jack Goldstein*, Riko Mizuno Gallery, 1972

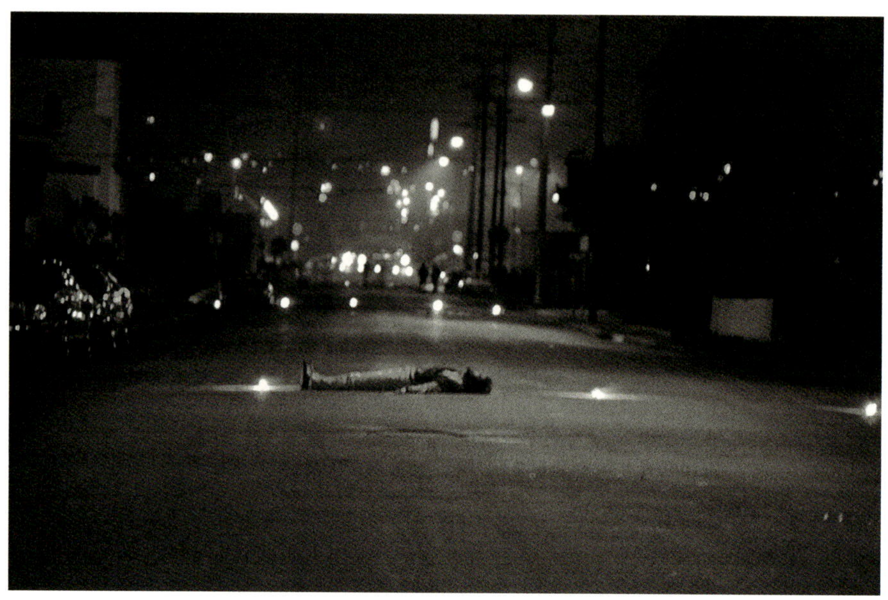

Harry Gamboa Jr., *Decoy Gang War Victim*, 1974, *from the Asco era*

1975

FEBRUARY

Burden performs *White Light/ White Heat* over the course of twenty-two days at Ronald Feldman Fine Arts, New York (Feb. 8–Mar. 1) (pages 74–77).

APRIL

Ader mounts a solo exhibition at Claire S. Copley Gallery in Los Angeles. Titled *Bas Jan Ader: "In Search of the Miraculous,"* the show consists of a performance and multi-part installation that includes the eighteen-photograph version of *In search of the miraculous (One night in Los Angeles)*, 1973. For the opening, nine UCI students form a choir and sing nineteenth-century sea shanties, such as "A Life on the Ocean Wave" by Epes Sargent and Henry Russell, with piano accompanist. The choir performs only once and is represented afterward in the installation by slide-projected photographs and sound recording. Framed musical scores of the shanties hang on the wall (Apr. 22–May 17) (pages 86–87 and 88–93).

JUNE

Ader purchases a used Guppy 13 sailboat. The boat is modified for his transatlantic voyage, and Ader names it *Ocean Wave*.

JULY

Ader sets sail on *Ocean Wave* from Chatham, Massachusetts, in Cape Cod (July 9) (fig. 2).

SEPTEMBER

Mary Sue Andersen Ader waits for the artist in Holland. Ader does not arrive as scheduled.

DECEMBER

After an extended delay and still no sign of Ader, Mary Sue Andersen Ader and the artist's brother, Erik Ader, notify embassies and the British Coast Guard of the artist missing at sea.

1976

Around 1976, when Goldstein is not in New York, he lives and works in a studio located in the Pacific Building at the intersection of Santa Monica Blvd. and Fifth St. in Santa Monica. Goldstein's friend and fellow artist James Welling moves into an office in the building the following year and takes the photographs of Goldstein and his studio that comprise the portfolio *Jack Goldstein's Studio*, 1977–78/2004.

APRIL

A Spanish fishing boat discovers Ader's capsized *Ocean Wave* off the coast of Ireland. Ader's body is not found. The Spanish crew brings the boat to La Coruña, Spain. Drydocked in the harbor, *Ocean Wave* mysteriously disappears sometime between May 8 and June 7.

MAY

Burden presents his first exhibition of performance relics at Ronald Feldman Fine Arts, New York (May 1–June 5). The installation includes *B.C. Mexico*, 1973, and *White Light/White Heat*, 1975.

OCTOBER

Burden completes *Death Valley Run*, crossing the Mojave Desert in Southern California (Oct. 14) (pages 108–13).

1977

FEBRUARY

Burden's relics are included in the Biennial at the Whitney Museum of American Art, New York (Feb. 19–Apr. 3). The installation includes *You'll Never See My Face in Kansas City*, 1971, and *White Light/White Heat*, 1975.

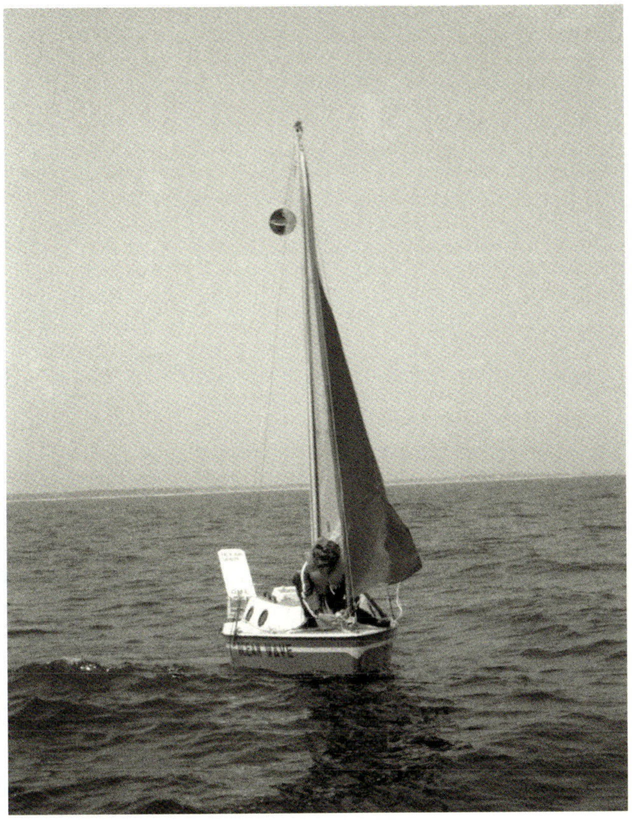

Bas Jan Ader, Still from the launch of the *Ocean Wave*, Chatham Harbor, Chatham, Massachusetts, July 1975

Installation view of Chris Burden's work in the 1977 Biennial Exhibition, Whitney Museum of American Art, New York, February 19–April 3, 1977

SEPTEMBER

Douglas Crimp organizes the exhibition *Pictures* at Artists Space, New York (Sept. 24–Oct. 29). Crimp's essay for the exhibition, which the critic later expanded and published in the journal *October*, opens with an extended description of Goldstein's then-in-progress film *The Jump*, completed in 1978. Crimp explains, "According to Goldstein, it is only through a distance that we can understand the world. Which is to say that we only experience reality through the pictures we make of it." *Pictures* includes films and photographs by Goldstein, along with works by the artists Troy Brauntuch, Sherrie Levine, Robert Longo, and Philip Smith. The exhibition travels to multiple venues, including the Los Angeles Institute of Contemporary Art (Apr. 15–May 12, 1978).

DECEMBER

Suzanne Lacy and Leslie Labowitz organize *In Mourning and In Rage* at Los Angeles City Hall (Dec. 13). One event in the larger series *Three Weeks in May*, which addresses violence against women and the role of the mass media, *In Mourning and In Rage* is equal parts protest and performance. The performance includes a hearse that circumambulates City Hall, out of which nine shrouded women and one speaker emerge for a press conference. The assembly of ten women protest the media's coverage of the Hillside Strangler and the erasure of the female victims, as well as the many other women murdered, raped, or assaulted during the same period that remain neglected in the media's reporting.

1979

In 1979, Goldstein makes an abrupt shift in his practice, which had consisted primarily of films, photographs, performances, and records. He begins painting at a prolific pace until 1993 (pages 124–31).

FEBRUARY

Burden realizes the first installation of *The Reason for the Neutron Bomb* at Ronald Feldman Fine Arts, New York (Feb. 28–May 28) (pages 120–23).

MARCH

Goldstein premieres *The Jump*, 1978, at the Foundation for Art Resources, Inc., Los Angeles (March 16–24) (pages 134–35).

1980

OCTOBER

On the Santa Monica bluffs overlooking the Pacific Ocean, Burden performs *Solaris* with then-studio assistant Jonathan Gold (Oct. 23) (pages 102–07).

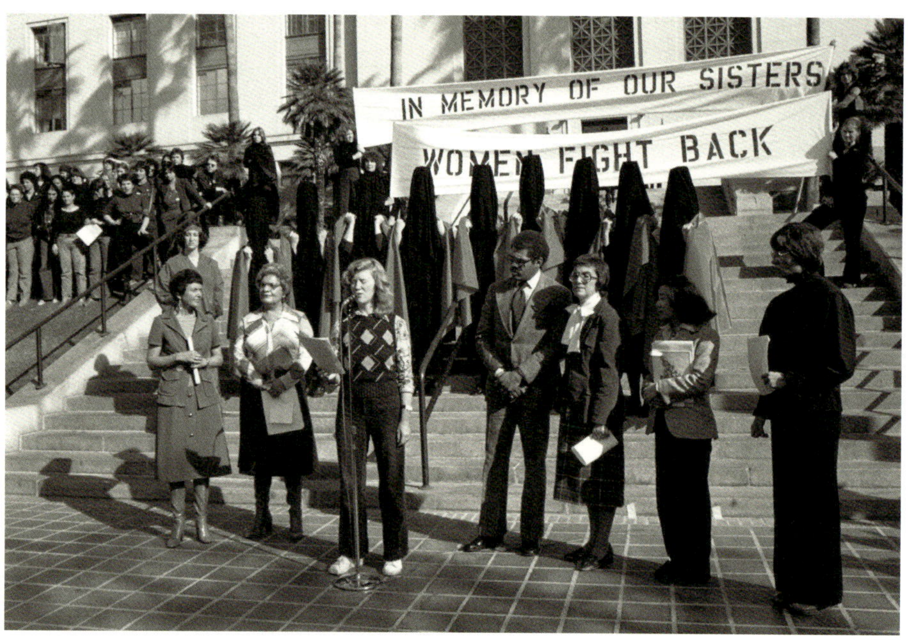

In Mourning and In Rage, 1977, Los Angeles City Hall. Performance by Suzanne Lacy and Leslie Labowitz

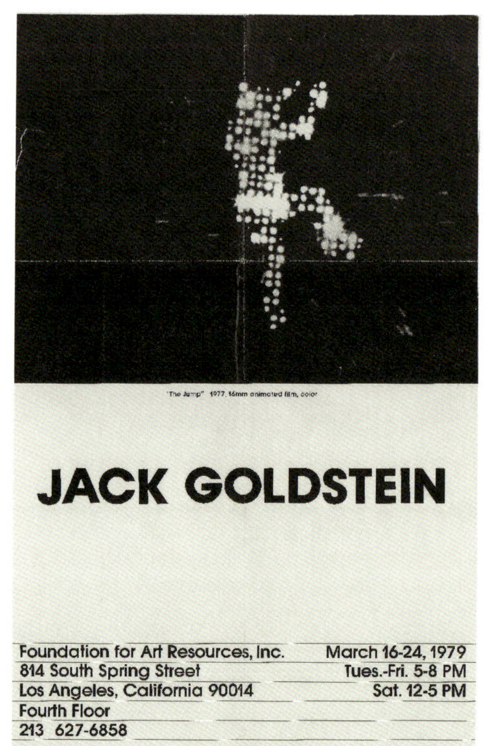

Exhibition poster for *Jack Goldstein*, Foundation for Art Resources, Inc., 1979

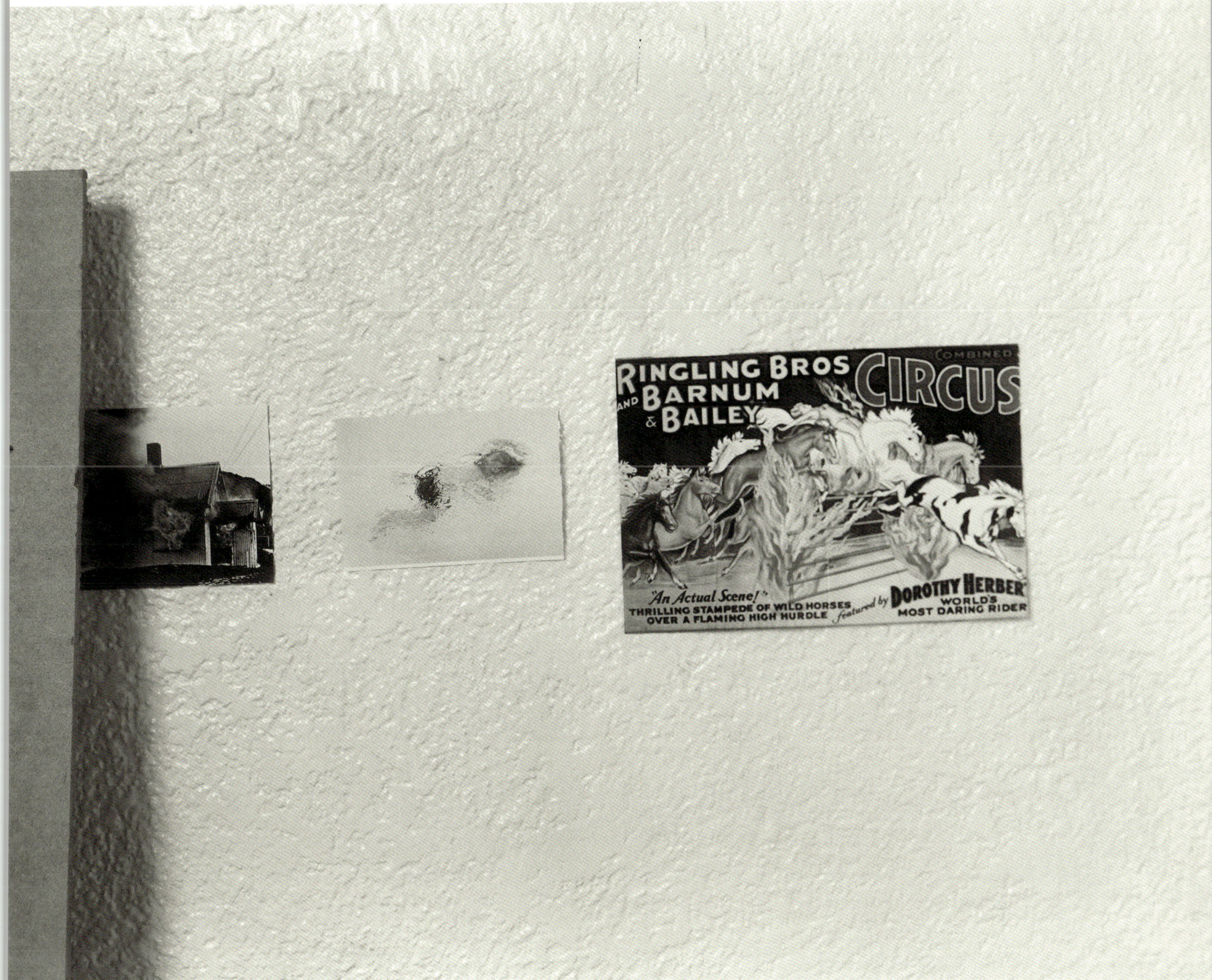

James Welling, *Jack Goldstein Studio Wall, Circus* from *Jack Goldstein's Studio*, 1977/2004

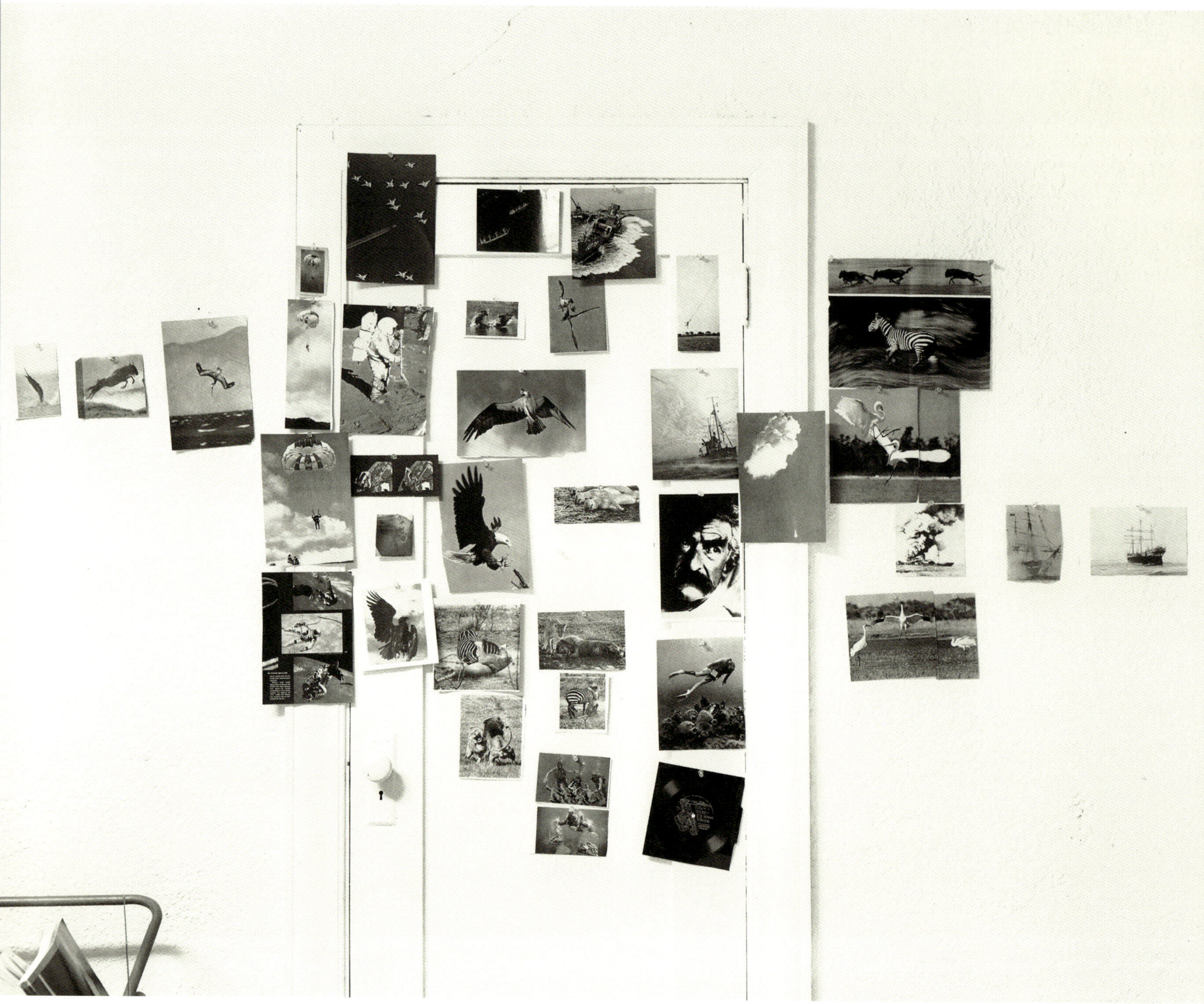

James Welling, *Jack Goldstein Studio Wall* from *Jack Goldstein's Studio*, 1977/2004

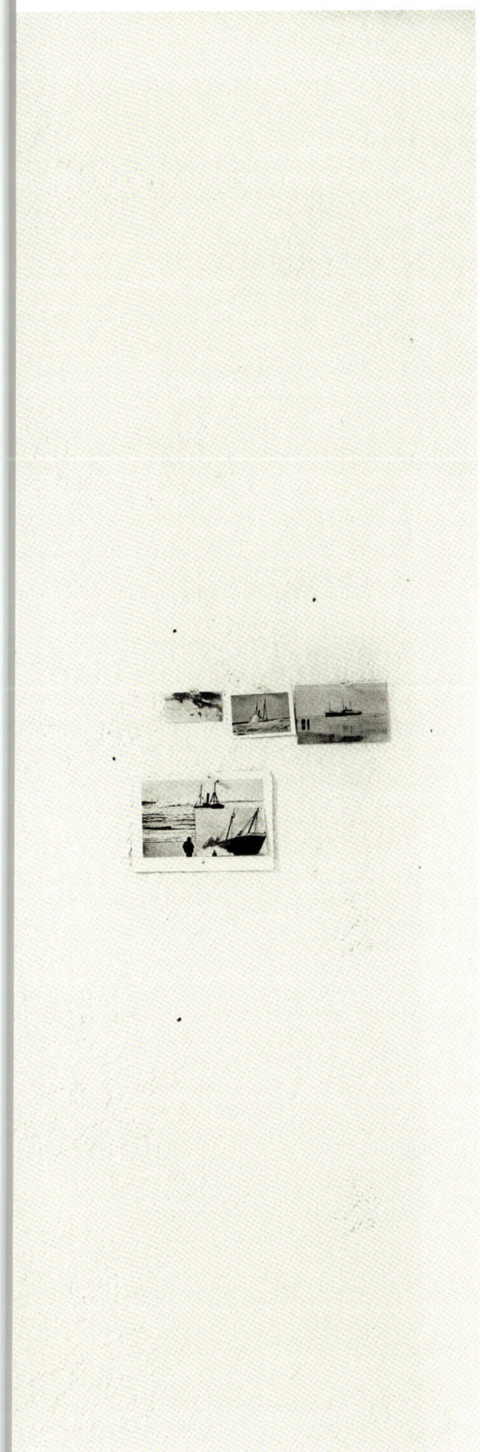

Bas Jan Ader

Please don't leave me, 1969
Paint, lightbulbs, and wire
Dimensions variable
The Estate of Bas Jan Ader
PAGES 36–37

All my clothes, 1970
Gelatin silver print
11 × 14 inches
Edition of 3
The Estate of Bas Jan Ader
PAGE 58

Fall 1, Los Angeles, 1970
16 mm film, black-and-white, silent; 24 seconds
Edition of 3
The Estate of Bas Jan Ader
PAGES 46–47

Fall 2, Amsterdam, 1970
16 mm film, black-and-white, silent; 19 seconds
Edition of 3
The Estate of Bas Jan Ader
PAGES 48–49

Farewell to faraway friends, 1971
Color C-type print
19½ × 22¼ inches
Edition of 3
The Estate of Bas Jan Ader
PAGES 40–41

Nightfall, 1971
16 mm film, black-and-white, silent; 4 minutes, 16 seconds
Edition 3 of 3
The Estate of Bas Jan Ader
PAGES 54–57

Untitled (Sweden), 1971
Projection of two 35 mm color slides
Dimensions variable
Unique
The Estate of Bas Jan Ader
PAGES 32–35

The boy who fell over Niagara Falls, 1972
Performance documented by video, sound recording, and black-and-white photographs
The Estate of Bas Jan Ader
PAGES 82–83

Untitled (Tea party), 1972
Color C-type prints
Six photographs, each 5 × 8 inches; overall, 34 × 8 inches
Edition of 3
Nicole Klagsbrun Gallery
PAGE 59

In search of the miraculous (One night in Los Angeles), 1973
Eighteen gelatin silver prints with hand-written text in white ink
Each photograph, 8 × 10 inches; overall, 30 × 75 inches
Unique
Collection of Philip Aarons and Shelley Fox Aarons
PAGES 86–87

In search of the miraculous, 1975
Installation and performance (unfinished), documented by 80 slides, audio tape, invitation card to Claire S. Copley Gallery, sheet music of sea shanties, *Bulletin 89* (published by Art & Project, Amsterdam), photographs, and Super 8 film material of the launch of the *Ocean Wave*
Dimensions variable
Collection of Philip Aarons and Shelley Fox Aarons
PAGES 88–93

Chris Burden

Disappearing, 1971
December 22–24, 1971
Relic: Void (empty case)
Case, 9¾ × 9½ × 14½ inches
The Chris Burden Estate
PAGES 30–31

Five Day Locker Piece, 1971
University of California, Irvine: April 26–30, 1971
Relic: Padlock
Case, 6 × 9¼ × 7¼ inches
Larry Gagosian Collection
PAGES 60–63

You'll Never See My Face in Kansas City, 1971
Morgan Gallery, Kansas City, Missouri: November 6, 1971
Relic: Ski mask
Case, 5½ × 17 × 12 inches
The Gilbert B. and Lila Silverman Collection, Detroit
PAGES 64–65

Deadman, 1972
Riko Mizuno Gallery, Los Angeles, California: November 12, 1972
Relic: Canvas tarpaulin
Tarpaulin (folded), 1 × 10 × 15 inches; tarpaulin (open), ½ × 53 × 70 inches; case, 9¾ × 19½ × 14½ inches
Schimmel Collection
PAGES 66–71

B.C. Mexico, 1973
Newspace, Newport Beach, California: May 25–June 10, 1973
Relic: Diary, seashell, stone
Case, 4¼ × 10¼ × 9¼ inches
Collection of Jasper Johns
PAGES 79–81

White Light/White Heat, 1975
Ronald Feldman Fine Arts, New York, New York: February 8–March 1, 1975
Relic: Section of board
Case, 7 × 15¼ × 10 inches
Courtesy Ronald Feldman Gallery, New York
PAGES 74–77

Death Valley Run, 1976
Death Valley, California: October 14, 1976
Relic: Customized bicycle
38 × 66 inches
Musee d'Art Contemporain, Marseille, France
PAGES 108–13

The Reason for the Neutron Bomb, 1979
50,000 nickels, 50,000 matchsticks, and signage
Dimensions variable
Collection Museum of Contemporary Art San Diego, Museum purchase, 1986.20
PAGES 120–23

Survival Kit, 1979
Tin box, red cloth, transistor radio, mirror, $100 bill, candle, matches, toothbrush, camping saw, fold out utensils, fishing hook and line, cigarette, printed text, and wood and glass case
11¼ × 20 × 20 inches
Kunsthaus Zürich, Vereinigung Zürcher Kunstfreunde, Gruppe Junge Kunst, 1989
PAGE 39

Solaris, 1980
Pacific Ocean, Santa Monica, California: October 23, 1980
Relic: Card table, walkie-talkie
36 × 30 × 30 inches
The Chris Burden Estate
PAGES 102–07

Three Ghost Ships, 1991
Three Micro 16 sailboats, one equipped with navigational satellite system, robotic sail and rudder controls, and concept drawing
Each ship, 276 × 192 × 72 inches
Nicolas Berggruen Charitable Foundation
PAGES 114–17

Chris Burden
Ode to Santos Dumont, 2015
7075 aircraft aluminum reproduction Erector parts, carbon fiber drive shaft, fiberglass propeller, nylon cable, hand-tooled ¼ scale replica of 1903 gasoline motor, polyurethane balloon, and 1,200 cubic feet of helium
192 × 720 × 720 inches
The Chris Burden Estate
PAGES 138–41

Jack Goldstein

Poster for the performance *Burial Piece*, California Institute of the Arts, Valencia, June 9, 1972
12 × 9½ inches
James Welling
PAGE 73

Rocking Chair, 1972
16 mm film, black-and-white, silent; 4 minutes
The Estate of Jack Goldstein
PAGES 44–45

Here, 1973
16 mm film, black-and-white, sound; 10 minutes, 42 seconds
The Estate of Jack Goldstein
PAGES 52–53

Jack, 1973
16 mm film, color, sound; 11 minutes, 24 seconds
The Estate of Jack Goldstein
PAGES 42–43

A Spotlight, 1972
16 mm film, black-and-white, sound; 8 minutes
The Estate of Jack Goldstein
PAGES 50–51

The Pull, 1976
Three chromogenic prints
Each photograph, 30 × 40 inches; overall, 90 × 119 inches
Galerie Bruno Bischofberger
PAGES 98–99

Suite of 9 Records with Sound Effects, 1976:
A German Shepherd, 45 rpm, red vinyl
The Lost Ocean Liner, 45 rpm, black vinyl
Two Wrestling Cats, 45 rpm, yellow vinyl
The Burning Forest, 45 rpm, red and white vinyl
Three Felled Trees, 45 rpm, green vinyl
A Swim Against the Tide, 45 rpm, blue vinyl
The Dying Wind, 45 rpm, translucent vinyl
A Faster Run, 45 rpm, orange vinyl
The Tornado, 45 rpm, purple vinyl
Vinyl records, sound
Dimensions variable
Private Collection, Fort Worth, Texas
PAGES 95–97

Burning Window, 1977/2012
Built-in window and red flickering lights
Dimensions variable
The Estate of Jack Goldstein
PAGE 133

The Jump, 1978
16 mm film, color, silent projection, and two black light tubes; 26 seconds
Dimensions variable
The Estate of Jack Goldstein
PAGES 134–35

Untitled, 1979
Oil on Masonite
89½ × 128⅞ inches
Brian Butler
PAGES 100–01

Untitled, 1981
Synthetic polymer paint on canvas
82¾ × 130 inches
The Museum of Modern Art, New York; The Sidney and Harriet Janis Collection (by exchange) and gift of Jill and Peter Kraus, 2015
PAGES 128–29

Untitled, 1981
Acrylic on canvas
84 × 132 inches
Collection of Raymond Learsy
PAGES 124–25

Untitled, 1981
Acrylic on canvas
96 × 60 inches
Collection of BZ + Michael Schwartz, New York
PAGE 131

Untitled (#61 Burning City), 1981
Acrylic on canvas
84 × 132 inches
The Broad Art Foundation
PAGES 126–27

Additional Works

James Welling
Jack Goldstein Studio, USC Poster from *Jack Goldstein's Studio*, 1977/2004
Inkjet print
38⅝ × 46½ inches
Courtesy the Artist and Regen Projects, Los Angeles

James Welling
Jack Goldstein Studio Wall from *Jack Goldstein's Studio*, 1977/2004
Inkjet print
38⅝ × 57½ inches
Courtesy the Artist and Regen Projects, Los Angeles
PAGES 152–53

James Welling
Jack Goldstein in my studio in the Pacific Building from *Jack Goldstein's Studio*, 1978/2004
Inkjet print
26½ × 22 inches
Edition 1 of 3, 1 AP
Courtesy the Artist and Regen Projects, Los Angeles

James Welling
Jack Goldstein's Apartment, East Village from *Jack Goldstein's Studio*, 1978/2004
Inkjet print
38⅝ × 63 inches
Edition 1 of 3, 1 AP
Courtesy the Artist and Regen Projects, Los Angeles

Andriesse, Paul, ed. *Bas Jan Ader*. Amsterdam: Stichting Openbaar Kunstbezit, 1988.

Ayres, Anne, and Paul Schimmel, eds. *Chris Burden: A Twenty-Year Survey*. Newport Beach, CA: Newport Harbor Art Museum, 1988.

Barron, Stephanie, Sheri Bernstein, and Ilene Fort, eds. *Made in California: Art, Image, and Identity, 1900–2000*. Los Angeles: Los Angeles County Museum of Art, 2000.

Bewley, Jon, and Jonty Tarbuck, eds. *Chris Burden*. Newcastle upon Tyne: Locus+ Publishing Ltd, 2007.

Broude, Norma, and Mary D. Garrard, eds. *The Power of Feminist Art: The American Movement of the 1970s, History and Impact*. New York: Harry N. Abrams, 1994.

Burden, Chris. *Chris Burden 71–73*. Los Angeles: Chris Burden, 1974.

Burden, Chris, and Peter Noever, eds. *Chris Burden: Beyond the Limits*. Vienna: MAK-Austrian Museum of Applied Arts, 1996.

Butler, Cornelia, and Lisa Mark, eds. *WACK! Art and the Feminist Revolution*. Los Angeles: Museum of Contemporary Art, Los Angeles, 2007.

Chavoya, C. Ondine, and Rita Gonzalez, eds. *Asco: Elite of the Obscure, A Retrospective, 1972–1987*. Ostfildern: Hatje Cantz, 2011.

Cherix, Christophe, ed. *In & Out of Amsterdam: Travels in Conceptual Art, 1960–1976*. New York: The Museum of Modern Art, 2009.

Crimp, Douglas, ed. *Pictures*. New York: Artists Space, 1977.

Crow, Thomas. *Modern Art in the Common Culture*. New Haven: Yale University Press, 1996.

Dumbadze, Alexander. *Bas Jan Ader: Death Is Elsewhere*. Chicago and London: University of Chicago Press, 2013.

Eklund, Douglas, ed. *The Pictures Generation, 1974–1984*. New York: The Metropolitan Museum of Art, 2009.

Fisher, Morgan. "Talking with Jack Goldstein." *LAICA Journal* 14 (1977): 44–45.

Fuchs, Rainer, ed. *John Baldessari: A Different Kind of Order*. Cologne: Museum Moderner Kunst Stiftung Ludwig Wien, 2005.

Goldstein, Ann, and Anne Rorimer, eds. *Reconsidering the Object of Art, 1965–1975*. Los Angeles: Museum of Contemporary Art, Los Angeles, 1995.

Goldstein, Jack, and John Miller. *Jack Goldstein: Films, Records, Performances and Aphorisms, 1971–1984*. Edited by Christopher Müller and Daniel Buchholz. Cologne: Walther König, 2003.

Grässlin, Karola, ed. *Kunst aus Los Angeles der 60er bis 90er Jahre*. Braunschweig, Germany: Kunstverein Braunschweig, 2007.

Grenier, Catherine, Howard Fox, and David James, eds. *Los Angeles, 1955–1985: Birth of an Art Capital*. Paris: Centre Georges Pompidou, 2006.

Grover, Andrea. *Radical Seafaring*. Water Mill, NY: Parrish Art Museum, 2016.

Guenther, Bruce. *Tony DeLap*. Newport Beach: Orange County Museum of Art, 2000.

Hertz, Richard. *Jack Goldstein and the CalArts Mafia*. Ojai, CA: Minneola Press, 2003.

Jones, Kellie, ed. *Now Dig This!: Art and Black Los Angeles, 1960–1980*. Los Angeles: Hammer Museum, University of California, Los Angeles, 2011.

———. *South of Pico: African American Artists in Los Angeles in the 1960s and 1970s*. Durham and London: Duke University Press, 2017.

Kaiser, Philipp, ed. *Jack Goldstein × 10,000*. Munich: Prestel, 2012.

Kennedy, Garry Neill. *The Last Art College: Nova Scotia College of Art and Design, 1968–1978*. Cambridge, MA: MIT Press, 2012.

Kienholz, Lyn, ed. *L.A. Rising: SoCal Artists Before 1980*. Los Angeles: California/International Arts Foundation, 2010.

Kraus, Chris, Jan Tumlir, Jane McFadden, and Oriana Fox, eds. *LA Artland: Contemporary Art from Los Angeles*. London: Black Dog Publishing, 2005.

Küng, Moritz. *Entropie: über das Verschwinden des Werkes*. Bozen: AR/GE KUNST Galerie Museum, 2004.

Lewallen, Constance, ed. *A Rose Has No Teeth: Bruce Nauman in the 1960s*. Berkeley: The University of California Press, 2007.

Lewallen, Constance, and Karen Moss, eds. *State of Mind: New California Art circa 1970*. Berkeley: The UC Berkeley Art Museum and Pacific Film Archive and the Orange County Museum of Art, 2011.

Lippard, Lucy. *Six Years: The Dematerialization of the Art Object from 1966 to 1972*. New York: Praeger Publishers, 1973.

Livingston, Jane, and Marcia Tucker. *Bruce Nauman: Work from 1965 to 1972*. New York: Praeger Publishers, 1973.

Morris, Frances, ed. *Chris Burden—When Robots Rule: The Two-Minute Airplane Factory*. London: Tate Gallery Publishing, 1999.

Müller, Christopher, ed. *Bas Jan Ader: Filme, Fotografien, Projektionen, Videos, und Zeichnungen aus den Jahren 1967–1975*. Cologne: Verlag der Buchhandlung Walther König, 2000.

Nittve, Lars, and Helle Crenzien, eds. *Sunshine & Noir: Art in L.A., 1960–1977*. Humlebæk, Denmark: Louisiana Museum of Modern Art, 1997.

Peabody, Rebecca, Andrew Perchuk, Glenn Phillips, and Rani Singh, eds. *Pacific Standard Time: Los Angeles Art, 1945–1980*. Los Angeles: Getty Research Institute and the J. Paul Getty Museum, 2011.

Phillips, Glenn, and Rebecca McGrew, eds. *It Happened at Pomona: Art at the Edge of Los Angeles, 1969–1973*. Claremont, CA: Pomona College Museum of Art, 2011.

Phillips, Lisa, ed. *Chris Burden: Extreme Measures*. New York: Skira Rizzoli in association with the New Museum, 2013.

Plagens, Peter. *Sunshine Muse: Art on the West Coast, 1945–1970*. Berkeley: University of California Press, 1999.

Ruppersberg, Allen. *One of Many—Origins and Variants*. Cologne: Kunsthalle Düsseldorf, 2005.

Schimmel, Paul, and Lisa Mark, eds. *Under the Big Black Sun: California Art, 1974–1981*. Los Angeles: Museum of Contemporary Art, Los Angeles, 2011.

Spence, Brad, ed. *Bas Jan Ader*. Irvine, CA: The Art Gallery, University of California, Irvine, 1999.

Teti, Matthew. "From Minimalism to Performance Art: Chris Burden, 1967–71." PhD diss., Columbia University, 2018.

———. "Occupying UCI: Chris Burden's *Five Day Locker Piece* as Institutional Critique." *RACAR (Revue d'art canadienne/ Canadian Art Review)* 43, no. 1 (Spring 2018): 39–52.

Verwoert, Jan. *Bas Jan Ader: In Search of the Miraculous*. One Work. London: Afterall Books, 2006.

Ward, Frazer. *No Innocent Bystanders: Performance Art and Audience*. Hanover, NH: Dartmouth College Press, 2012.

Weschler, Lawrence, and Ursula Ströbele. *The Sense of Movement: When Artists Travel*. Ostfildern: Hatje Cantz Verlag, 2015.

Wijk, Marion van, and Koos Dalstra. *In Search of the Miraculous: Bas Jan Ader, Discovery File 143/76*. Amsterdam: Veenman Publishers, 2007.

Wilding, Faith. *By Our Own Hands: The Women Artist's Movement, Southern California, 1970–1976*. Los Angeles: Double X, 1977.

Wolfs, Rein, ed. *Bas Jan Ader: Please Don't Leave Me*. Rotterdam: Museum Boijmans Van Beuningen, 2006.

Philip Aarons and Shelley Fox Aarons

The Estate of Bas Jan Ader

Nicolas Berggruen Charitable Foundation

Galerie Bruno Bischofberger

The Broad Art Foundation

The Chris Burden Estate

Brian Butler

Larry Gagosian

The Estate of Jack Goldstein

Jasper Johns

Nicole Klagsbrun Gallery

Kunsthaus Zürich

Raymond Learsy

Musee d'Art Contemporain, Marseille, France

Museum of Contemporary Art San Diego

The Museum of Modern Art, New York

Regen Projects, Los Angeles

Ronald Feldman Gallery, New York

Schimmel Collection

The Gilbert B. and Lila Silverman Collection, Detroit

BZ + Michael Schwartz, New York

James Welling

and those lenders who wish to remain anonymous

LENDERS TO THE EXHIBITION

UNLESS OTHERWISE NOTED:
Artworks by Bas Jan Ader are © The Estate of Bas Jan Ader / Mary Sue Andersen Ader, 2019 / The Artists Rights Society (ARS), New York. Images courtesy of Meliksetian | Briggs, Los Angeles

Artworks by Chris Burden are © 2019 Chris Burden / licensed by The Chris Burden Estate and Artists Rights Society (ARS), New York. Images courtesy of The Chris Burden Estate

Artworks by Jack Goldstein are © The Estate of Jack Goldstein. Images courtesy of The Estate of Jack Goldstein

COVER Photograph by Alfred Lutjeans

16 John Baldessari, *Cremation Project*, 1970. Bronze urn (with ashes) in shape of book, bronze plaque, affidavit on board, and six color photographs. Urn: 9½ × 6⅛ × 3⅛ inches; plaque: 9½ × 16⅛ inches; affidavit: 10⅛ × 8 inches; photos: 20 × 24¼ inches. Courtesy of John Baldessari and Marian Goodman Gallery

22–23 Allen Ruppersberg, *Where's Al?*, 1972. 110 typed index cards, 3 × 5 inches; 160 instamatic prints, 3½ × 3½ inches; 55¼ × 85⅜ × 1⅜ inches installed. Courtesy the Artist and Greene Naftali, New York

24 Tony DeLap, *A Spatial Occurrence, the Levitation of a Human Being*, 1971. Performance at Duchamp Festival, University of California, Irvine. Courtesy of the Artist. Photograph by Alfred Lutjeans

27 Photograph courtesy Suzanne Lacy Studio

31 Photograph by Brian Forrest

32–33 Installation view, *Bas Jan Ader, William Leavitt, Ger van Elk*, Pomona College Art Gallery, Claremont, California, 1972

34–35 Installation view, *Bas Jan Ader*, Simon Lee Gallery, London, 2016. Courtesy of Simon Lee Gallery, London

39 Courtesy of Kunsthaus Zürich

60 Barbara Burden feeding Chris Burden during *Five Day Locker Piece*, 1971. Archival photograph. The Chris Burden Estate

61 Photograph by Diana Zlotnick

63 Photograph by Gene Ogami

65 Photograph by Daniel Zimbaldi

66–69 Photographs by Gary Beydler

71 Photograph by Joshua Nefsky

73 Courtesy James Welling, Los Angeles/New York

74–75 Photograph by Eeva Inkeri

79 Photograph by Barbara Burden

81 Photograph by Eeva Inkeri

103 Chris Burden, *Solaris* script, 1980. Typed script on paper. 11 × 8½ inches. The Chris Burden Estate

107 Photograph by Brian Forrest

108 Chris Burden, *Death Valley Run* map, 1976. Annotated map. 17 × 11 inches. The Chris Burden Estate

109–11 Photographs by Alexis Smith

113 Image © RMN-Grand Palais / Art Resource, New York. Photo: Benjamin Soligny / Raphaël Chipault

114–15 Installation view, *Chris Burden: Three Ghost Ships*, Portland Art Museum, Portland, Oregon, October 1, 2011–January 15, 2012. Courtesy Portland Art Museum. Photograph by Robert DiFranco

117 Chris Burden, *Three Ghost Ships I*, 1990. Ink on paper. 8½ × 13 inches. The Chris Burden Estate

120–21 Photograph by Chris Burden

138–39 Installation view, *Chris Burden: Ode to Santos Dumont*, Los Angeles County Museum of Art, May 18, 2015–June 21, 2015. Image © Museum Associates/ LACMA

141 Installation view, *Chris Burden: Ode to Santos Dumont*, Los Angeles County Museum of Art, May 18, 2015–June 21, 2015. Image © Museum Associates/ LACMA

142–43 Bas Jan Ader, *Fall 2, Amsterdam*, 1970. Color production still from making of 16 mm black-and-white film. Color photograph

144 (LEFT) Bas Jan Ader, *Implosion/The artist contemplating the forces of nature*, 1967. Offset lithography on paper. 16¾ × 10¾ inches. Edition size unknown, estimated at approximately 100

144 (RIGHT) Bas Jan Ader, *Landslide: A quarterly journal of underground art*, 1969. Six mimeographed sheets in acetate cover and one offset lithograph sheet, in an envelope. Publication, 11¾ × 9 inches; letter, 9½ × 8½ inches. Edition size unknown, maximum of 25

145 (LEFT) Photograph by Barbara Smith

146 (LEFT) California Institute of the Arts Institute Archives: Feminist Art Materials Collection

146 (ABOVE RIGHT) Photograph by Robert Boss

146 (LOWER RIGHT) Courtesy the Artist and Pomona College Museum of Art

147 (LEFT) Getty Research Institute, Los Angeles (2010.M.84). © J. Paul Getty Trust

147 (RIGHT) Barbara T. Smith, *Deadman* courtroom sketch, 1973. Ink on paper. 10¾ × 13½ inches. The Chris Burden Estate

148 (LEFT) Getty Research Institute, Los Angeles (2010.M.84). © J. Paul Getty Trust

148 (RIGHT) Harry Gamboa Jr., *Decoy Gang War Victim*, 1974, *from the Asco era*. Chromogenic print. 16 × 20 inches. Edition of 10. Printed 2010. ©1974, Harry Gamboa Jr. Image courtesy of Marlborough Contemporary

149 (RIGHT) Photograph by Geoffrey Clements

150 (LEFT) Photograph by Maria Karras

150 (RIGHT) Courtesy of Jonathan Monk

151 James Welling, *Jack Goldstein Studio Wall, Circus, 1977* from *Jack Goldstein's Studio*, 1977/2004. Seven digital chromogenic prints. 15 × 19 inches. Edition of 10, 5 AP. © James Welling, Courtesy Regen Projects, Los Angeles and 1301PE

This book was published on the occasion of the exhibition
DISAPPEARING—CALIFORNIA, C. 1970: BAS JAN ADER, CHRIS BURDEN, JACK GOLDSTEIN,
curated by Philipp Kaiser, with assistance from Jamin An, and organized by the Modern Art Museum of Fort Worth, on view May 10 to August 11, 2019.

Support for the exhibition is generously provided by the Kleinheinz Family Endowment for the Arts and Education.

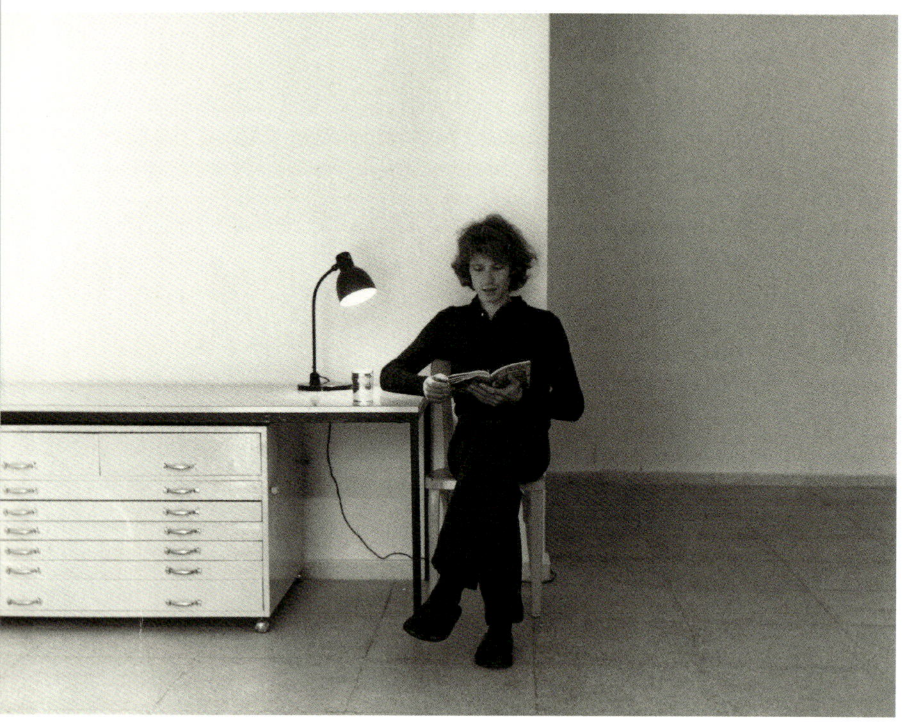

COVER
Chris Burden, *You'll Never See My Face in Kansas City*, 1971
Morgan Gallery, Kansas City, Missouri: November 6, 1971
Performance documentation

BACK COVER AND PAGES 8–9
Jack Goldstein, *The Pull* (details), 1976

END PAPERS
Jack Goldstein, *Untitled* (details), 1979

TITLE PAGE
Exhibition announcement for *Bas Jan Ader: "In Search of the Miraculous"* (detail), Claire S. Copley Gallery, Los Angeles, 1975

TABLE OF CONTENTS
Chris Burden, *Solaris* (detail), 1980
Pacific Ocean, Santa Monica, California: October 23, 1980
Performance documentation

ABOVE
Bas Jan Ader, *The boy who fell over Niagara Falls*, 1972
Performance at Kabinett für aktuelle Kunst, Bremerhaven, Germany

Published in 2019 by the Modern Art Museum of Fort Worth and DelMonico Books•Prestel.

Modern Art Museum of Fort Worth
3200 Darnell Street
Fort Worth, TX 76107
817.738.9215
1.866.824.5566 toll free
www.themodern.org

DelMonico Books, an imprint of Prestel,
a member of Verlagsgruppe Random House GmbH

Prestel Verlag
Neumarkter Strasse 28
81673 Munich

Prestel Publishing Ltd.
14–17 Wells Street
London W1T 3PD

Prestel Publishing
900 Broadway, Suite 603
New York, NY 10003

www.prestel.com

Edited by Leslie Murrell, Modern Art Museum of Fort Worth, and Sheryl Conkelton

Translation by Elizabeth Tucker

Designed by Lorraine Wild and Xiaoqing Wang, Green Dragon Office, Los Angeles

Printed and bound in Germany

ISBN: 978-3-7913-5854-3

A CIP catalogue record for this book is available from the British Library.

Library of Congress Cataloging-in-Publication Data
Names: Kaiser, Philipp, 1972, author. | Modern Art Museum of Fort Worth, organizer, host institution.
Title: Disappearing-California c. 1970 : Bas Jan Ader, Chris Burden, Jack Goldstein / Philipp Kaiser.
Description: Fort Worth, TX : Modern Art Museum of Fort Worth ; Munich ; New York: DelMonico Books•Prestel, 2019. | Includes bibliographical references.
Identifiers: LCCN 2019002166 | ISBN 9783791358543 (paperback)
Subjects: LCSH: Performance art--California, Southern--Exhibitions. | Absence in art--Exhibitions. | Ader, Bas Jan, 1942-1975--Exhibitions. | Burden, Chris, 1946-2015--Exhibitions. | Goldstein, Jack, 1945-2003--Exhibitions. | BISAC: ART / Individual Artists / Monographs. | ART / Performance. | ART / History / Contemporary (1945-).
Classification: LCC NX456.5.P38 K35 2019 | DDC 702.81--dc23 LC record available at https://lccn.loc.gov/2019002166

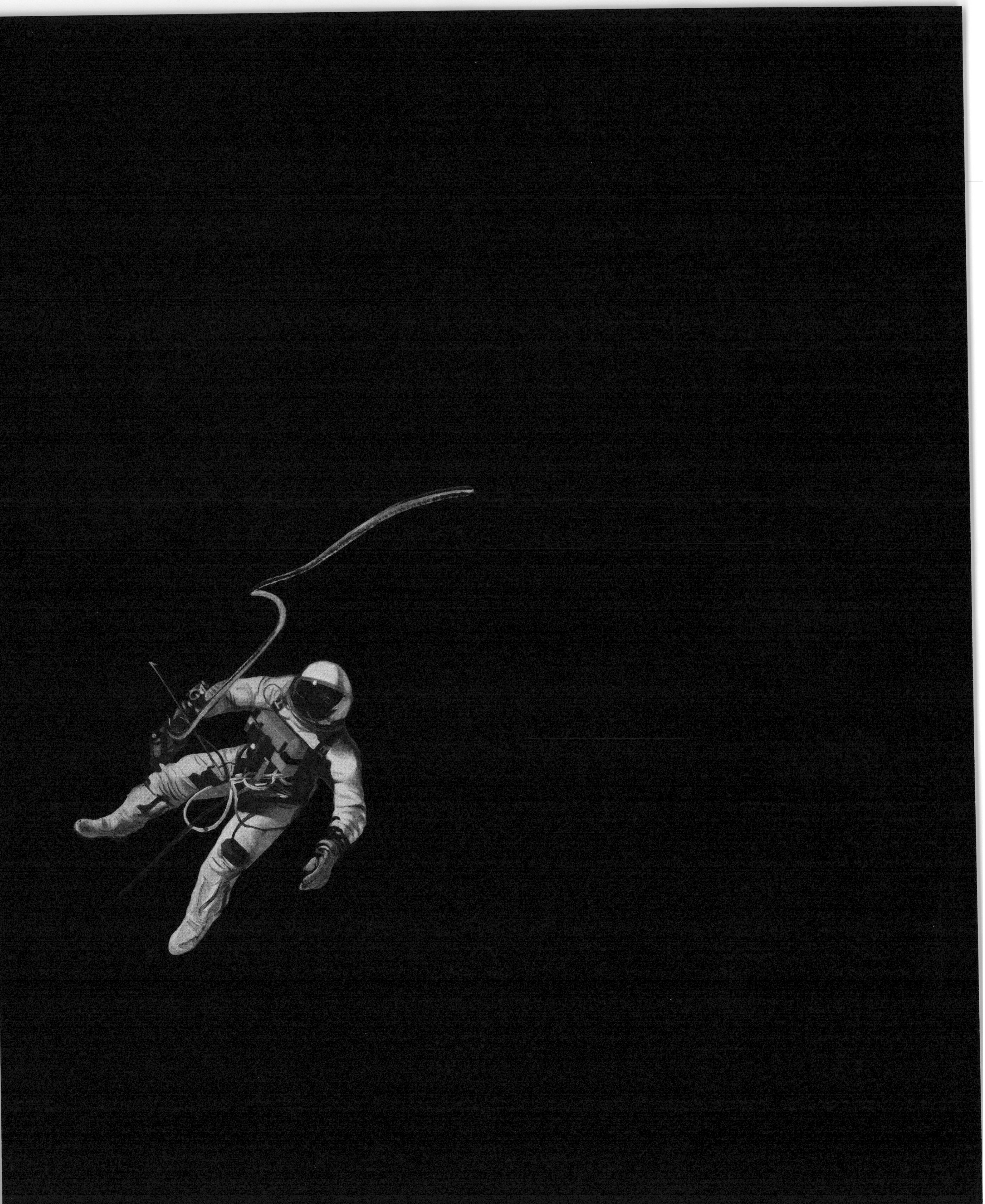